Saints Alive

Saints Alive

EDITED BY

HAL M. HELMS

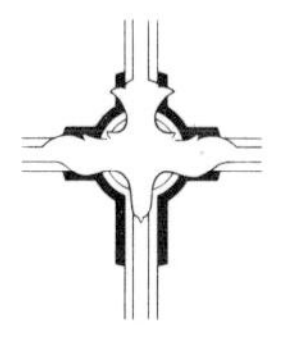

PARACLETE PRESS
Orleans, MA

Third Printing, October, 1993

Library of Congress #: 85-71758
ISBN: 0-941478-44-0

Published by Paraclete Press
Orleans, Massachusetts
Printed in the United States of America

Dedication

For all the saints, who from their labors rest
Who Thee by faith before the world confessed,
Thy Name, O Jesus, be forever blest,
Alleluia.

William Walsham How, 1864

Contents

APOSTLES

EARLY SAINTS

JUST FOLKS

TEACHERS AND PREACHERS

MISSIONARIES

ROYAL SAINTS

YOUNG PEOPLE

NATIONAL SAINTS

GREAT MYSTICS

LEADERS

CONFESSORS AND CONTENDERS

PATRONS OF SPECIAL CAUSES

Introduction

What is a saint? Probably there is no better definition than that of a child, who remembered seeing pictures of them in the stained glass windows of his church. "Saints," he said, "are people that the light shines through."

And that is just what they are. People of almost every imaginable description. Some of them were very brilliant people, some were very simple. Some were high born — kings, queens, princes, princesses, noble men and women; others were peasants, humble fisherfolk, shepherds, laborers, housewives. Some felt called to remain single and celibate; others were married and reared families. Some were sweet and even-tempered; others were by nature easily provoked, excitable or even "difficult to live with." But through them all the Light shines through, the light of God's love, the light of His presence, the light of Jesus Christ.

And so they are given to encourage and inspire us to become more Christlike ourselves. C. S. Lewis wrote, "The great sinners are made of the very same material as . . . the great saints." That is something to ponder. Out of the same clay, the same emotions, the same temptations, the same twenty-four hours of each day, some fashion sainthood while others fashion emptiness and waste. The difference seems to be in the inner heart attitude.

God even uses some of the very things that would seem negative and turns them to good. The willful child Teresa becomes the indefatigable foundress of Carmelite reform. Matthew the tax collector becomes Matthew the careful chronicler of the life of our Lord Jesus Christ. The dissipated young Augustine becomes the ardent lover of Christ and of His Church. As they rubbed up against trials, adversity, difficulties of all sorts, the glory within shone forth all the more brilliantly.

Sometimes people have engaged in the vain question, "Who are the greatest saints?" Thomas à Kempis had heard such discussions in his day (the 15th century), and he writes, "Do not inquire or dispute about the merits of the saints, which of them is more holy than the other, or which shall be the greater in the kingdom of heaven . . . . Am I not He who made all the saints? Moreover, I gave them grace and bestowed glory on them. I know what every one has deserved, and I have gone before them with the sweetness of my blessing . . . . I am to be praised in all My saints . . . . Whoever despises one of the least of My saints, therefore, does not honor the greatest, for I made both great and small . . . . They are all one through the bond of love. Their thought is one, their will is one, and they all love each other as one. " (Book III, Chapter 58).

In this book we have selected eighty-four saints representing twelve different categories to show the tremendous variety of faith and devotion with which God has blessed His people. Their special recognition by the Church is meant to edify all of us in our faith and obedience to Him. But we know that besides these, there are myriads of others, many of them known only to God, whose faith and devotion have been without measure.

The writer of the Book of Hebrews, looking back across the generations of old, referred to the faithful, the martyrs, the overcomers, as those "of whom the world was not worthy." As we celebrate God's light coming through these faithful women and men, old and young, may we be inspired to follow their good examples, that with them we may be made partakers of the same joy.

Their joy unto their Lord we bring
  Their song to us descendeth.
The Spirit who in them did sing
  To us His music lendeth:
His song in them, in us, is one;
  We raise it high, we send it on,
The song that never endeth!

(Thomas Hornblower Gill, 1868)

Hal McElwaine Helms
Feast of St Augustine of Hippo
August 28, 1985

Acknowledgements

This book is the product of many hands and many hearts. We have drawn freely on those whose painstaking research has resulted in a dependable body of information about the saints. In particular, we have found Butler's *Lives of the Saints* to be an invaluable resource. *The Catholic Encyclopedia* also yielded much help, while the Oxford *Dictionary of Saints,* and Donald Attwater's *Penguin Dictionary of Saints* did their part in helping clarify points from time to time. Late in the growth of the book we discovered Mary Reed Newland's *The Saint Book,* published by Seabury Press. An old favorite was *A Year Book of Saints* by Christine Chaundler, concerned mainly with English and British saints. *The Saints of Scotland,* by E. S. Towill, concentrated on Scotland, but contained some valuable information on St Andrew and some of the early Celtic Irish/Scottish saints. The Daughters of St Paul (Hyde Park, Massachusetts) have an attractive set of two books called *Saints for Young People for Every Day of the Year,* which is much enjoyed by some of the young people I know. Any of these books are well worth reading and reference. We have sought carefully to avoid infringement of any copyright.

Beyond our acknowledgement of sources, I wish to thank the members of the Community of Jesus, Orleans, Massachusetts, for their help in research and original drafts of some of the biographies. Special thanks go to the Sisterhood and to Sister Clare Schmidt, Ph.D., who not only helped with the research, but also added her personal touch to many of the stories, adding life and sparkle to many of them. The illustrations are by Roger Snure, a man of many parts — artist, printer, sculptor.

Special thanks are due to M. Cay Andersen and M. Judy Sorensen, Directors of the Community of Jesus, who have encouraged this project from the beginning; to my wife, Helen, who read my drafts and insisted that I re-write some of them; to Miss Gertrude Andersen, Miss Barbara Booth and Mrs. Susie Kanaga, for checking our copies for errors; and to Sisters Martha Clark and Mary Lane, and Paul Mitman, who did the layout design.

All of us have been blessed in working on this book, and offer it to the greater glory of God and the upbuilding of His Church.

H.M.H.

Apostles

And when it was day, He called unto Him
His disciples, and of them He chose twelve,
whom He also named apostles.
Luke 6:13

And many signs and wonders were done
by the apostles.
Acts 2:43b

And they continued steadfastly in the apostles'
teaching and fellowship.
I John 1:3a

The princes of the Church are they,
Triumphant leaders in the fray,
In heaven's hall a victor band,
True lights that lighten every land.
St Ambrose, 340-397

St Peter

First Century

"Peter!" The man in the prison cell stirred restlessly, listened drowsily, and then settled more deeply into his sleep. "Peter!" In his half-doze he heard it again. It sounded a little like a voice he knew. He started in his sleep, remembering the sparkling Galilean lake, the fishing boats drawn up on the shore, and the Master. "Follow me," He had said that day, "and I will make you a fisher of men." Peter and his brother Andrew and their friends James and John had left everything that day and life for them had never been the same. "You shall no longer be Simon, but Peter — a Rock."

There it was again, "Peter!" This time he awoke fully and looked around. His cell radiated with light. Was he dreaming? There lay the guards, sleeping on the floor, but now he was no longer chained to them. He was standing free. Turning, he saw where the light was coming from — a dazzling angel. "Get dressed and put on your shoes," said the Vision. "Put on your cloak and follow me!" Peter followed the angel past the first and second cell blocks, and to the iron gates leading to the street. These opened of their own accord. After they had walked a little way, the angel left him.

"It's really true," Peter said to himself. "The Lord's angel has rescued me from Herod's hand." He hurried through the Jerusalem streets to the home of Mary, where the little band of Christians had gathered to pray for his safety and release. At first they could not believe it had really happened. "You're seeing things," they told the girl who answered the door and left him standing outside. But Peter kept knocking, and finally he was let in and told them his amazing story.

"You are a Rock," Jesus had told him. And after receiving the promised Holy Spirit at Pentecost, Peter had acted like a Rock. Called to remain in Jerusalem while the others were scattered by persecution, Peter kept witnessing before the Jewish Council and performed many miracles. He was recognized as the leader of the twelve.

Later he went to Samaria, to assist Philip in his mission there, and to pray for those who had become believers.

Following that, Peter took missionary journeys into Syria. During one of those, he saw a sheet let down from heaven with every kind of animal, and a voice telling him, "Rise, Peter; kill and eat." But Peter refused, saying, "I have never eaten anything unclean." Then the Voice said, "What God has cleansed, you shall not call unclean." Peter understood that this meant that the gospel was not to be confined to the Jewish people, but was to be carried to all nations. Just then he saw messengers approaching, asking for him to come and bring the gospel to a Roman centurion, Cornelius. He obeyed, and a large group became Christian believers.

We do not know when Peter went to Rome, but very reliable and early tradition says that he was there, concluding that when time came to be crucified, he requested that he be crucified upside down so that his death would not appear to rival that of Jesus.

He is honored as "Prince of the Apostles," and over his tomb has been built the magnificent Basilica of St Peter's in Vatican City, Rome. His feast day with St Paul is June 29, and there is also a subsidiary feast on August 1, St Peter in Chains, commemorating his miraculous escape from prison.

St James

First Century

James, the son of Zebedee, is called "St James the Great," to distinguish him from another apostle named James, who is called St James the Less. It probably meant that James, the son of Zebedee, was the older of the two.

The name "James" is the English form of "Jacob," a very common name in Jesus' time. Some confusion remains about these names, but of one thing we are very certain: James and his younger brother John were early disciples of Jesus, and they were so fiery and spirited that He called them "Boanerges," "Sons of Thunder."

James and his brother were fishermen, as were Peter and Andrew. They lived near the Sea of Galilee in

Capernaum, and worked with their father Zebedee. But when Jesus paid a visit to their business one day, they left their father's nets to follow Him. From now on James would be a "fisher of men." James was one of the "inner circle" of disciples — Peter, James, and John. He was present when Jesus raised Jairus' daughter from the dead. He also witnessed the Transfiguration, when Jesus was bathed in light brighter than the sun; he went with Jesus to Gethsemane on the night He was betrayed, and was there when Jesus appeared to all of the apostles in the Upper Room.

About fourteen years after Jesus' crucifixion, James was arrested along with Peter during the persecution of Herod Agrippa I. Tradition tells us some of the particulars of that time of suffering.

The man who had accused James before the court stood and watched as James was questioned about his faith. All attempts to get him to deny what he believed, to turn from Christ, were useless. James stood his ground, and answered every question clearly and courageously. He was still a "Son of Thunder"! The accuser began to wonder what it was that made James so strong in the face of death. Surely nothing like that had ever moved him. "Why did I bring this suffering on this good man?" he asked himself. As the trial went on, he could stand it no longer. He drew himself up and cried out, "I, too, am a believer! I believe that Jesus is the Messiah, the Son of the Living God."

"Seize him," commanded the judge. "He will die with the fisherman." And so the two of them were marched off together to be beheaded.

"James, I beg of you, please find it in your heart to forgive me."

Forgiveness did not come easily, even to a saint, and especially to a Son of Thunder! It took a little thinking, and a little praying. He could not forget what the Lord had said, "If you do not forgive others when they sin against you, neither will your Heavenly Father forgive you your sins."

At length he spoke. "I do forgive you, with all my heart. Peace be with you."

The two men embraced, and together they went to their death.

Spanish tradition says that James' body was later transferred to Spain, and his shrine became a famous place of pilgrimage during the Middle Ages. He is the patron saint of Spain. In art he is often pictured with a sword, and sometimes with a pilgrim's staff, because he is also patron of pilgrims. His feast day is July 25.

St John

First Century

Ignatius sat spellbound in Church that Sunday morning. He watched, wide-eyed, as the guest preacher, an old man, walked in slowly and took his place near the front. Beneath a shock of white hair, and framed by a long, white beard, was the kindliest face he had ever seen. The presbyter welcomed the guest, and asked him to say whatever was on his heart.

"My little children, love one another," began St John, as was his custom. "Love is of God, and he who loves is born of God." On and on the words flowed out, and Ignatius knew that he would never be the same after that day. He wanted to know the man with the kind face better, and soon became a disciple, listening for hours to the saintly apostle's words.

"I recall," said John, "how the Lord came walking by Galilee where we were mending our father's nets. There was such a majesty and power in Him that we immediately knew that here was One whom we would have to follow, no matter what. Andrew and Peter had already joined him, and James and I were the next to follow. He had said He would make us 'fishers of men.'

"We traveled all around Galilee and Judea with Him. We even went through Samaria. When one of the villages wouldn't receive Jesus, James and I wanted to call down lightning from heaven to destroy it. But the Lord looked at us and said, 'You don't know what spirit you belong to! I did not come to destroy people's lives, but to save them!' I never forgot those words, nor the look of disappointment in His face when He said them to us."

Ignatius found that John was the youngest of the Twelve Apostles, and was the only one still alive. When Jesus was being crucified, John had been given the special commission of caring for His Mother, and she had lived in his own house for years and years. Now John was continuing his teaching and preaching to the young churches in Asia Minor, and instead of being known as a Son of Thunder, he was called The Apostle of Love. Many young men like Ignatius sat at his feet and learned firsthand from him what it was like to follow Jesus when He was on earth. And some of them, like Ignatius, went willingly to their deaths as martyrs for Christ.

Toward the end of John's long life, a new persecution broke out against Christians, and John was exiled to the island of Patmos. But he was not left alone there. He was given a vision of the majesty of God, and was shown that, although the powers of Rome and all the evil forces in the world were lined up against Jesus, God would triumph over them all. The kingdoms of this world will become the Kingdom of our Lord, and He will reign for ever and ever. You can read about those visions in the Apocalypse (Revelation), the last book in the Bible.

The closing prayer of John, the beloved disciple, and the closing prayer of the New Testament are the same: "Come, Lord Jesus."

One story about St John tells that some enemies of his succeeded in getting him condemned to death. The manner of death was to be a particularly gruesome one — being dipped into a cauldron of boiling oil. But John was miraculously delivered and came forth unharmed. After this, he was banished to Patmos. Still another legend tells of him being made to drink poison, and being unharmed by it. He is patron of theologians, writers, and all who work at the production of books. His feast is celebrated on December 27.

St Matthew

First Century

Tax collectors are never popular. In Jesus' time, they may have been even more unpopular than they are today, because the Jews were living under the iron fist of Rome. The tax collectors were employed by the Roman government, and they were told to collect as much as they wanted from the people. They only had to give a certain amount to the government, and could keep the rest for themselves. Because of their disloyalty to the national honor, along with their shady dealings, tax collectors were despised and belittled by their countrymen.

Matthew (also called Levi) was a tax collector. Day by day he would sit with his account books at a certain spot, waiting for people to come in and pay their taxes. If they did not pay — Rome would see to them!

One day, as Matthew sat in his usual place on the outskirts of Capernaum, Jesus walked by with His little band of followers. Matthew looked up. His eyes met those of the Lord. Then he heard Jesus say, "Matthew, follow me." That was all Matthew needed. Something in the face and eyes of Jesus said more than words, and Matthew got up, left his tax table and books, and followed Him. That night he gave a great party in his beautiful home to introduce Jesus to all his friends. There was a great crowd of social outcasts and "sinners" eating there with Jesus. The religious leaders judged Jesus in their hearts.

"Why do you eat and drink with tax collectors and sinners?" they asked. But Jesus said, "I didn't come to call the righteous, but sinners to repent."

After that, Matthew became one of the Twelve and followed Him everywhere. He saw Jesus' miracles and heard His teaching. Yes, life was so much better than when he had earned thousands of shekels collecting taxes, though now the little band usually had only enough for a day's needs.

Three years quickly sped by. Jesus once more came into Jerusalem for the Passover, against the advice of many. The disciples had eaten the Passover with Him in the upper room. Matthew had followed Him to the garden of Gethsemane afterwards. Jesus had seemed especially upset, and taking some of the other disciples, He had gone to another part of the garden to pray. Matthew didn't understand what was happening, but he knew what the clanking and heavy footsteps which followed meant: Roman soldiers! They had come to arrest his Master. Matthew fled, terrified. He lurked in the city's shadows that night, hardly daring to breath. Then he found some of the other disciples, and together they listened to the reports of what had happened. Jesus had been crucified. They had buried Him. Now it was all over. Matthew could hardly believe it; but then an even more incredible report reached them. Jesus was alive! Some of the women had seen Him. Their little band went back to the upper room and waited, bolting the doors for fear of the officials. Suddenly, there was Jesus, standing right among them. "Peace be with you," He said. Overjoyed, Matthew and the others experienced a whole new beginning. Then Jesus ascended to heaven after promising that the Holy Spirit would come and give them power and lead them into all truth.

Pentecost came, and with it, the promised Holy Spirit. The Church suddenly had three thousand new members! In a few years, churches had sprung up all over the country. Most of the new Christians had to learn about Jesus directly from those who had known Him. But there were so many wonderful things Jesus did, and someone needed to write down as much as could be remembered of what Jesus had done and said. So Matthew decided to write it down in order. He started with a careful account of Jesus' ancestry, because it was important that people know that He fulfilled the Scriptures in being a descendant of David, the promised Messiah. With the same care he had used in keeping his tax records, he wrote the famous Sermon on the Mount, the Beatitudes, and the Our Father, and many, many other wonderful stories, so that people who had not known Jesus when He lived on earth could know what He said and did. Matthew's account, which is named after him, had an honored place when the Church put together the New Testament. It is the very first book.

Tradition says that Matthew spent his last days in Ethiopia, where he had gone to carry the gospel to others. There he was martyred. The symbol of his gospel is a winged man, because he emphasized the human lineage of Christ. He is sometimes pictured writing his gospel, and sometimes with a money-bag or money-box, recalling his life before he became a disciple of Jesus. His feast day is September 21.

St Philip

First Century

"Nathanael, come and see the long-awaited Messiah that Moses and the prophets wrote about! It is Jesus of Nazareth." Philip's voice was brimming with excitement as he paused to catch his breath.

Nathanael looked at him quizzically. "Can any good thing come out of Nazareth?" he asked. Everyone knew that the Messiah would come from Bethlehem, for that, too, was in the prophecies of old. But Philip would not be put off. He waited insistently, until finally his brother, more to please him than to satisfy any curiosity of his own, agreed to go and see for himself.

As Nathanael walked with him, Philip thought of the message he had heard from John the Baptist. "Repent! The Kingdom of heaven is at hand," John had preached, from one side of the Jordan River to the other. Philip had heard him gladly.

Then one day, he saw two of his townsmen, Andrew and Peter, with a stranger. The Man turned and looked at Philip. "Follow me," He said. After just a few hours with this Teacher, Philip knew that Nathanael needed to know him, too.

When the two of them caught up to Jesus, Philip knew his hunch had been right about Nathanael. "You are the Son of God!" Nathanael exclaimed in awe.

But Jesus said to him, "You shall see greater things than this." Philip caught his breath. More than anything else in the world, he wanted to follow this Person and be a part of the "greater things."

Philip became one of the Twelve who went with Jesus up and down the country. He saw His healings, the miracles and signs which He did, and heard the words of the Beatitudes and the parables of the lost sheep and the runaway son who came back home. He loved Jesus and loved to be with Him. But sometimes Philip blurted out things that sounded like what we might say. And we can love him all the more for it. When the five thousand hungry people needed to be fed, Jesus had asked, "Where can we get bread for these people?" Philip said, "A whole year's wages is not enough that every one could have even a little." He had forgotten the power of God he had already seen.

Again, after the Last Supper, Jesus was talking with all His disciples about His death, preparing them for what would lie just ahead of them. Philip blurted out, "Lord, show us the Father, and it is enough for us." Jesus answered, "Philip, have I been with you so long, and yet you have not known me? Whoever has seen me has seen the Father. How do you say then, 'Show us the Father'?" Philip was still growing in his understanding of who Jesus was.

After the Resurrection and Pentecost, Philip spent the rest of his life carrying the Gospel to others. Early traditions say that he was martyred, although we do not know the exact whereabouts of his death. His feast is now celebrated with St James the Less (the Younger) on May 3.

St Thomas

First Century

Certainly in choosing His disciples, Jesus did not want or expect them all to think or act alike, and Thomas proves that. He is called Doubting Thomas, and his name has become a byword in our language for anyone who insists on proof before believing something.

The few glimpses we have of him in the Gospels indicate that he may have been a negative or pessimistic person by nature. Many people are like that, and tend to look on the dark side of things. But this did not mean that Thomas did not love the Lord. He was ready to die for Him, and when Jesus insisted on going to Jerusalem, against the advice and urging of Peter and others,

Thomas said simply, "Let us go, that we may die with Him."

For some reason, Thomas was not in the Upper Room on the first Easter, when the risen Jesus miraculously appeared to the others. In their great excitement they told him every detail of that meeting. But Thomas was a disappointed man. His hopes had been shattered on Good Friday, and he had forgotten all the times Jesus had reminded them that He would be crucified and would rise from the dead on the third day. Thomas did not want to be duped or have any false hopes raised. His was a practical, down-to-earth turn of mind. "No!" he said. "If I do not see the nail prints in His hand, and put my hand in His wounded side, I will not believe that it is really the Lord."

The next Sunday Thomas was present. Nothing would have been able to keep him from the meeting that day! And just as it had happened the previous Sunday, Jesus was suddenly in their midst. He first greeted them with the familiar, "Peace be with you." Then He looked straight at Thomas.

"Thomas," He said, "reach out your finger here. See my hands. Reach your hand here and put it into my side, and don't be unbelieving any longer, Thomas, but believe."

Thomas didn't wait to put his hand in the sacred wounds. He simply fell on his knees and said, "My Lord and my God!" He had all the proof he could ever require.

Then Jesus said a wonderful thing. "Because you have

seen me you have found faith. Happy are they who never saw me and yet have found faith." That can be all of us who find faith today.

After the great persecution which scattered the apostles, Thomas is said to have gone to India to take the Word of God there. When St Francis Xavier, the pioneer missionary to India in the 16th century, arrived in India to tell the people about Christ, he found an ancient Church in Malabar which called itself "Church of St Thomas." Their own tradition said that they were descendants of those who had first heard of Jesus from St Thomas, and had passed the faith on from generation to generation. He died a martyr's death, and his body was reverently entombed there.

His feast day is now celebrated on July 3.

St Jude

First Century

St Jude is also called Thaddeus or Lebbeus, in order, many believe, not to get him confused with Judas Iscariot.

He is not mentioned often in the Gospels, and the information we have about him is very scanty. Tradition says that after Pentecost, when the Apostles were scattered abroad by the persecution of Herod Agrippa I, Jude went with Simon to Persia (modern Iran). There he is said to have been martyred.

The symbol used in picturing Jude is usually the halberd or club, indicating how he was killed. He is also pictured holding a ship, along with St Simon, who holds a fish.

In recent times, Jude has been popularly known as the patron of hopeless cases. You can often see little classified ads in newspapers thanking him for answers to certain prayers, indicating that his intercessions are greatly appreciated by people facing dire need. It has been suggested that this patronage grew out of the fact that nobody invoked him for any cause, because his name is so similar to Judas Iscariot, who betrayed the Lord. He is therefore thought to have special regard to those who find themselves in desperate or hopeless situations.

His feast day, with St Simon, is October 28.

Early Saints

Hold fast the form of sound words which you heard
from me, in the faith and love which are in
Christ Jesus.
I Timothy 1:13

And in Antioch [of Syria], the disciples were
for the first time called Christians.
Acts 11:26

The Son of God goes forth to war,
A kingly crown to gain;
His blood-red banner streams afar:
Who follows in His train?
Who best can drink his cup of woe,
Triumphant over pain;
Who patient bears his cross below:
He follows in His train.
Reginald Heber, 1812

The Blessed Virgin Mary

First Century

"Hail, Mary, full of grace, the Lord is with thee!" Thus the angel Gabriel saluted the lowly maid of Nazareth, and promised that all generations henceforth would call her blessed.

And his word was true, for from the earliest days, the Church has called her Mother: Mother of our Lord Jesus Christ, *theotokos*, God-bearer, Mother of God.

It is good to remember, however, that in the Gospel records, her role is a modest, background role. Her "yes" to the angel's word initiated the earthly beginning of our salvation. She gave her willing cooperation with God's eternal plan to bring forth His Son, born of woman, born in David's line, of Adam's race, that He might redeem all who live under the curse of sin, disobedience and death. Her response was simply, "Be it unto me according to thy word."

She is the first among the saints. By her godly example, she was used in the earthly training and rearing of the Lord Himself. When told of the wonders that would come and the pain she would bear personally, "she kept these things and pondered them in her heart." In her outwardly simple life in Nazareth, she carried Heaven's best secret, and in her inner relationship to God, she is an example to all of us who would follow her Son.

Mary was a Jewish peasant-woman, the wife of a working man. Of her one writer says, "Her hands were scored with labor, her bare feet dusty, not with the perfumed powder of romance, but with the hard stinging grit of Nazareth" from walking the paths leading to the well, the olive grove, the synagogue. And then, after those years, her feet were dusty from other roads, but now with following her divine Son from afar as He began public life. From the rejoicings of the wedding-feast at Cana to the steep ascent of Calvary, they plodded, then stood, when the sword prophesied by Simeon pierced her very heart.

At two points in the Gospels, Mary appears with concern for her Son. One incident is the only childhood incident recorded in the Gospels. It is found in Luke 2:41-51.

Jesus' family went to Jerusalem every year at the feast of the Passover, and when He was twelve years old, they went up according to custom. After the feast was ended, as they were returning, the boy Jesus stayed behind in Jerusalem. His parents did not know it, but supposing Him to be in the company, they went a day's journey and sought Him among their kinsfolk and acquaintances; and when they did not find Him, they returned to Jerusalem, seeking Him. Three days passed before they found Him in the temple, sitting among the teachers, listening to them and asking them questions. Everyone who heard Him was amazed at His understanding and His answers. One can almost feel the relief His Mother must have felt when they finally located Him. "Son," she said, "why have you treated us so? Your father and I have been looking for you anxiously."

"How is it that you sought me? Did you not know that I must be in my Father's house?" was His reply.

Although His Mother did not understand the meaning of it all, she "kept all these things in her heart."

In the second incident, recorded by Matthew and Mark, Mary appeared with Jesus' brothers on the fringe of a crowd while Jesus was "still speaking to the people." They asked to talk with Him. Mark adds that when Jesus was told this, He looked around on those who sat about Him and said, "Here are my mother and my brothers! Whoever does the will of God is my brother and sister and mother" (Mark 3:31ff). In this case, the Lord used the concern and visit of His blessed Mother to show the family relationship which exists among all His people, and the tender care He has for us all, calling us by such intimate terms.

Mary's attitude toward her Son is clearly shown at the Wedding Feast at Cana. When the wine had run out, she went to Him and told Him about the need. Then she spoke to the servants: "Do whatever He tells you," and left it at that. We know that Jesus instructed them to fill the great wine jars with water, and then to draw some out and carry it to the steward, and that the first public miracle of His ministry occurred. This great sign is related in John 2. The words of Mary linger on in the heart of the Church: "Do whatever He tells you."

In the many apparitions under many different names and circumstances, Mary's message has always been the same: "Do what He tells you." She has pointed us to her beloved Son, who is the Savior of the world. As we have been incorporated in Him through baptism, we have been privileged to call her not only His Mother, but ours as well.

At the Crucifixion of our Lord, His Mother stood by the tomb, and from the Cross, He said to the beloved disciple, John, "Behold thy Mother." To Mary He said, "Behold thy son." From that day, she made her home with John. Christian devotion has often stood with her as she witnessed the torture and death of Her Beloved, and many of the great hymns and pictures have centered around this scene. One of the most famous says,

> Who, on Christ's dear Mother gazing,
> Pierced by anguish so amazing,
> Born of woman, would not weep?
> Who, on Christ's dear Mother thinking,
> Such a cup of sorrow drinking,
> Would not share her sorrows deep?

Her greatest solemnity of the year is August 15, the Feast of the Assumption, celebrating her reception into the glory of heaven after her life of suffering and faithfulness on earth. Other feasts honoring her are as follows: Immaculate Conception, December 8; Annunciation, March 25; Visitation to Elizabeth, May 31, Birthday of the Virgin, September 8, Solemnity of the Mother of God, January 1 (formerly called Circumcision), and February 2, Feast of the Presentation in the Temple (formerly called Purification). In addition there are memorials of her apparitions at various times and places, and the month of May has been devoted to her special honor.

Here is a prayer which is used on one of her feast days: "Eternal Father, we honor the holiness and glory of the Virgin Mary. May her prayers bring us the fullness of Your life and love. We ask this through our Lord Jesus Christ, Your Son, who lives and reigns with You and the Holy Spirit, one God, for ever and ever. Amen."

St Joseph

First Century

The choice of Joseph to be the husband of Mary and the foster-father (sometimes called "legal father") of our Lord Jesus Christ says a great deal about the man himself. The Church therefore honors him, giving him a place second only to the Virgin herself in the roll call of the saints.

Joseph was a descendant of King David, perhaps originally from Bethlehem of Judea. But he was a carpenter, which means that he was a poor man, and when we first learn of him in the New Testament, he lived in Nazareth of Galilee. How old he was when he became engaged to Mary we do not know, but early tradition says that he was not a young man. He was, however, strong and vigorous enough to support his family and to protect Mary and the infant Jesus as they fled to Egypt. The nobility of Joseph's character is seen in the way he handled the strange and baffling events leading up to the birth of Jesus. He was espoused to Mary — which meant that there was a legal, binding agreement to marry her. Learning that she was to have a child, he was upset and thought he would divorce her secretly to avoid the unfavorable publicity. As he turned these things over in his mind, however, he dreamed a dream so brilliant and real that he never forgot it. An angel stood by him with a message from God: "Don't be afraid to take Mary as your wife. Her child was conceived by the Holy Spirit. She shall bear a Son and you shall call Him Jesus, for He shall save His people from their sins." Joseph awoke with joy in his heart and a new sense of purpose. From now on, he would be a protector and provider for Mary and this Child.

We see him only briefly again in Matthew 13:55 and Luke 4:22, when people asked in astonishment about Jesus, "Is not this the carpenter's son?"

In his everyday work, Joseph shows us that we can serve God; this included being the kind of father any man ought to be. St Bernardine of Siena wrote about him, "Whenever divine favor chooses someone to accept a lofty vocation, God adorns the person chosen with all the gifts of the Spirit needed to fulfill the task at hand. This is especially true in the case of St Joseph." As the foster-father of our Lord, he carried out this vocation with complete fidelity until at last God called him, saying: "Good and faithful servant, enter into the joy of your Lord."

Joseph also had the special vocation of caring for Mary as well as our Lord Jesus. He not only showed her all the consideration and respect a man owes his wife, but also honored her beyond the way women were regarded in his time. For instance, when he and Mary found the child Jesus in the temple, it is Joseph who assumes a background role, while Mary speaks to her Son. When the wise men visited the infant Jesus, Joseph is so much in the background that he is not mentioned at all in the account. Mary is permitted to have the pre-eminent place. "And going into the house they saw the child with Mary his mother . . . ." (Matt. 2:11)

Presumably, Joseph died before Jesus began His earthly ministry. Tradition confirms this, and he does not appear again in the Gospel records. When Jesus died on the cross, He gave the care of His mother to one of His disciples.

Joseph was declared Patron of the Universal Church by Pius IX. He is also patron of fathers of families, of manual workers, of carpenters, and of all who desire a good death. Many churches and hospitals bear his name, as well as a great many Christians. He is usually pictured with the Child Jesus, or as part of the Holy Family. Two feasts are dedicated to his honor: March 19, St Joseph the Husband of Mary, and May 1, St Joseph the Worker.

St Stephen

First Century

When the Church was very young, people shared all their goods in common, and ate together daily, in addition to worshipping together. St Luke describes this in the Acts of the Apostles.

Even then, however, Christians did not always get along perfectly with one another. The Hellenists were jealous of the Hebrew Christians, and complained "because their widows were neglected in the daily distribution." The Hellenists were people who came from other countries, and the Hebrews were those who were native to Jerusalem. The apostles were troubled by this situation, and in order to prevent serious divisions they told the Church, "Choose seven men of good repute, full of the Spirit and of wisdom." These they put them in charge of organizing and serving the food and caring for the needs of the various groups in the Church. When they were chosen, Stephen's name headed the list.

Almost immediately Stephen's role in the church grew in importance and visibility. "Full of grace and power, he did great wonders and signs among the people." This provoked the enemies of the Church to single him out and try to get rid of him, so they accused him of speaking blasphemous words against Moses and God. This stirred up the people. Led by the scribes and elders they caught Stephen and dragged him before the Sanhedrin. The false witnesses from his enemies were there. They repeated the accusations, "We heard this man say that Jesus of Nazareth will change the customs which Moses delivered to us and will destroy this place." The members of the Council looked steadfastly on him, and as he began his defense, they saw that his face shone like that of an angel.

Stephen began by recounting God's dealings with the Jews from the time of Abraham; he reminded them of how many of the prophets their fathers had rejected. "Moreover," he said, "they killed those who told beforehand the coming of the Just One, the One you have now betrayed and murdered."

Incensed at his words, the crowd began to shout and rail, and gnash their teeth at him. But Stephen was given a vision at that very moment. "Behold I see the heavens opened, and the Son of man standing at the right hand of God," he said.

At that they stopped up their ears, rushed upon him, dragged him outside the city and stoned him. And as they were stoning him, Stephen prayed, "Lord, do not hold this sin against them," words which remind us of what the Lord Himself prayed when He was being crucified.

St Fulgentius said of him, "The love that brought Christ from heaven to earth raised Stephen from earth to heaven; shown first in the King, it later shone forth in His soldier. His love of God kept him from yielding to the ferocious mob; his love for his neighbor inspired him to pray for those who were stoning him. Love inspired him to reprove those who erred, to make them amend; love led him to pray for those who stoned him, to save them from punishment."

His feast has been celebrated at the latest since the fourth century in both East and West. He is patron of deacons and of many ancient churches including several French cathedrals. He is usually depicted with a stone, and sometimes with a palm as a symbol of his victorious martyrdom. His feast is celebrated on December 26.

St Joseph of Arimathea

First Century

Joseph was an important man from the town of Arimathea. It was the custom in those days to identify people by the name of their father (Simon bar Jonah, which meant Simon, son of John) or by the name of their home town, as in the case of Joseph of Arimathea. Even our Lord Himself was called "Jesus of Nazareth," when He was crucified. Arimathea was a tiny village in the northwest corner of the central hill country of Judea. Very little is known about Joseph of Arimathea, except that he was a member of the Jewish Council or Sanhedrin, which means that he was a man whose religious sincerity earned him the high regard of his fellowmen. St Matthew tells us that he was rich, and Mark adds that he was "looking for the kingdom of God."

The Gospels tell us that Joseph was a disciple of Jesus. John adds, "But secretly, for fear of the Jews." During Jesus' earthly ministry, Joseph was drawn to His message, but it seems he was afraid of losing his reputation. When the Lord was crucified, however, he was moved with compassion. With Nicodemus, another ruler of the Jews who was also a secret disciple, he obtained the body of Jesus for burial. Lovingly they anointed the Body with spices Nicodemus had brought and laid Him in Joseph's own tomb, newly hewn out of the rocks. There they wrapped Him in a linen shroud which Joseph had purchased for his own burial. (This burial cloth is believed to be the same Holy Shroud now preserved in Turin, Italy, and venerated as one of the most holy relics of Christendom.)

By risking everything to care in this way for our Lord, Joseph became instrumental in the fulfillment of an Old Testament prophecy about Jesus: "They made his grave . . . with a rich man in his death." (Isaiah 53:9)

His name is associated with an intriguing legend concerning the foundation of the first Christian community at Glastonbury, England. There a hawthorn, called the Holy Thorn, blossoms out of season at Christmas time, and was reputed to have sprung from the staff of Joseph of Arimathea. We do not know if the legend is true, but it still evokes a sense of wonder and appreciation for those who did plant the faith in the far-distant reaches of the

Roman empire, even in the first century. His feast is celebrated in the East on July 31, and was formerly observed in the West on March 17.

St Mark

First Century

Our knowledge of St Mark is sketchy, which makes it all the more challenging to find mention of him in different parts of the New Testament. Since his name appears at the beginning of the second Gospel, it is not surprising that we find him somewhere in the story. An interesting incident told only by him in connection with the last night of our Lord's earthly life is found in Mark 14:51: "And a young man followed him, [i.e., Jesus] with nothing but a linen cloth about his body; and they seized him, but he left the linen cloth and ran away naked." Since that does not seem to have any particular relationship to the story, it has been conjectured that the young man was none other than Mark, the writer, who remembered it painfully and vividly when he wrote many years later.

Mark's mother's home was a meeting place for the apostles. Mark must have known Jesus then, and later on, he joined his older cousin Barnabas along with Paul to go with them on their first missionary journey. Things were going fine, and many people were being converted through the preaching of Paul and Barnabas, but at some point, Mark decided to leave the team. Paul must have been furious with him.

The tour was completed without Mark, and Paul and Barnabas then returned to Antioch, where they spent some time, preaching the Word of God and teaching the people. They began to feel it was time to make a second missionary trip, and Barnabas suggested that they take Mark with them again. Paul was adamant, and their disagreement was so deep that they decided to separate and go in two different teams. Barnabas left with Mark, and Paul chose Silas to accompany him. After that, we hear no more of Mark until we read some of St Paul's letters. In one, he tells the Church to receive Mark if he should come to them. In another, he asks that Mark come to him in Rome. "Take Mark and bring him with you," the aged apostle writes to Timothy, "for he is profitable to me in the ministry." So we know there was reconciliation and healing of the broken relationship between Paul and Mark.

Tradition carries us further than the New Testament, and tells us that Mark went on to found the Church of Alexandria and that he was its first Bishop. At that time, Alexandria was one of the most important cities of the empire, and the Bishop of Alexandria would have great power and influence in the future.

Tradition also tells us that Mark was a disciple of St Peter, and in I Peter 5:13 he is called "my son Mark." This means that the primary source of Mark's Gospel is none other than St Peter himself. St Mark's symbol is the lion, and his feast is celebrated on April 25.

St Luke

First Century

St Luke's is the third of the four Gospels. He is the only evangelist who was a Gentile. We know very little about his life, except that he was a companion of St Paul on his third missionary journey, and that he remained with him after Paul was taken to Rome as a prisoner. From Rome Paul wrote, with some discouragement, that others had left him. "Only Luke is with me," he says. The beloved physician (Luke was a medical man) was staying with him to the end.

It is probable that the Gospel bearing his name was not written until after Paul's death, since we have no mention of it in any of the apostle's letters. The Gospel is unique in several ways. For instance, his is the only Gospel which tells us the story of the angel's announcement to the Blessed Virgin Mary that she would bear a Son. He alone records the immortal *Magnificat* which Mary sang when she visited her cousin Elizabeth. It is he who tells us of John the Baptist's miraculous birth, of Simeon in the temple who sang *Nunc dimittis*. He relates six miracles and eighteen parables which are not included in any of the other three Gospels, including the parable of the Good Samaritan and the parable of the Prodigal Son. It has been noted that in his Gospel he pays special attention to the role of women and is very sensitive to the importance they play in the story of our salvation.

In addition to the Gospel, Luke wrote the Acts of the Apostles, recording the wonderful miracle which occurred on Pentecost, "the Birthday of the Church," and the miracles which attended the earliest days of the infant community. He recorded the story of St Stephen, the first martyr and the beheading of James, the leader of the Jerusalem Church, and tells how the Church handled an important controversy by holding a Council at Jerusalem, attended by the apostles themselves. (Acts 15).

The book of Acts shifts over to focus mainly on the apostle Paul following his conversion, and in the 20th chapter, the story suddenly changes from "he" to "we." Obviously Luke has included himself in these passages, such as "we were gathered together to break bread," "when we had finished the voyage," and so on. Not only was Luke reporting firsthand experiences, but there is good evidence that he heard and wrote down many other stories straight from the Apostles. His special information concerning the Blessed Virgin Mary indicates that he must have had close contact with her and those around her.

He was a careful researcher, and in the prologue of his Gospel says, "It seemed good to me also, having followed all things accurately for some time past, to write an orderly account for you . . . that you may know the truth concerning the things of which you have been informed."

He is patron of physicians and surgeons, and, because early tradition also told of his work as a painter, he is patron of artists, too. He is believed to have lived to a ripe old age and to have been unmarried. His feast, celebrated from very early times, takes place on October 18.

St Polycarp

c. 69-c. 155

What we can learn about St Polycarp makes us wish that we could learn much more. But the information and records of his life are enough to give us the picture of one of the greatest and most important saints from the earliest days of Christianity. About his early life we know very little. He was born about the year 69, was taught by the apostles and lived in close fellowship with many who had seen Christ. Himself a disciple of St John the Evangelist, he became the teacher of others who would lead the church after him, including Irenaeus and Papias. Writing a friend who had begun to embrace false teaching and teach false doctrine many years later, Irenaeus said:

"These things were not taught you by the bishops who preceded us. I could tell you the place where the blessed Polycarp sat when he discoursed, and describe his goings out and his comings in, his manner of life and his personal appearance, and the sermons which he delivered to the people, how he used to speak of his intercourse with John and with the rest of those who had seen the Lord, and how he would relate their words. And everything that he had heard from them about the Lord, about His miracles and about His teaching, Polycarp used to tell us as one who had received it from those who had seen the Word of Life with their own eyes, and all this in perfect harmony with the Scriptures. To these things I used to listen at the time, through the mercy of God vouchsafed to me, noting them down, not on paper but in my heart, and constantly by the grace of God I brood over my accurate recollections."

Polycarp, then, is a very important link between the apostles and those who followed them. As such, he was a strong and vigorous upholder of the true faith. One of the earliest heretics, Marcion, taught a combination of the New Testament and his own ideas, rejecting the Old Testament entirely. He used his wealth and brilliance to start communities of followers all over the Roman empire. His teaching caused much pain and confusion in the infant Church, and Polycarp stoutly opposed it. While on a visit to Rome, Polycarp accidentally met Marcion in the street. Marcion was offended that Polycarp did not seem to notice him at all.

"Do you not know me?" he asked indignantly.

"Yes, I know you," said Polycarp. "I know you, the first-born of Satan!"

Polycarp lived a long and useful life as bishop of Smyrna, but was not to be spared the fate which so many Christians of that time met: martyrdom. A persecution against the Church broke out in greater-than-usual fury, and a young Christian, Germanicus, was killed at a pagan festival. His bravery in the face of death so incited the crowd, that they demanded more blood.

"Away with the atheists," they shouted, referring to the Christians, who refused to worship the Roman gods. "Bring Polycarp." So soldiers were dispatched to bring him. When they found him, he neither invited nor resisted arrest. Instead, he urged them to eat a meal while he prepared himself by prayer for what was to come.

Taken to the place where the crowds waited, Polycarp was led before the proconsul, who urged him to call Caesar "Lord," and thus save himself. "Swear by Caesar, and I will discharge you!" he said. "Revile Christ!"

"For eighty-six years I have been His servant and He has never done me wrong. How can I blaspheme my King, who has saved me? . . . I am a Christian, and if you wish to study the Christian teaching, choose a day, and you will hear it."

When the proconsul urged him to persuade the people, the saint refused, saying that rage had made them incapable of hearing him.

The proconsul wanted out of the tight spot. He knew that Polycarp was a holy man, yet he feared the crowd. "I have wild beasts," he threatened.

"Call for them," replied Polycarp. "We are resolved not to change from good to evil. It is only right to pass from evil to good."

Finally the sentence was pronounced: death by fire. At Polycarp's request, instead of being lashed to a stake, he merely had his hands tied behind his back. He met the ordeal with a look of radiance and joy on his face. And it was said by some who observed it that the flames encircled the body of the martyr, forming themselves like the sails of a ship swelled with the wind. Since then, he has often been pictured with the flames surrounding him like a halo.

After his death, his body was burned to ashes since some feared that so holy a man might be worshipped. But the disciples gathered up his ashes and buried them reverently and decently, awaiting the sure hope of the resurrection of the body and the life of the world to come.

His death took place at 2 o'clock in the afternoon on February 23. The exact year is not known, but believed to have been 155 or 166. His feast is celebrated on the anniversary of his death, February 23.

We give thanks to God always for you all,
constantly mentioning you in our prayers,
remembering before our God and Father your work
of faith and labor of love and steadfastness of hope
in our Lord Jesus Christ.
I Thessalonians 1:2, 3

Just Folks

Consider your call, brethren; not many of you
were wise according to worldly standards, not many
were powerful, not many were of noble birth;
but God chose what is foolish in the world to shame
the wise, God chose what is weak in the world to
shame the strong, God chose what is low and
despised in the world, even things that are not,
to bring to nothing things that are, so that
no human being might boast in the presence of God.
I Corinthians 1:26-29

He has scattered the proud in the imagination
of their hearts, he has put down the mighty
from their thrones, and exalted those of low degree.
The Magnificat: Luke 1:51, 52

Disposer Supreme and judge of the earth
Who choosest for Thine the weak and the poor
To frail earthen vessels and things of no worth
Entrusting thy riches which ever endure.
I. Williams, from the Latin

St Martha

First Century

Martha lived with her sister Mary and her brother Lazarus in the little village of Bethany, about two miles from Jerusalem. They were special friends of Jesus, and He used to visit them when He was in the area. St John's Gospel says, "Jesus loved Martha and her sister Mary and Lazarus."

Martha was probably the oldest of the three and seems to have been responsible for running the household. She was a good hostess, and loved to take care of the needs of our blessed Lord when He was at their home. Sometimes He would teach the people who had gathered, while Martha would be busy getting food ready and trying to be a good hostess. On one occasion, however, she became very upset with her sister Mary, who stayed in the room where Jesus was talking, while Martha continued to get the food ready. Nothing was too good for Jesus, and Martha may have been afraid that things were not getting done well enough or fast enough, because she went in and blurted out, "Lord, do you not care that my sister has left me to serve alone? Tell her then to help me." But the Lord answered, "Martha, Martha, you are anxious and troubled about many things; one thing is needful. Mary has chosen the good portion, which shall not be taken away from her."

Then a great sadness came into this home that Jesus loved. Lazarus, Martha's brother, became very sick, and Martha sent word as quickly as possible to Jesus. She knew that if He came, her brother could be healed. But Jesus did not come at once. And during the delay, Lazarus died. When the Lord finally did arrive in Bethany, she left immediately and went out to meet Him.

"Lord," she said, "if you had been here, my brother would not have died. Even now I know that whatever you ask from God, God will give to you."

Jesus intended that Martha should learn a great lesson. "Your brother will rise again," He said.

Not knowing what He meant, she went on, "I know that he will rise again in the resurrection at the last day."

But Jesus continued, "I am the resurrection and I am life. If a man believes in me, even though he die, he shall come to live; and no one who is alive and has faith will ever die. Do you believe this?"

"Lord, I do," said Martha. "I now believe that You are Christ, the Son of God who was to come into the world."

Jesus then made His way to the tomb where His friend was buried. "Lazarus, come forth!" He shouted.

Suddenly Lazarus stood at the door of the tomb, still wrapped in his burial clothes. "Unbind him," said Jesus.

Mary and Martha and all His friends were astonished beyond words. And so St Martha learned that those who believe in Jesus do not need to fear death. Lazarus was brought out of the tomb alive, and then the whole family gave a great feast in Jesus' honor. Guess who served the food to Jesus and the guests? You're right. Martha!

We celebrate St Martha's feast on July 29.

St Mary Magdalene

First Century

The Gospel tells us about a woman, a great sinner who came into a feast given for Jesus in the home of Simon the Pharisee. In those days people could come into a house where a feast was going on, even if they were not invited. There are several instances of this in the Bible. This woman, though, wanted to see Jesus, because He had done something very wonderful for her. He had forgiven her sins. So when she came into the feast, she began to wash his feet with her tears, and dry them with her hair. Then she kissed His feet and anointed them with expensive ointment. This was a special act of love, because feet got very dry and rough walking in the dirt roads with nothing but open sandals.

Those who watched were indignant that a woman like this should do such a thing, and they said to one another, "Look! If this Jesus were really a prophet, He would know what kind of woman this is who is touching Him, for she is a sinner."

Jesus, knowing what they were saying, said to His host, "Simon, you did not wash my feet when I came in, but this woman has washed them with her tears. You gave me no kiss, but she has kissed my feet; you did not anoint my head with oil, but she has anointed my feet with ointment. I tell you, her sins, which are many, are forgiven, for she loved much; but he who is forgiven little, loves little."

St Luke also tells us that Jesus cast "seven devils" out of Mary Magdalene. She joined the group of women who helped Jesus in His ministry and became a faithful follower of our Lord. The night before His arrest, she again took ointment, and anointed both His head and His feet. Again people found fault, but Jesus said, "Let her alone! She has prepared my body for burial, and wherever the Gospel is preached in all the world, this story will be told about her."

Mary stood with the blessed Mother of our Lord and several others, watching as He was crucified. With some other women, she hurried to His tomb on that first Easter morning. They were carrying spices to anoint Him because they had not been able to finish preparing His body for burial on Friday before the Sabbath began at sunset. But the tomb was empty! Some of them ran back to tell the other disciples, but Mary stood weeping outside, saying, "They have taken away the Lord and I do not know where they have laid Him."

A Stranger appeared and asked, "Why are you weeping?"

Thinking he was the gardener, she answered through her tears, "Sir, if you have carried Him away, please tell me where He is, and I will take Him away."

Jesus said, "Mary!"

Immediately she recognized who He was and cried, "Rabboni! Master!" Thus she was allowed to be the first person to see the risen Lord.

Mary Magdalene has always been a favorite saint of many, because we can see how a person who has many problems, who has done many things wrong, can change and become holy. This happened because St Mary Magdalene was grateful for all that the Lord had done for her. Her feast day is July 22.

Sts Priscilla and Aquila

First Century

In the days of the Apostles, every Jewish rabbi had a trade. St Paul, for instance, was a tent-maker. Aquila was a Jewish rabbi, and like St Paul, was a tent-maker. His wife was named Prisca (or Priscilla). We do not know when Aquila and Priscilla became Christians. It may have been when they first heard St Paul preach, or it may have been before they met him. At any rate, he found them in Corinth on his missionary journey, and decided to live with them during his stay there. They were hospitable people, very devoted to the Lord and they became Paul's co-workers. Whenever they are mentioned in the New Testament, they are about the Lord's business.

They went on with Paul when he went to Ephesus, and stayed there when he continued his missionary travels. In Ephesus they met another Jewish teacher, Apollos of Alexandria. Alexandria was a great center of learning, and Apollos was well-grounded in the Holy Scriptures. He had not been thoroughly instructed in the Christian faith, however, so Aquila and Priscilla became his teachers, teaching him more about Jesus, the promised Messiah, His crucifixion and resurrection, and about God's plan to take the Good News to the whole world.

They returned to Rome later on, possibly because their trade required that they go where they could make a living. When St Paul wrote the Letter to the Romans, he remembered his old friends, and said, "Salute Prisca and Aquila, and the church which is in their house." Christians met in homes wherever they lived, since there were no church buildings as yet. St Paul also remembered how much help Priscilla and Aquila had been to him in his missionary work. He called them "My helpers in Christ Jesus, who have laid down their own necks for my life."

Priscilla and Aquila remind us that all of us can serve God, whatever our profession or occupation may be. If we are faithful to do all we can, the best we can, we will be serving God. They remind us of a little verse about saints which says,

JUST FOLKS

They lived not only in ages past,
There are hundreds of thousands still
The world is bright with joyous saints
Who love to do Jesus' will:
You can meet them in school, or in lanes, or at sea
In church, or in trains, or in shops, or at tea,
For the saints of God are just folk like me,
And I mean to be one too.

(L. Scott, 1929)

Early tradition says that they died in Asia Minor. St Priscilla's obvious role in teaching is an early example of the Church's high regard for women, and of St Paul's own recognition and appreciation of her spiritual gifts and wisdom. Their feast day is July 8.

St Benezet

d. 1184

Nowadays we think very little about the bridges which cross little streams and big rivers. But such was not always the case. Bridges were very special building projects, and often cost the lives of some of the men who built them, especially if they crossed a stream which was wide, rapid and deep. The story of Benezet is the story of a remarkable young man and his bridge.

Benezet was a peasant boy who lived in the twelfth century. We do not know just when he was born, because his parents were poor peasants. His father died when he was very young, and as a boy, Benezet had the job of looking after his mother's small flock of sheep. They lived in France, near one of France's great rivers, the Rhône, which has its source in the great Rhône Glacier in the Swiss Alps, includes the 45 mile length of Lake Geneva, and continues 500 miles to the Mediterranean Sea. It is noted for its rapid flow, and for its rise during the winter rains and the summer melting of the Swiss snows.

As Benezet watched his flocks near the shores of Lake Geneva, he could see how hard it was for travelers to make their way from one side of the Rhône to the other. He saw, and remembered.

One day, a fearsome storm arose. The sun was obscured in the sky, and sudden cold seized the air. Benezet heard a voice like thunder, and at first he thought his fear was causing his imagination to work overtime. But the voice came again, louder, telling him to go to Avignon, and build a bridge over the Rhône.

Benezet was shocked. Why would God ask him, an untrained shepherd, to do such a work of mercy — such an impossible task as building a bridge over the dangerous Rhône? How could it be done? Doubtless he had heard the story of what happened to Moses, when Moses saw a bush burning without being consumed, and heard a voice telling him to go back to Egypt to deliver the people of Israel from Egyptian slavery. "Who am I to go?" Moses had asked. And God had answered, "Certainly I will be with you!"

But Benezet must have received the assurance that God would go with him, for soon afterward he took leave of his mother, his sheep, and his home, and set out for

Avignon, many miles down the river. When he arrived, he found the Bishop first and told him his story.

The Bishop looked at him with a kindly but questioning glance. He had known other people who claimed special visions and voices, and sometimes they turned out to be delusions, but he could not so easily put off this poor shepherd. Benezet had come a long way; he trusted God would not fail him now, so he earnestly prayed that God would show the Bishop. Several miracles occurred in answer to Benezet's prayers, which convinced the Bishop to back his unusual project. So with the blessing of the Church, Benezet began. The year was 1177.

"Little Benezet," as he was called, set to work with such determination and faith that word began to spread. "A shepherd has been given a mission from God to build a bridge across the Rhône." Others began to join him, contributing money for stones and working along with him. Soon they had laid graceful arches across the swift stream. With no training or engineering experience whatever, Benezet guided the builders as stone by stone, and arch by arch the bridge grew.

For seven years Benezet worked on his bridge. Miracle after miracle occurred, convincing even the most skeptical that God had truly sent him to do this.

When Benezet died in 1184, the major difficulties had been overcome, and the completion of the bridge was assured. It took four more years to complete, and when it was done, the city fathers decided that a little chapel on the bridge should be built as a resting place for Benezet's body. There his body remained until, in 1669 a great flood washed away part of the bridge, including the chapel. The coffin containing Benezet's body was recovered and when it was opened, his body was found to be undecayed after 500 years. Recognizing this as a sign of his special sanctity, the city placed Benezet's body in a nearby church and he was declared to be one of the patron saints of the Avignon.

He is affectionately remembered as "Little Benezet, the Bridge Builder," and the Order of Bridge Brothers regards him as their founder. His Feast Day is April 14.

St Zita

c. 1218-1278

"It is very hard to send her away when she is so young," said the young mother.

"Yes, my dear. But, much as we love her, I cannot earn enough to feed her. At Lucca, the Fatinellis have food enough and to spare; she'll have a position that may last her the rest of her life. And after all it's only eight miles away. So it's all for the best."

Zita was only twelve years old, but she loved God and wanted to be obedient. Her new master, Pagano di Fatinelli had a wool and silk weaving business and he needed another servant for his busy household. Although he had a bad temper, at heart he was a good man.

JUST FOLKS

The year was 1230 when Zita went off, determined to do her very best. She made up her mind to get up every night and pray, and early every morning she went to Mass. But these were not the only things she did to please God. The food she was given to eat was so much better than she was used to at home, she would often give it to others who were poorer than she. Sometimes she would give up her bed to beggars who came by, while she slept on the bare ground for the night.

Her willingness to work hard and long made the other servants look lazy by comparison, and they resented it. Their bad language and their gossip did not please her, and this made them dislike her even more. Her patience and good heart attitude finally won out, however, so that even those who had resented her most came to love and appreciate her. The Fatinellis began to realize what a good servant she was. One day Señora Fatinelli called her into her study.

"Zita, the Señor and I have been talking about you. We have watched you grow since you came to work for us. You're not only taller, but you're more mature as well. We're very pleased with the fine job you're doing, so we think it's time to increase your responsibilities. Do you think you would like to begin taking care of our children?"

"Oh, I love the children, and I would enjoy taking care of them," Zita replied. "Only, if you please, I would like to talk to them about God."

"Of course, Zita," said her mistress. "We know you love the Church and love to go to Mass. You can take them with you from time to time if you like."

And so Zita started caring for the children. In time, she became the head housekeeper as well, and in that capacity she had many responsibilities, including supervision of the food supplies and distribution of gifts to the poor who came to the door begging.

One day Pagano decided to check the supply of beans, because he had a chance to sell some of them at a good price. Zita's heart sank when she heard his plans, because she had given a large amount of their beans to the beggars, and she knew the supply was almost gone.

"Oh, mistress!" she cried, running to Señora Fatinelli, "what shall we do? The master will be very angry when he learns how many of the beans I've given away!"

"Say nothing until we've seen what will happen," said the Señora.

Together they went to the place where the beans were stored, and to their amazement, there were more beans than Zita had given away. The containers were overflowing. God had made up for what had been given away!

One bitterly cold Christmas Eve, no one wanted to leave the warm house to attend Mass. No one, that is, except Zita.

"Well," said Pagano, "if you must go, then I will give you my fur coat to wear so you won't freeze to death. But for heaven's sake, don't lose it on the way!"

Arriving at the church, Zita saw a poor man at the entrance clad only in rags, shivering from the cold. What could she do? Quickly she took off the beautiful warm coat and put it over his shoulders, telling him he could wear it until she came out.

Zita left the Christmas Mass filled with deep peace and joy. But where was the beggar? She could not find him anywhere.

"How can I face my master? He was so kind as to let me have his coat, and now I've given it away!"

Pagano was furious when she came into the house and told him what had happened.

"I might have suspected it!" he shouted. "You're always giving things away!"

It looked as though Christmas might be spoiled by the incident, but a little while later, as they sat down to dinner, there was a knock at the door.

"I'll go," said Pagano gruffly. "Probably more beggars wanting handouts from Zita." A moment later, he returned, with a shamefaced look, holding the missing coat.

"He never spoke a word," he said. "Just turned and disappeared into the darkness."

The people of the town called the church door where Zita met the stranger, "Il porta del angelo: The Angel Door."

Her hard and faithful work, her saintly attitude, and her openheartedness towards the poor won Zita a warm place in the hearts, not only of the family she served as a servant for forty-eight years, but of the townsfolk as well. In her later years, as her duties in the house grew lighter, she spent much time visiting the poor, the sick, and those in prison. She had learned that it is indeed more blessed to give than to receive, and, like her Lord, lived "not to be served, but to serve." She said, "Work-shy piety in people of our position is sham piety." And she lived what she believed.

She died in 1272, and was buried in the Church of Frediano in Lucca, which she had so often attended. It is no wonder that she has been named Patron of Domestic Workers. She was often invoked for aid by housewives and servants, especially when they needed to find their keys or were in danger from crossing streams. Her name was added to the Roman Martyrology in 1748 by Pope Benedict XIV, and her feast day is April 27.

St Nicholas von Flue

(Brother Klaus)

1417-1487

If you were a boy or girl living in Switzerland, you would know all about the story of Brother Klaus. There he is even more famous and beloved than the fabled William Tell.

Klaus was born in 1417. His family owned a farm in the Alps, and his mother, especially, was a deeply spiritual person. She belonged to a group called *The Friends of God*, a fellowship of people trying to live a very obedient Christian life. Even as a child, Nicholas showed signs that he took his faith seriously and wanted to follow Christ.

After serving in the army, Nicholas married, and he and his wife Dorothea had ten children. One of his sons later related how after they had all gone to bed, his father would get up again, and could be heard praying in his room. Sometimes he would go to the old Church in the night, or would visit some other holy place.

One day Nicholas told his family that God was calling him to a special work of prayer. Since his wife was a devout Christian, she did not object when he went to dwell alone as a hermit. He put on a special grey-brown robe, took his staff and started out barefooted to find a place to stay. A kind peasant gave him shelter and persuaded him not to leave Switzerland to pursue his vocation. Being convinced that this was the right advice, Nicholas started back home. That night, under a tree, he suffered such pains in his stomach that he thought he was going to die. From then on, he lost all desire for food or drink, and actually became unable to eat. For the rest of his life he lived on the Host he received at daily Mass. Eventually he was persuaded to go to the little village of Ranft, in the same valley where he had been staying. The people of Ranft built him a little cell with a chapel attached to it near the center of the valley. There he lived for 19 years — praying from midnight till noon, and spending the afternoon giving counsel to people who came looking for help.

Not only individuals sought his advice, however, but whole towns and governmental bodies believed that he had wisdom from God that would help them solve difficult questions. One time, for instance, the authorities of two Swiss Cantons could not agree on a matter. Soon everyone was involved in the argument, and a civil war nearly broke out. Representatives of the two Cantons went to Brother Klaus and laid the problem before him. His answer was so wise that it pleased everyone and the matter was settled at once without any fighting.

He lived to be 70 years old. The little room in which he dwelt as a hermit still exists in Switzerland. When news of his death came, all Switzerland honored him both as a patriot and a saint.

He was honored there for many years, but in 1917, the whole country celebrated the 500th anniversary of his birth. Brother Klaus was canonized in 1947, and his Feast Day is March 23.

St Rose of Lima

1586-1617

The first saint from the Americas to be canonized was born in 1586 in Lima, Peru, of Spanish parents. She was christened Isabel de Flores. But finding a rose one day in the little one's cradle, her mother exclaimed, "Rose! My little Rose!" That name stuck, and today we know her as St Rose of Lima.

At a very early age, Rose wanted to belong completely to God. She spent a lot of time talking with Him in a little shack in the garden. Like her mother, she was timid and afraid of the dark. But she did not think about her fears when she was praying. One day she stayed after dusk in the little shack, and when she did not return to the house, her mother became worried. Fearful of searching for Rose in the garden after dark, she called her husband, and together they found her.

"I'm very sorry for taking so long," Rose said as they made their way back to the house. "Since you are not afraid and feel safe when Father is with you, Mother, the thought came to me, how can I be afraid when Jesus is with me?" From that day on, she was never again afraid of the dark.

As she grew a little older, Rose undertook fasts and other forms of penance. She had begun to understand that suffering can become an avenue for God's grace. One day, while she prayed in the garden, she saw a vision of Jesus as a child her own age. At another time, she saw her guardian angel encouraging her and praying with her. These visions were very important to her.

When she became a teenager, she asked permission to enter a cloister.

"Of course not!" her parents replied. "You know that your Father's business has failed and if we didn't have you to help with your flowers and gardening, where would we be?"

Rose listened with her heart and obeyed. Then God gave her an idea. "I could live alone with God, just like in a cloister, only right here in our garden." At the age of twenty she became a member of the Third Order of Dominicans and donned the white habit. Her parents gave her permission to live alone in the garden shed, where she made herself a bed of bricks and roots. Often she was kept awake by her uncomfortable bed, but she always asked the Virgin to awaken her in time for morning Mass. Sometimes she would see a vision of Mary in the rays of the morning sun when she first opened her eyes. During the day she worked hard, weeding and tending the flowers in the garden.

Rose wanted to imitate the sufferings of Christ as much as possible. She remembered how Jesus wore a crown of thorns for our sins. "I want to wear one, too," she said. Plaiting a circlet of brambles, she placed it on her head.

But her mother objected. "I can't stand the way you look with that thing," she told Rose.

Rose found a way to obey. She made a circlet of roses to cover the crown, and wore these over her veil, with the brambles underneath.

Soon she was led to help others. She made a small infirmary in one room of the house where she cared for destitute children and sick elderly people. The kind of modern social services available in Peru today trace their origin to this humble beginning.

Rose began to be known and loved throughout the city for her piety and works of charity. But some religious leaders were concerned about the validity of her visions and other experiences. They were especially worried about reports that the devil had fought with her and tried to hurt her. Rose bore all the questioning patiently. Finally, the commission of priests and physicians announced their conclusion, that she was directed by "impulses of grace." She continued her work of ministering to the poor and interceding for the citizens of her city. When a pirate attack threatened them with grave danger, her prayers were credited with averting it.

In 1617, after a long and painful illness, she died at the age of thirty-one. In that illness, Rose had prayed,"Increase Thy love in my heart." After her death, everyone who had known her wanted to visit her home. The funeral had to be postponed several days because of the crowds. Finally, she was buried privately in the cloister of St Dominic's Church, as she had requested, with the town officials taking turns carrying her body to its grave.

We are warned that St Rose's mode of life and ascetical practices are not meant for everyone to copy. Rather, we should aim at her spirit of holiness and her desire to serve God and her fellow man. In this way, her saintly life can inspire us to try to live more nearly according to God's will for us.

She was canonized in 1674, the first person born in the Western Hemisphere to be declared a saint. She is patroness of South America and the Philippines. Her feast day is August 23.

Teachers and Preachers

Hear, O sons, a father's instruction, and be attentive,
that you may gain insight; for I give you good precepts:
do not forsake my teaching.
Proverbs 4:1, 2

Now you have observed my teaching, my conduct,
my aim in life, my patience, my love, my steadfastness,
my persecutions, my sufferings . . . .
II Timothy 3:10-11a

O blest teacher, light of holy Church,
blessed lover of God's law:
plead with the Son of God for us.
Antiphon for the Common Feast of Doctors

St Justin Martyr

c. 100-165

St Justin is one of the earliest saints and martyrs. Born about 100 A.D. in Nablus (the Shechem of the Bible), Samaria, of Greek, pagan parents, he was brought up in the religions and philosophies of his people.

In school Justin studied literature, history and what was called rhetoric. Rhetoric trained people to think logically and speak effectively. He is regarded as the first Christian philosopher, and his writings which are still extant "reflect the outlook of a Christian intellectual" of the first generation after the Apostles.

One day he was walking by the sea, pondering one of Plato's maxims, when, turning, he saw an old man following him. They fell into conversation, and as they talked, the old man began to tell him of a philosophy which was nobler and more satisfying than any he had heard. That philosophy had been revealed by God through many prophets of old and had been fully revealed in Jesus Christ, His Son. He urged the young Justin to pray for light and knowledge from God in answer to his inner need. As a result, Justin decided to study the Scriptures and to become more closely acquainted with Christians and their teachings.

He had already noticed that under the increasing persecution they were suffering, Christians were willing to die for their faith, and that made a profound impression on him. He was about thirty years old when he embraced the Christian faith as his own.

Since most Christians were still recruited from the lower classes, he felt that no one had explained their faith so that educated people could see how truly wonderful it was. So he set about, after his own conversion, to try to make Christianity attractive to other sincere unbelievers who thirsted for the Truth. Still wearing the cloak of a philosopher, he set out to make his faith available to others, traveling through various countries, and finally coming to Rome.

One of his writings, addressed to the Emperor Antoninus and his two sons, sought to vindicate Christians from accusations of atheism and immorality, insisting that their religion, far from making them a danger to the Empire, actually makes them better, more loyal citizens.

Antoninus was succeeded by his adopted son, Marcus Arelius, who had been trained as a Stoic philosopher himself. Although in many ways, Marcus Arelius was a good ruler, he considered Christians superstitious, revolutionary and immoral. Although the bravery of Christians under torture should have commended itself to his Stoic outlook, he judged their courage mere obstinancy. His prejudice may have come from one of his mentors, the philosopher, Fronto, who had a special hatred for Christians, or from the Stoic, Epictetus, who considered them fanatics, or from counsellors who poisoned his mind against them. His own loyalty to the old Roman gods made him resent the growing success of Christianity as it continued to spread across the Roman world.

In the year 165, Marcus Arelius had launched one of the severest and cruelest persecutions the Church had experienced. Torture was a normal part of the effort to force Christians to deny their faith and conform to the old ways. Refusal to sacrifice to the old gods meant suffering and almost certain death. Justin, continuing his teaching and writing, went to Rome, perhaps one of the most dangerous of all places for a Christian to be found. There he was brought with a number of other Christians before Rusticus, prefect of Rome, and ordered to sacrifice to the gods. They all refused.

The record of the trial that followed has been termed "among the most valuable and authentic which have come down to us." Justin took the occasion to present a bold argument, saying that as a philosopher he had studied all the philosophies and had concluded that the Christian way is the true one. "We believe in one Creator, not many gods. We confess His Son, Jesus Christ, who was foretold by prophets of old and who came to bring salvation to all men everywhere."

"Where do these Christians hold their meetings?" asked Rusticus.

"Wherever they can," replied Justin. "The God of the Christians is not found in any particular place. He is everywhere in Heaven and earth, and His faithful praise and worship Him anywhere they can."

"Are you a Christian?" Rusticus asked solemnly.

"Yes, I am a Christian," said Justin firmly.

"And do you think that if I have you beaten and beheaded that you will then go to Heaven?"

"I don't think it, I know it," said Justin. "I have no doubt about it whatsoever."

His tormenter barked, "Very well! We'll see! Come here and sacrifice to the gods."

"Nonsense!" replied Justin. "Nobody gives up truth for falsehood if he has his senses about him!"

So Justin and six others, five men and one woman, were then put to death.

Justin was the first Christian apologist known to us by works of any considerable length. He devoted his life to making the faith not only known, but put into a language that educated pagans could understand and accept. He believed that the truth of it would convince them, once they saw it for what it is.

His feast day, formerly April 14, is now celebrated on June 1.

St Bernard of Clairvaux

c. 1090-1153

Born in 1090, Bernard was the third son of Tescelin Sorrel, a nobleman of Burgundy, and was sent to school under secular canons at Châtillon-sur-Seine. But in addition to the studies from books, Bernard learned to listen with his heart, to be taught inwardly by the Lord. That was a very important part of his training for what lay ahead. One Christmas Eve during his boyhood, he fell asleep as he waited to go into the Matins service with his mother. He dreamed that instead of entering the church, he was in Bethlehem about to go into the stable where the Infant Jesus lay. Tiptoeing over, he gazed at the Baby's face. That glimpse so influenced him that he became especially devoted to the mystery of God as shown in the human Jesus.

In young adulthood, noted for his charm, wit and eloquence, Bernard was in great danger of losing his earlier devotion to Christ. The death of his mother, to whom he was very close, left him grief-stricken and confused. Gradually, though, the diversions of the world failed to satisfy him, and he began to think of entering the monastery of Cîteaux, which had a reputation for demanding complete commitment to God. In fact, the abbot there, St Stephen Harding, had gone without a single novice in the last two years. Still undecided, Bernard entered a roadside church and prayed to know God's will. He rose from his knees with all his doubts resolved. No amount of persuasion could make him change his mind. In fact, the very opposite happened. When he arrived at Cîteaux, Bernard brought no less than 31 others with him — relatives and friends — to the discouraged monastery and abbot!

But Bernard was not destined to stay at Cîteaux, even though he had gone there determined to die to the world and to remain in obscurity. The abbot saw his leadership potential and his spiritual zeal, and after three years sent him with twelve monks to the Valley of Wormwood, an area with poor soil, surrounded by woods. There the little group built themselves a house and eked out a bare living from the soil, with the help of the local bishop and others living in the area. The reputation of the monastery grew; so did the numbers of novices coming to join them. Soon the name of the valley (and their monastery) was changed to "Clairvaux," "Clear Valleys," because the darkness had been driven away.

At first Bernard was too strict with his monks, and they almost lost heart. Sensing this, he gave up preaching for a time, improved the food and saw to it that the brothers had enough sleep. He learned to stop magnifying small transgressions, to concentrate on the more important work of forming devoted followers of Jesus Christ. The work grew and prospered and it was not long until their number had risen to 130 members.

Bernard became renowned as a worker of miracles. A certain nobleman had his power of speech restored during Mass in response to a prayer of Bernard. Others said that they had been cured when he made the sign of the cross over them. But as people came for help, for prayer and counsel, "they do not leave me even the time to pray," Bernard wrote. His life became so overrun with the trials and cares of others, "that scarcely an hour is left free," he said, "but I have no power to stop their coming and cannot refuse to see them."

Bernard lived to see one of his former monks chosen to be Pope, Eugenius III. By this time he was intimately involved in many of the concerns and controversies that plagued the Church of his time. He wrote to Eugenius a long, detailed letter about the dangers of his high office, warning him to keep alive his love of God and tenderness of heart.

Unfortunately, in that period, even bishops and archbishops sometimes went to war against one another. They were very powerful and had great wealth and even controlled armies. Bernard sought over and over again to bring peace between enemies — not at the cost of betraying the truth, but for the sake of Christ.

His many years of eating very rough (sometimes unsuitable) food, and his personal sacrifices took their toll on him and he became seriously ill. There is reason to believe that he really wanted to die and get out of the many conflicts that were raging throughout France and all of Europe at that time. "I confess myself to be overcome by the violence of the storm for lack of courage," he had said. However, when his monks implored him to stay with them, he cried, "I am torn between the two, and what to choose, I know not. I leave it to the Lord; let Him decide."

When he died at the age of 63, he had been abbot for 38 years. Clairvaux had been the mother house from which sixty-eight monasteries had been founded, and the Cistercian Order went on to become one of the great influences in European life of the 13th century. He was canonized in 1174, and in 1830 was declared a doctor of the Church. His popular title is *Doctor mellifluus*, the Honey-sweet Teacher. His writings are still read, and have had great influence on other teachers and theologians. His feast day is August 20.

St Francis of Assisi

1181-1226

In the Italian city of Assisi in 1192, Pai Bernadone, the wife of a wealthy cloth merchant, was about to give birth. Suddenly a stranger knocked on the door, and gave the servant an even stranger message: "If you wish everything to go well, tell Peter Bernadone's wife to go to the stable at once."

Obeying, Señora Bernadone went immediately to the stable, and there was suddenly taken with labor pains so severe she had to remain there until she had delivered a fine baby boy. The child was christened "John," but his father named him "Francis," to commemorate his latest trip to France — "A very profitable venture," he said.

The name stuck. Peter Bernadone's cloth business flourished, and little Francis grew up to be the toast of the town. He loved going to parties with his friends and singing romantic ballads far into the night. So popular was he that he was proclaimed "king of the festivities."

When he was about seventeen years old, war broke out between the towns of Perugia and Assisi. Francis enthusiastically helped repair the city wall and joined others in defending it. But the Perugians captured him and carried him away. Because he was dressed in such fine clothes, they threw him into a prison reserved for nobles. Even in prison, however, he remained undaunted.

"How can you be singing in here?" his fellow prisoners asked him.

"Why, this is nothing," he replied. "One day I shall be venerated throughout the world." He was joking, as usual, not having the least idea that he had spoken the truth.

After a year, the cities came to terms and Francis was released. He and the others marched back into Assisi singing, but Francis was too sick to celebrate. He went home to bed. He had barely recovered from his illness when his father came home with the big news that all the nobility were arming for a battle against the German emperor.

"I will fight in this big war and become a famous knight," Francis declared. Riding out of Assisi, he looked the part better than any of the nobles, with his fine silken tunic and armor gleaming in the sun. On the road not far from the city wall, he noticed a battle-scarred knight riding near him, and began to be ashamed of his own finery. Then he had an idea.

"Why not change clothes with me?" he said. The knight happily agreed, and they rode on together. That night Francis dreamed that his home had been transformed into a great palace, filled with beautiful banners, swords, shields and fine armor. All the arms were emblazoned with a glittering red cross. "All this is for you and your companions," a voice said. "Take up arms."

However excited Francis may have been from the dream, he never reached the battle front. At Spoleto, his old illness recurred. "Go on without me," he told the others. "I'll catch up later."

As he lay on his sick bed one day, he heard a voice questioning him, "Is it better to serve the Master or the servant?"

"The Master," Francis replied.

"Then why are you leaving the Master for the servant?"

Francis from that moment on knew that his call was not to serve in any army of this world, but rather to fight for the kingdom of God.

As soon as he was well enough, he rode back to Assisi, to be ridiculed by those who had seen him ride forth in his finery. Now, however, he ignored their laughter, and spent days wandering over the hills near the town, thinking about becoming a knight in the service of Lady Poverty.

One day while riding along, he met a leper covered with repulsive sores. At first, Francis shrank back from the loathsome sight and smell. Then he remembered the words of Jesus, "As you have done to the least of my brothers, you have done to Me." Getting down from his horse to give alms, he reached out and kissed the leper in Christ's love.

"There must be others like that," he thought. And so he sought them out, visiting the hospitals and caring for the sick and needy. He gave away his money and often his own clothes.

Returning from one of his trips, his father confronted him angrily. "What's this I hear about you?" he demanded. "From now on you're to work like your brother and me, or else . . . " he paused, ". . . or else leave!"

Francis left. He wandered out of town and found the little, tumbled-down Church of St Damian, outside the walls of Assisi. There he waited and prayed, and the old priest of the Church fed him from his own meager resources. One day, praying before the crucifix in the Church, Francis heard the Lord speaking from it. "Francis, go and repair my house, which you see, is falling down." He decided right away that he should build St Damian's, which was in bad need of repair. Going back home, he went into his father's warehouse, took a bolt of cloth, and sold it and his horse, and took the money back to the Church.

"Here," he said to the priest. "Use this to repair the Church."

But the priest would not take the money. "It isn't ours," he said gravely.

Meanwhile, his father discovered what Francis had done. He dragged him home, beat him unmercifully, and locked him up. Then he left for another business trip, leaving Francis imprisoned. His mother took pity on him and released him, only to bring her husband's wrath upon her own head when he returned. The father then appealed to the bishop for help.

"My son has been associating with the scum of the earth," he complained. "And now he has stolen my property."

"Return the money," the Bishop told Francis. "Trust God for what you need. The Church should not profit from unjustly gained goods."

"Francis can have all the money he wants to give to the poor," said his father, "as long as he gives up his crazy life!"

"I appeal to your protection," Francis told the bishop.

"In that case, I advise you to give up your inheritance," the bishop replied.

Francis then made this statement: "I no longer call Peter Bernadone my father. Here is everything that is his." With that, he stripped off all his clothes and handed them to his father.

"From now on," said Francis, "I will say 'Our Father who art in heaven.' "

Quickly, they found an extra tunic and Francis put it on, and went off in great joy and simplicity, following Jesus as the poorest of the poor. From house to house in Assisi he begged bread for himself and stones for rebuilding the Church. Although he was the object of much ridicule, he also received scraps of food and bricks and mortar for the Church wall.

St Damian's was rebuilt into a fine little Church. Then Francis began repairing another old Church, St Peter's. In the meantime, a young nobleman named Bernard Quintavalle joined Francis. At a nearby Church they asked the priest, Peter Cattani, to open the Scriptures three times to give them a message in the name of Jesus.

"Go sell what you have and give to the poor. . . take nothing for your journey. . . Do not possess gold. . . nor two coats, nor a staff," they read. With these words burning in their hearts, Francis and Bernard set out to live out these instructions. "I want to go with you also," said the priest. As followers gathered around him, Francis began to understand that the words "rebuild My house" meant for him to preach the gospel and live the life of Christ among his fellow men. Soon there were twelve in the little band.

"From now on," said Francis, "We shall call ourselves the Friars Minor because we are the smallest of all, and so that we may be good bridegrooms of Lady Poverty, no matter where we come from, I have made a Rule. We will go to Rome and ask the Pope to approve us."

So in 1210, Francis and his band of twelve ragged followers made their way to Rome and Pope Innocent III. At first the Pope did not want to recognize them. "There are too many orders already," his advisors said. But that night he dreamed that St Francis was propping up the Church of St John Lateran (the Pope's own Church). He sent for the Little Brother. "I will conditionally approve your Rule. Go into the countryside and preach repentance. When the Lord increases your number, come back and see me." Then he gave Francis and his companions the tonsure.

Francis never wanted to be a priest. He felt that the call of the Little Brothers was to be helpers and servants of the Church. The abbot of Monte Subasio handed over the Chapel of our Lady of the Angels at Portiuncula to Francis in 1212. For rent, Francis agreed that once a year they would send the monks a basket of fish caught in the nearby river. As their numbers increased, the Little Brothers built huts of clay and wood around the chapel. Francis called the spirit of holy poverty the foundation of the order. They wore the brown tunics of Italian peasants, tied about the waist with rough cords. In twos and threes they roamed the countryside, sleeping in haylofts or in the open, preaching, begging, ministering to the sick and to lepers, sometimes working as servants to pay for food. Their most distinctive mark was their happiness. Gloom and depression, Francis thought, were akin to sin.

TEACHERS AND PREACHERS

Always they sought to imitate the spirit of Francis, who taught them that they were brothers, not only to all mankind, but to nature as well. The animals loved and obeyed him. "All creatures of our God and King, Lift up your voice and with us sing," he would sing. When he was ready to preach to his brothers at Alviano, he quieted the birds, whom he called, "my sisters, the swallows." Later they perched around him when he told them to praise their Creator.

Meanwhile, at St Damian's, Francis had started an enclosed order for women under the direction of St Clare. Called "The Poor Clares," they became a bulwark of prayer support for Francis and his wandering brothers. The Friars helped keep their convent in repair and did other heavy work for the sisters.

Francis longed to carry the gospel to those who did not know the faith. The Saracens followed the religion of Islam, and he decided to go on mission among them. His health, however, again intervened, and he had to return home. A few years later he went again with a dozen brothers, and joined the Crusaders, only to be shocked at their unchristian way of life. He sternly denounced their sins, and somehow managed to get through enemy lines to the Sultan himself. The man was deeply impressed with Francis' spirit and message, but refused to be converted. Francis then returned to the Christian armies and spent some time in the Holy Land, making pilgrimages to places where Christ had lived.

The number of Franciscans had grown incredibly large. Francis was called back from the Holy Land to attend the first general chapel held at the Portiuncula during Pentecost in 1217, where five thousand were present. With their growth, however, new problems had arisen, and Cardinal Ugolino had to help them become organized. There were many who felt that Francis was very impractical in his insistence that no Friar Minor could own anything. This became a serious issue, but Francis stood his ground. Eventually he developed a revised Rule, but which compromised nothing of the original principles of poverty, humility and evangelical fervor. In its final form it was approved by the Pope in 1223.

It was after he had resigned his office in the Friars Minor that Francis inaugurated the famous Christmas crib at Grecchio. This was the beginning of our Christmas creches, and at the first one, prepared by Brother John, Francis read the Christmas story to the people with such devotion that men wept when they heard it. In 1224 Francis retired to Mount Alvernia and made there a little cell. While praying there, he received the Stigmata, a physical sign of Christ's suffering in his body.

"You may be My standard bearer," the Lord said to him. Francis was filled with inexpressible joy as he painfully made his way down the mountain with his close companion, Brother Leo. The rest of his life he spent at the Portiuncula, nursing a painful disease in his eyes.

There he composed his Canticle of the Sun, a hymn of praise for all God's creation.

When he realized that his death was near, he said, "Welcome, my Sister Death," and called Brother Angelo and Brother Leo to come and help him sing the Canticle, adding some new verses on Sister Death. He died on October 3, 1226, praising God to the end.

Just two years after his death, he was canonized by his old friend and supporter, Gregory IX, formerly Cardinal Ugolino. In 1230, his relics were moved into the New Basilica, decorated with the famous frescos by Giotto, himself a Friar Minor.

His order went on to become one of the best known and largest in the world, exercising great influence on the Church in various periods. Francis became one of the most loved, if not *the* most beloved saint of all time. His feast is celebrated on October 4. A second feast commemorating the Impression of the Stigmata is observed on September 17.

St Bonaventure

1221-1274

Born in Italy in 1221, Bonaventure, as a young man, joined the Franciscans, who were founded only a few years before his birth. He studied at the University of Paris and taught there himself from 1248 to 1257. And although he was a sharp, effective teacher, this was not to be his life-time work. He and St Thomas Aquinas received their doctorates of theology together from the University of Paris in 1257.

That same year, Bonaventure was chosen to be Minister-General of the Friars Minor (the Franciscans). The order had been in a turmoil ever since the death of St Francis, and it was actually divided into two sharp factions — the Spirituals (who wanted an extreme interpretation of Franciscan life) and the Moderates or Regulars, who wanted certain changes in the Rule by which they lived. Bonaventure sought to reconcile the two, but the Spirituals could not be appeased. They eventually went on their own, and even fell into error and disobedience.

At the request of the Friars, Bonaventure wrote a life of St Francis, and it is from him that we learn most about that beloved figure.

The Pope decided to appoint him Archbishop of York, but Bonaventure succeeded in persuading him to withdraw the appointment. Later, however, the Pope made him Cardinal-Bishop of Albano, and instructed him to come to Rome at once. The messengers arrived to present Bonaventure with the cardinal's hat, the greatest honor that the Pope could bestow. They found Bonaventure washing dishes in the monastery. He asked them to hang the hat on a nearby tree, because he could not take it with greasy hands! When he had finished with the dishes, he joined the papal messengers in the garden.

The time had come for a General Council of the Church, planned by Pope Gregory X in the hope of working out a reconciliation with the Eastern Orthodox Church. The Church of the East (Orthodox) and the West (Catholic) had divided in 1054 AD in the midst of bitter quarrels and mutual excommunications. The Emperor, who lived in Constantinople, in the East, was anxious to have the Church reunited. To such an important gathering, all the best theologians were called. St Thomas Aquinas would have been a major voice but died en route, leaving Bonaventure to be the outstanding voice in the council. It lasted for three sessions, during which his loving and conciliatory spirit helped to heal old wounds and bring about an agreement for the reunion of the Church. The Council ended with the belief that it was an accomplished fact.

St Bonaventure died before learning that the agreement had been repudiated by the bishops in Constantinople, dashing the Church's hopes for reunion for centuries to come. Bonaventure died in 1274, and was canonized in 1482. He was made a Doctor of the Church in 1588, and is known as the Seraphic Doctor ("angelic teacher"). His writings have been read and admired by many people since his death.

His feast day is celebrated July 15.

St Thomas Aquinas

1225-1274

If you were living in Paris in the 13th century (1269) and got up early enough, you might see a tall, stocky Dominican priest on his way to say Mass. And if you checked him closely on one particular morning, you might notice a parchment carefully tucked in his sleeve. The person was St Thomas Aquinas, and the scroll contained his ideas on the nature of the Blessed Sacrament. No less a person than King Louis IX of France had asked Thomas's opinion to settle these questions, so his answer was very important indeed. But Thomas was more concerned to be true to God than to have the King's approval, or anyone else's, for that matter. Thus, when he emerged from the sacristy robed for Mass, he still had the precious scroll with him. Laying it carefully on the altar, he began the service, As he prayed, he received assurance that what he had written was true, and later both the Church and the University where he taught accepted it.

Thomas always knew that reasoning could take him only so far. "Faith. . . pierces through the veil" of mystery surrounding the Blessed Sacrament, and faith alone is all a pure heart needs. As an oblate at the famous monastery of Monte Cassino in Italy, and later as a student in Naples, he felt drawn to that mystery. The Dominican friars had often found him in prayer in their little church. When he was 18 years old, he joined them as a novice, but over the strong objections of his family. His upper-class family felt that it was beneath their son to belong to an order that begged for a living! (This is what the Dominicans did at that time). So the friars tried to prevent trouble with Thomas' family by transferring him to Bologna. But on the way Thomas and the friars were suddenly surrounded by a troop of soldiers led by two of his brothers. "Grab his habit!" said one, and with that Thomas felt himself being pulled and yanked from several directions at once. But being large, and strong as an ox, he resisted stoutly.

"I'm not going to change from being a Dominican," he shouted. Soon, however, he was overpowered, tied up, and dragged off to a castle near his family home. There his family kept him for two years, using every means to get him to change his mind.

Thomas persisted, however, and spent his idle hours memorizing the Bible and writing about philosophy. At last one of his sisters took pity on him and helped him escape. Rejoining the Dominicans, he set out with them to Cologne (Germany) and spent several years there studying under St Albert the Great. Albert soon recognized what a brilliant mind Thomas had been given, and prophesied, "We call Brother Thomas, 'the dumb ox,' but I tell you, he will yet make his lowing heard to the ends of the earth."

After his ordination, Thomas was sent to Paris to teach at the University of Paris, the oldest and most famous university in Europe. His reputation as a teacher and thinker grew, and he was often invited to dine with famous persons, though usually he said, "No, thank you." But there was one invitation he could not refuse: a state luncheon with the King. Accompanied by his superior, Thomas went. Course followed course during the meal, while Thomas sat in silence. He started thinking about his work. All of a sudden an idea struck him. "And that's the end of the Manichean heresy!" he exclaimed out loud, banging his fist so hard on the table that the goblets rocked. Everybody stopped talking, and in the awkward silence that followed, his prior tugged at Thomas' sleeve. Then, remembering where he was, Thomas bowed shamefacedly toward the king, saying, "My apologies to your Majesty." King Louis looked fondly at his absent-minded subject, and motioned to the court recorder. "Do take down his idea before he forgets it," he said.

Lecturing, debating and writing filled Thomas' days in Paris, but the Sacrament was the thing he loved most. Often he would be found kneeling before the altar, and it was while doing so on St Nicholas' Day (December 6), he received one final revelation. We do not know its content, but it completely changed his outlook. "All my work seems like so much stubble," he confided to a friend afterwards. He wrote no more, gave up teaching, and devoted himself to the worship of God. When asked why, he said, "I can write no more. The end of my work has come."

He was summoned to attend the General Council at Lyons, but had to stop at an abbey on the way because he was too sick to travel farther. There he died peacefully on March 7, 1274, still telling others about how good and wonderful God is to those who love him. Here are some words of a hymn he wrote about the Blessed Sacrament:

Taste and touch, and vision, to discern Thee fail
  Faith, that comes by hearing, pierces through the veil
I believe whate'er the Son of God hath told,
  What the truth hath spoken, that for truth I hold.

Jesus, whom now veiled, I by faith descry,
  What my soul doth thirst for, do not, Lord, deny:
That Thy face unveiled, I at last may see,
  With the blissful vision blest, dear Lord, of Thee.

He was canonized in 1323, and his body was removed to Toulouse in 1368. Pope Pius V declared him a Doctor of the Universal Church in 1567, and the Council of Trent gave special honor to his great theological work, the *Summa Theologica.* His work experienced some eclipse in the ensuing centuries, but was given new prominence in 1879 when Pope Leo XIII enjoined his study on all theological students. In 1880 he was made patron of all Catholic Universities, and in 1923, Pius XI reaffirmed his writings as an authoritative source of Catholic teaching. No other single Catholic writer has enjoyed greater influence on the theological teachings of the past four centuries. His feast is observed on January 28 since 1970.

St Anthony of Padua

1195-1231

Saint Anthony was actually from Portugal. He is called St Anthony of Padua (which is in Italy) because that is the last place he lived, and that is where he is buried.

The Franciscans were still a young order when he was growing up, and their missionaries were spreading in all directions, eager to carry the gospel to people who did not know about it. Some of them had gone over to Morocco to preach to the Moors. Unhappily, the Moors rejected their message and murdered the messengers. When Anthony heard this, he was filled with a desire to become a Franciscan, even though he had already joined the Augustinians. He even longed to be martyred, but that was not God's will. He had been continuing his studies in the Augustinian priory at Coimbra, the capital of Portugal, when the mutilated remains of the missionaries were lovingly enshrined in their chapel. He confided his desire to become a missionary to some Franciscan brothers who came to beg at their door, and after some difficulties, succeeded in being admitted to their order in 1221.

"Go," said one of the Augustinians kindly. "You will make a great saint."

When he put on the brown robe of a Franciscan, he took the name Anthony in honor of the great St Antony, patriarch of monks, in whose chapel he took his vows.

Filled with zeal to preach the Gospel to the heathen, and to be martryed for Christ, Anthony arrived in Morocco that very same year. But shortly after his arrival, he fell ill and had to spend that winter in bed. When he failed to get better, he had to take a ship back for Europe. Their ship, however, was blown off course by a storm, so instead of arriving back in Portugal, Anthony found himself in Sicily. The Franciscans there gave him shelter and invited him to go with all the Franciscans to the last General Chapter of their order. The revered Francis himself was in attendance.

After the meeting was over, and all were leaving for their various labors, Anthony stood alone with nowhere to go. Seeing the Provincial of Romagna, he entreated him to take him.

"Are you a priest?" the official enquired.

"I am," said Anthony.

Impressed by the devout life he observed in the young friar, the Provincial assigned him to say masses for the small convent of lay brothers at Monte Paulo in Tuscany. So Anthony lived there in a small cave hewn out of the rocks for nearly a year, fasting and praying. He did his share to help the brothers, too; after their meals he would wash their dishes and sweep the floors.

No one suspected Anthony's brilliance or learning until he and his brothers attended the ordination of a group of Franciscans and Dominicans at Forli. Because of some confusion, no speaker had been arranged for the ceremony, so the superior called on Anthony to give a message to the guests who were present. One bishop wrote about him, "He began in the fear of God, with simple words," but was so enlightened by Heavenly grace that he soon captivated the minds of his hearers with his eloquence. Everyone present agreed, "Never a man spoke like this man!" Soon after this, Francis gave him a special appointment to lecture the brothers in theology. "To my beloved brother Anthony," Francis wrote. "I desire that you instruct the brothers in sacred theology, provided that this study does not quench the spirit of holy prayer and devotion according to our Rule."

For nine years Anthony preached in France and Italy. Wherever he went, crowds flocked to hear him. Hardened criminals, indifferent folk and heretics alike were brought to conversion and confession. People closed their shops and offices to hear his sermons. Women rose early or remained overnight in the church to secure their places. Often the churches could not hold the numbers who came to hear him, so he preached in the squares and marketplaces.

Because of his wonderful speaking ability and his deep love of God, there have been many stories about his miracles. He is called St Anthony the Wonder Worker, however, more because of the miracles that have been wrought after his death than during his lifetime.

Of all the cities Anthony visited in his travels, Padua was his favorite because of the lively faith the people there had. Even though he spent only the last two years of his life there, Anthony is still revered in that city as its own. At the age of 36, he suddenly fell ill from dropsy and asked to be carried back to Padua. They reached the outskirts of the city, and he had to be taken into an apartment reserved for the chaplain of the Poor Clares, where he died on June 13, 1231. After receiving the last rites, his eyes filled with tears and he murmured, "I see my Lord!" Then he calmly passed into the next life.

Anthony is often pictured holding the Infant Jesus in his arms. A legend tells us that late one night, while he was on a visit, his host looked through his window and saw him holding the Infant Jesus and gazing at Him in deep devotion. Anthony is also frequently invoked to help in locating missing objects. A story recounted about his miracles that may be connected with this tells of a runaway novice who stole a valuable psalter he was using. After Anthony prayed for its recovery, the book was quickly returned. The frightened youth admitted the theft and explained that he had returned it when compelled by an alarming apparition of the saint himself.

His love of the poor and his labor in their behalf earned him the title of patron of the poor. He was canonized within a year of his death by Pope Gregory IX, in 1232. His feast is celebrated on the anniversary of his death, June 13.

St John Bosco

(Don Bosco)

1815-1888

A crowd of angry, swearing, fighting children surrounded John Bosco. Shouting to be heard above the noise, he urged them to be at peace. But they continued, and in frustration, he began to strike them with his fists. Suddenly, a mysterious lady appeared. "Softly, softly . . . if you wish to win them," she said. "Take your shepherd's staff and lead them to a pasture."

This dream called nine year old John Bosco to help poor and needy boys in his native Italy. He is known today throughout the world as Don Bosco, founder of the third largest religious community, the Salesian Order. Although he also built churches, wrote, published, and worked miracles, he is best known and loved as "the children's priest."

Born in 1815 in Turin, Italy, John Melchoir Bosco was the youngest son of a peasant farmer and a devout mother. He had become accustomed to hardships at an early age. John was two years old when his father died, and after that his mother, Margaret Occhiena Bosco, had to struggle hard to keep the family together. There was no money for the education that young John desperately wanted. On visits with his aunt who kept house for a priest, John learned to read, and this kindled his heart's desire to become a priest too. So great was his desire that he left home at the age of twelve to earn money for this education.

Eventually, at sixteen, he was able to enter the seminary. His tuition and clothes were provided by charity. Indeed, his hat came from the mayor, his cloak from the parish priest, his cassock and shoes from other church members. After he began studying at the theological college of Turin, his superiors encouraged him to start a ministry with the boys of that city. Each Sunday, he gathered many of the neglected apprentices and young ruffians to play games and hear the Gospel. From this beginning the work expanded to a full-time ministry which provided hundreds of boys with love, shelter, schooling and recreation.

As his work with the boys expanded, Don Bosco used his own home for some classes, such as grammar, as well as for workshops in trades such as shoemaking, tailoring and printing. For other schooling, he sent the boys to teachers from some of the best schools in the city, who donated their time to help. His mother served them as housekeeper, and they affectionately called her, "Mamma Margaret."

The next step was to construct a church for his flock. The money came in almost miraculously. Then he set to work to build a home for the boys who were living with them, and oratories, which served as schools. All this he placed under the patronage of his favorite saint, Francis de Sales. By 1856 there were 150 resident boys, with four workshops, four Latin classes and other classes taught by ten young priests in addition to the oratories, which by that time had 500 students.

One might suppose that with the kind of undisciplined boys who came, he would find it necessary to use corporal punishment, then so common in discipline. But Don Bosco employed quite a different means to bring about the wholesome, disciplined life that he desired for them.

"The practice of my system," he said, "is wholly based on the words of St Paul who says, 'Charity is patient, is kind. It bears all things, hopes all things, endures all things.' Let the boys have full liberty to run, skip and play . . . ." He made gymnastics, music and outings an important part of their lives. With these activities, he added frequent confession of sin, instruction in the Catholic faith, and Communion. All that he combined with his fatherly guidance, to give the kind of nurture and support that helped these youths grow into fine young men, many of whom went on to become priests themselves.

For years, John Bosco had trouble getting the right kind of help for his work. Enthusiastic young priests would offer their services but then give up because they did not have his patience with the undisciplined youngsters or because of their lack of money. In 1854, he assembled a group of young men whom he had trained himself, and suggested that with God's help they should begin a time of doing practical works in assisting their neighbors. At the end of the time, "we might bind ourselves by a promise," which later would become a vow; those who did so received the name "Salesian Brother," in honor of St Francis de Sales. In that way a new apostolate was formed. They started with the ministry to the boys but grew into a religious congregation which eventually numbered in the thousands, sending missionaries all over the world. Although mainly concerned with educational work, the Salesians have founded hospitals, and seminaries, and carry on extensive mission and pastoral work. In 1872, he helped St Mary Mazzarello, a peasant woman from near Genoa, to begin a new congregation for work among girls, similar to the Salesians. He called them Daughters of Mary, Help of Christians, and they, too, had marked success.

Although his work was beset by many difficulties, some of them instituted by anticlerical officials and unsympathetic church officials, he was sustained by a steady vision of purpose and spirit of sacrifice. A large number of miracles are recorded in connection with his work, including the miraculous multiplication of food.

On January 31, 1888, at the age of seventy-three, John Bosco died after a long illness. He refused to rest or spare himself right to the end. Forty thousand people attended his funeral. He left behind a wonderful legacy: the Salesian Order which by 1964 numbered more than 40,000 priests, lay brothers and sisters in all parts of the world. Numbers alone are not enough to describe the countless lives enriched by his lifetime dedication to caring for unwanted children. He was beatified by Pope Pius XI on June 2, 1929, and canonized on April 1, 1934. He is patron saint of Catholic publishers and young apprentices, and his feast is celebrated on January 31.

Missionaries

Go therefore and make disciples of all nations,
baptizing them in the name of the Father and
of the Son and of the Holy Spirit, teaching them
to observe all that I have commanded you;
and lo, I am with you always, to the close of the age.
Matthew 28:19, 20

You shall be my witnesses in Jerusalem and in all Judea
and Samaria and to the end of the earth.
Acts 1:8b

These men who have turned the world upside down . . .
Acts 17:6

Send forth, O Lord, thy strong Evangel
By many messengers all hearts to win;
Make haste to help us in our weakness;
Break down the real of Satan, death and sin:
The circle of the earth shall then proclaim
Thy kingdom, and the glory of Thy name.
Karl Heinrich von Bogatzky, 1749

St Paul

First Century

"Saul, Saul, why are you persecuting me?" The Voice was loud and clear in the ears of the young man who lay sprawled on the ground beside the Damascus Road. Others with him thought it was thundering, and were bewildered by the whole thing.

"Who are you, Lord?" meekly asked the zealous young Jew who had been hastening to Damascus to seize all those who admitted to being followers of Jesus.

"I am Jesus, whom you are persecuting!" came the unexpected answer.

The zealous young man was Paul (as he would later be called), and this was his first encounter with our Lord

Jesus Christ. Afterward he would tell of this meeting over and over again, even before kings and governors.

After his conversion, Paul was introduced to the Christians by none other than St Barnabas, and together Paul and Barnabas made their first missionary tour of the eastern end of the Mediterranean Sea. They made many converts, established churches, and spent many months training people in their new faith. Later, Paul had another companion, Silas (St Silvanus), who went with him, visiting the churches and preaching the Gospel to all who would receive it.

To keep in touch with the new converts and to make sure they had a full understanding of their new faith, he wrote many letters. The letters were treasured and preserved. Later they were gathered together and became a part of the New Testament.

St Paul was given many visions and revelations. He says in one of his letters that he had been "caught up into the third heaven . . . into Paradise," and that he had heard "things that cannot be told, which man may not utter." (II Cor. 12:2-4). Luke tells us in the Book of Acts that "God did extraordinary miracles by the hands of Paul, so that handkerchiefs or aprons were carried away from his body to the sick, and diseases left them and the evil spirits came out of them." (Acts 19:11,12).

Although he was unflagging in his enthusiasm and zeal for the Faith, he never stopped being sorry for having persecuted Christians. He called himself "the chief of sinners," but never tired of telling people that they could have new life by their faith in Christ. One of his greatest words was this:

"I am not ashamed of the Gospel; it is the power of God for salvation for every one who has faith, to the Jew first and also to the Greek." (Romans 1:16).

He called himself Apostle to the Gentiles (non-Jews). At a time when there was a famine in Israel and the Christians there were in great need, he took up an offering from the new non-Jewish Christians and carried it back to Jerusalem to aid them in their need. But there he was arrested, and would have been killed, but as a Roman citizen, he claimed his right to appeal his case before Caesar himself. And so he was carried to Rome, with many adventures — and even a shipwreck — on the way.

Tradition says that eventually he was condemned to death, and, as a Roman citizen, was beheaded rather than crucified. The place of his death outside the ancient walls of Rome now has a beautiful church, "St Paul's Outside the Walls," where there are many relics associated with his martyrdom. His feast day, with St Peter, is June 29, and the commemoration of his conversion is January 25.

St Columba

c. 521-597

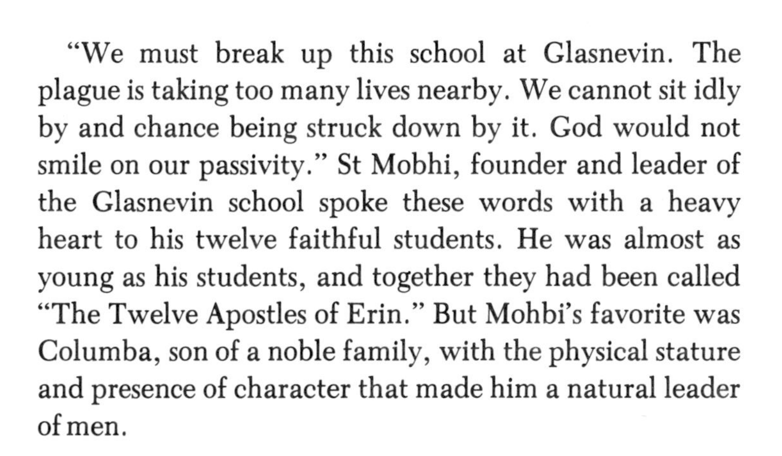

"We must break up this school at Glasnevin. The plague is taking too many lives nearby. We cannot sit idly by and chance being struck down by it. God would not smile on our passivity." St Mobhi, founder and leader of the Glasnevin school spoke these words with a heavy heart to his twelve faithful students. He was almost as young as his students, and together they had been called "The Twelve Apostles of Erin." But Mohbi's favorite was Columba, son of a noble family, with the physical stature and presence of character that made him a natural leader of men.

The students agreed, and with the closing of the school, Columba's formal education ended. But his heart had always burned with a desire to serve God as long as he could remember. His earliest memory was that of the old priest to which his family sent him, after the custom of noble families of the time. He knew that serving God was the only kind of life worth living.

Now that he was no longer a student, Columba tramped all over Ireland preaching the beauty of a life lived for Christ, with a voice, so it was said, that could be heard a mile away. He was instrumental in founding several monasteries: Derry, Durrow, Kells and others — because so many wanted to follow his way of life.

His desire to have and read books never left him. But books were very rare, because they had to be hand-copied and were usually illuminated with colors and drawings. He borrowed a book of Psalms from his old master, Finnian, and proceeded to copy it himself. Finnian was displeased, however, and demanded the copy as well as the original. An ugly dispute followed, with a trial before the king, who ruled that Columba was wrong and should return both the original and the copy. Other disputes followed, and Columba decided that it was time for him to leave his beloved Ireland and all the disputes behind.

With twelve others (all kinsfolk) he sailed in a little leather-covered boat towards Scotland, and landed on the island of Iona. There they founded a monastery with the object of winning as many people to the Christian faith as possible. From Iona, Columba and his monks spread the gospel all over Scotland to the Picts and other tribes. Iona became a place where even kings came to seek good advice, and eventually a favorite burial place for many kings.

The story is told that when Columba was old, and knew he was soon to die, the faithful community horse came and placed his head on Columba's shoulder as a kind of farewell.

Iona would eventually become a "mother of monasteries," and its fame would spread over all the British Isles. Lindisfarne, one of its most famous daughter houses, is credited with the spread of Christianity throughout northern England. The monastery of Iona is still famous, and people make pilgrimages there. Columba was born about 521, and died on Iona in 597. His feast is June 9.

St Kenneth

c. 525-c. 600

Kenneth was born in Derry, Ireland, the son of a bard, or poet. Bards were called upon to make up a poem on the spot, and often sang it rather than merely reciting it. Bards were often poor, and Kenneth's parents had difficulty even finding food for their young son. A wandering cow stopped by their little hut, and became the answer to their needs for milk for Kenneth. It was also the custom of that time for sons to be sent away to school at a monastery, and Kenneth studied under St Finnian, the same teacher who taught St Columba. Columba and Kenneth, together with St Kieran and St Comgall were known as "The Apostles of Ireland."

After helping establish monasteries and churches in Ireland, Kenneth moved over to nearby Scotland to preach the Word of God among the Picts and Scots. A close friend of Columba, he planted his most important church on the island of Mull, near Columba's holy island of Iona. Together Columba and Kenneth went across Scotland to carry God's Word to Brude, the Pictish King at Inverness. Brude closed the castle gate, but it opened miraculously in answer to the prayers of the two saints. When Brude threatened them with his sword, Kenneth made the sign of the cross, and Brude's hand was paralyzed.

At one time Columba was crossing the sea, and a violent storm blew up, threatening to capsize his boat. "Don't worry!" he told his companions. "Kenneth is running to church with only one shoe on to pray for us, and God will hear him." Sure enough, at just that moment, St Kenneth had felt an urgent impulse to leave the table and rushed to the church to pray — leaving one shoe behind him!

The fame of St Kenneth's holy life and zeal for the Faith spread throughout Ireland and Scotland, and lives on today in villages and churches bearing his name in both countries. His feast is celebrated on October 11.

St Boniface of Mainz

c. 675-754

"Crash!" The giant oak fell smashing to the ground almost as soon as Boniface's axe hit its trunk. It splintered into four parts, and the people breathlessly awaited the wrath of their gods to fall on this impious intruder. But no wrath fell. The sacred oak, long worshipped as a dwelling place of the god, Donar, lay before them in a pitiful heap.

"Thus is the power of the gods you feared so much," shouted Boniface. "But we have come to tell you of the true God, who created heaven and earth, and everything in them, and who sent His Son to save you from belief in these terrible demons you call 'gods.' "

St Boniface of Mainz

Boniface is known as "the Apostle of Germany." Born in England, and dedicated from his youth to the service of Christ, he had longed to carry the Word of God to the people in Europe who still lived under the evil spell of their old beliefs. He knew that the English and the Germans were closely related peoples, and it grieved him that so many still lived in fear and hate, when Jesus Christ could change their whole outlook on life.

His first job had been teaching in the monastery where he himself had been trained. He had written the first Latin grammar produced in England, and had a wonderful gift for making the teachings of the Bible plain. But the missionary zeal burned in his heart, and eventually he was allowed to join an older man, St Willibrord, who was waging an uphill battle of faith among the Frieslanders who lived in what is now northwest Germany and the Netherlands. Boniface was then known by his baptismal name, Winfrid, and after finding that he could get nowhere in his attempts to aid Willibrord, he went to Rome to consult with the Pope. There he was given the name, Boniface, and sent with papal commission to carry the Word of God to the heathen. He made his way over the Alps to Germany and began his work.

His work was so successful that the Holy Father called him back to Rome, made him a bishop and gave him power to establish other bishops in the German area. In each of these areas where he set up a new bishop, he placed one of his English disciples.

His task was not easy, however, because there were already some stubborn and unworthy men who claimed the right to lead the few Christians that already lived there. These Boniface had to depose and replace, and it caused much conflict and controversy for him. One of his greatest achievements was the establishment of a monastery at Fulda, which became a kind of German Monte Cassino. Monte Cassino was the great foundation of St Benedict, the motherhouse of all Benedictine monasteries.

After many years of establishing the faith among the Germans, Boniface still wanted to evangelize the stubborn Frieslanders whom he had worked with many years before. So, having retired from his episcopal duties, Boniface sailed down the Rhine for Friesland at the age of 73. He and his group of helpers began to preach and teach; now many more could be brought into the Church. Their mission was going to be a success this time. A sizeable group of converts were ready to be baptized; Boniface had arranged for them to meet him at Dokkum on Whitsun Eve for an open-air ceremony. Quietly reading, he waited in his tent for the group to gather. Suddenly they heard angry shouts outside. A band of men had gathered with knives and swords to attack them. His followers rushed forward.

"No!" shouted Boniface. "Trust in God and be willing to be martyred if that's His will!"

Boniface himself raised the Gospel book he was reading over his head. The leader of the mob brought his sword down upon Boniface so vigorously that the book bears deep slashes from every side. The attackers killed the entire group and left. The book Boniface was holding, still bearing the marks of the sword, is preserved at Fulda, where his body rests.

As a missionary and reformer, a man of holiness and simplicity, loveable and gracious in personal relationships, and as a faithful martyr, Boniface is recognized as one of the greatest of English saints. He is lovingly remembered and venerated throughout Germany and the Netherlands. His feast day is June 5.

St Columban

(Columbanus)

c. 543-615

Two men were quietly talking in the serene garden. Flowers were bursting out in beauty and a nearby stream gurgled playfully down a mountainside. The young man dressed in fine robes with a small crown on his head was pouring out his heart to the older man. The face of the elder was lined with years of toil and suffering, but softened by a look of tenderness. "My king, that is entirely wrong, and you know it," he said plainly. "Far better for you to marry and gain for your kingdom a queen who would be held in honor and whose children would be acknowledged as your legitimate heirs." The young King, Theodoric II agreed, thanked the aged monk for his stern but wise words of counsel, and set out, determined to follow all that the saint had told him.

Columban was elated that the young king of the Franks was willing to listen to his godly advice. Theodoric had always been reserved with him, but Columban's warmth had finally won his heart. Columban still had a sense of dread, however, because he knew that Theodoric was actually under the domination of his wicked grandmother, Brunhild. Ambitious and heedless of the good of the people, Brunhild encouraged her two grandsons to do whatever they liked, knowing that this would make them weak rulers and strengthen her own hand.

Sadly, Columban's fears were realized in a short time, when Brunhild managed to make a shambles of Theodoric's marriage and send his young wife packing. Because Columban had advised Theodoric to marry, Brunhild was able to use this to turn her grandson against the saint.

The king ordered Columban to leave Burgundy, and sent the old monk out across the country toward the sea under armed guard. Arriving at the coast of France, they put him safely on board. But the ship in which he was to sail stayed stuck in the mud despite the rising tide. The sign did not go unnoticed by the captain. Undoubtedly the story of Jonah had been told and retold to many a Christian seaman.

"Father, I'm afraid we must ask you to go ashore again," he said to Columban. "My ship seems to be unmoveable as long as you are on board. This has never happened before, and since I know you were put aboard against your will, I think God is speaking to us."

"I am ready to sail or go ashore," said the old saint. "Only let God's will be done."

And so they put him ashore, and immediately the ship floated and sailed away! Columban was now free, both from the ship and from his guards, who had already returned to the king to assure him that he was rid of the old monk.

Columban now made his way back across the land of the Franks to Austria where Theodoric's brother encouraged him to preach about Christ to the heathen in the southern part of his province. Columban set to work around Lake Constance (Switzerland) and Lake Zurich. The resistance of the heathen was so fierce that he could not convert many of them. But he established monasteries on the pattern of Irish monasteries like Iona and Kells. Some of them became large and famous in later times.

Again he was forced to leave and find another place of service because of the opposition of the people and the hostility of the king of Burgundy. So, at the age of seventy, he made his way over the Alps and into Italy. A kindly king and queen there deeded him an old ruined church at Bobbio and he labored there with others to rebuild it until the day he died. In later years it, too, became a great center of learning. Its celebrated collection of early manuscripts, many of them dating from the tenth century, is now in the Vatican Library, the Ambrosiana at Milan and Turin.

He was one of the great Irish missionary saints, whose work helped spread Christianity and civilization over Europe during the Dark Ages. In addition to his work as a missionary abbot, he wrote several poems and a *Rule of Life* for his monasteries. His feast is November 21.

St Francis Xavier

1506-1551

One of the greatest missionaries of all time, St Francis Xavier was born in Castle Xavier in the Basque section of Spain. At the age of 18 he went to the University of Paris, where he met Ignatius of Loyola, and before they had finished their studies, they had launched one of the great Orders of the Church, the Jesuits.

The little Society got off to a slow, difficult start, but in 1540, Ignatius appointed Francis to join Father Simon Rodriguez on a missionary journey to the East Indies. When Francis arrived in Lisbon for the journey, the King required them to stay and minister there for almost a year before he would send them to the Far East. He wanted them to serve not only the Church but the interests of Portugal as well. When they finally left, Francis Xavier had been appointed apostolic nuncio in the East. This gave him something of an ambassadorial status, and he used that office to achieve much good.

His destination was Goa, a Portuguese colony in India, where there were already many Christians. However, the spiritual state of the people was very poor, and immorality was everywhere. Those who claimed to be Christians were the worst enemies to St Francis' mission. The suffering of the native people from the Europeans made, he said, "a permanent bruise on my soul." But he continued to work with the sick in the hospitals, the prisoners, lepers, slaves and children. In order to make the gospel understood, he made up songs to the popular tunes the people knew. His greatest success was among the Paravas, a low-caste people; he was much less successful with the Brahmans — at the end of a year he had only one Brahman convert!

He lived as one of the people — sleeping on the ground in his hut, eating the same simple food the people had, and speaking to them as one of them. As time went on, he widened his work, going to Ceylon and many other islands off the Indian coast. He eventually was able to make a trip to Japan, and there he labored a year, studying the language and preaching. Leaving his converts in charge of others, he continued his missionary work.

His last great hope was to go to China with the Word of God, but this was not to be. After several frustrating attempts, he was on board a ship waiting to be taken to Canton, when he developed a high fever. He was put ashore and left without protection on the sand, with a chilling north wind blowing. Taken into a little hut by a Portuguese merchant, Francis lay for about two weeks, growing weaker and often delirious from his high fever. His young Chinese companion, Antony, realized that he was dying. Later Antony wrote, "With the name of Jesus on his lips, he rendered his soul to his Creator and Lord with great peace."

He died on December 3, 1552, only forty-six years old. Two or three months later, it was decided to remove his body and take it back to Goa. It was found to be flesh-colored and undecayed, and has remained so till the present time. His feast day is December 3.

St Elizabeth Seton

1774-1821

The covered wagons set out from Baltimore carrying their precious cargo, a handful of teenage girls who wanted to become nuns, several nuns, and their leader, Mother Elizabeth Seton. Barely five feet tall, she hardly seemed strong enough for the ordeals that awaited them in their new home in the country.

Ordeals, however, were no stranger to this sturdy woman. Her life had already had many unexpected turns and sorrows enough and to spare. Life had begun pleasantly enough. Born in New York City, in 1774, the year before the Declaration of Independence was drawn up, she was too young to remember much of the Revolutionary War period. She was the daughter of a wealthy and famous physician, and had been brought up in all the refinements of her class. Her family were members of the Protestant Episcopal Church, (her mother's father was rector of St Andrew's Episcopal Church on Staten Island). Her mother's death when she was very young had left her sensitive to others' needs, and her writings, even as a child, showed a marked spiritual character. Her concern for the poor and the sick earned her the nickname of Protestant Sister of Charity. She was a talented girl, spoke French fluently, played the harpsichord skillfully and was an able horsewoman. Popular at parties and balls, she was twenty years old when she married a wealthy young merchant, William Seton.

They were deeply in love with each other. They moved into their home on Wall Street and life went on happily for them for a number of years. Five children were born to them before financial disaster struck William's shipping business, following the death of his father. Already showing signs of ill health, the shock precipitated in him visions of impending doom, and his health declined more rapidly than ever. In less than three years the young couple were bankrupt, and Elizabeth had to take the children back to her father's home. An epidemic of yellow fever struck New York, claiming her father's life. Grief-stricken Elizabeth turned more than ever to God, spending much time in reading the Bible and prayer.

In 1803, William's health had deteriorated so much that his doctor suggested a sea journey. Selling the last possessions she had inherited from her father, Elizabeth and William and their oldest child, Anna Maria, set sail for Italy. Their friends, the Filicchis, had invited them to stay with them in Leghorn. But once they arrived, they were quarantined in a tower outside the city because of fear of yellow fever, and during the next forty days the Setons suffered untold agony. The tower was so cold that Elizabeth and Anna Maria had to skip rope to keep warm. Elizabeth tended William, whose condition was growing steadily worse. He died, two days after Christmas in Pisa, and was buried there. Elizabeth was twenty-eight years old, a widow with five children to support.

Attending church with her friends in Italy, Elizabeth felt drawn more and more to Roman Catholicism. Their belief in the Real Presence in the Sacrament, the praying of the Rosary and their veneration of Mary had a special appeal to her. The warmth and sacrificial charity of the Filicchis reinforced this. Following her return to New York she went through an intense personal struggle; converting would mean giving up her friends, most of her family and what little inheritance she had left. Acting against the advice of friends and against the strong urging of her pastor, Dr. Henry Hobart, she made her decision and was received into the Catholic Church on March 15, 1805. Opposition against her redoubled when her sister-in-law Cecilia joined her. The boarding-house for schoolboys which Elizabeth had opened soon failed because parents feared her religious influence and withdrew their sons.

At this point the president of St Mary's Seminary in Baltimore came to her rescue and invited her to become a teacher in that institution. In 1808 she left New York City, and in no time, had a house full of girls in Baltimore. That fall, a girl arrived who wanted to become a nun, and soon she was joined by four others. Bishop Carroll and Father DuBourg made plans for uniting them into a religious community, and the following year Elizabeth made her vows before Bishop Carroll. At first these women took simple vows to bind them for a year, and that June they wore religious habits for the first time. Soon there was not room enough for all who wanted to join them, and Mother Seton was given property in Emmetsburg, Maryland, where she and her company could go to carry out their religious life and mission.

It was a drafty lodging that awaited them in Emmetsburg, and when winter came, snow had to be shoveled from *inside* the house! Their provisions were so meager that the strictest economies had to be practiced. Bad colds grew worse, and before long their little cottage looked like a hospital. In spite of these hardships, though, they kept up their spirits. They learned to enjoy carrot coffee, buttermilk soup (made from milk given by a kind neighbor), and stale lard.

Hardships were not over when spring came. They rejoiced when their permanent home was finally completed, and then even more when first a chapel, then an infirmary, refectory, school and workroom were added. Their numbers were growing, but death seemed never far away. Her two sisters-in-law died, bringing fresh accusations from New York, and during the next few years, Elizabeth nursed two of her daughters in their dying days, as tuberculosis ravaged their bodies. Her grief was deep and lasting.

The infant community which St Elizabeth was founding was the American Sisters of Charity. She patterned her rule on that of St Vincent de Paul, and in spite of her setbacks and personal tragedies, she laid the foundation for the American parochial school system, trained teachers and prepared textbooks, wrote spiritual treatises and translated other works from French into English. In addition, she visited the sick of the neighborhood, and was instrumental in the conversion of many to the Catholic Church. Her work was especially effective among minority groups. Through all her trials and difficulties, she had found strength in God to carry on. Someone has said, "We call it coping — and we need a patron saint for coping."

Always thinking the best and hoping for the best for her sons, she was always ready to overlook their faults. To the very end of her life she continued to send them money, trying to help them in their business ventures, and worrying about their spiritual welfare. One son, who had been living a wasted life, saw the error of his ways and began to change, only to be lost at sea a short time later. The other son, William, eventually married, and one of his sons later became a bishop.

Elizabeth lived long enough to see her community blossom into a useful and much needed arm of the Church. She sent Sisters to open orphanages in Philadelphia and New York. But tuberculosis, which had stricken the whole family, finally took its toll on her. Her illness was slow and painful, but she dreaded being a burden to others, and felt that the kindnesses the Sisters poured out on her were spoiling her. On the night of January 4, 1821, sensing that the end was near, having no priest nearby, she began the prayers for the dying herself. As the Sisters watched anxiously, she bade them repeat with her a prayer she had loved and often used. Then she said one word with the last strength she had. Very distinctly she said, "Jesus."

St Elizabeth Bayley Seton, or Mother Seton as she is more popularly called, is our first American-born saint. Her Sisters of Charity picked up the wounded on Civil War battlefields; they teach in schools at every level, are found in hospitals, homes for the aged and schools for the deaf. These Sisters of Charity walk in the steps of Mother Seton, their founder, by serving others, sometimes at great cost. They serve in North and South America, in Italy and on foreign mission fields.

One thousand nuns from her Order were present at her canonization by Pope Paul VI in 1975. Impressive cures were credited to her intercession. Pope Paul praised her contributions as wife, mother, widow and consecrated nun. The Church remembers her in the celebration of her feast on January 4.

And He said to them, "Go into all the world
and preach the gospel to the whole creation."
Mark 16:15

Royal Saints

In Thy strength the king rejoices, O Lord,
in Thy help how greatly he exults!
Psalm 21:1

For the king trusts in the Lord and through the steadfast
love of the Most High he shall not be moved.
Psalm 21:7

In your majesty ride forth victoriously for the cause
of truth and to defend the right!
Psalm 45:4

Christ is the King! O friends upraise
Anthems of joy and holy praise
For his brave saints of ancient days,
Who with a faith forever new
Followed the King, and round him drew
Thousands of faithful men and true.
George Kennedy Allen Bell

St Helen Empress

c. 250-330

One day, about the year 275 A.D., a young Bithynian maiden named Flavia Helena was helping her parents to manage their inn in the little village of Drepanum, a region of present-day Turkey. A Roman legion arrived in the village. The young general, Constantius Chlorus, looked over the inn and said to his senior officer, "We'll make our headquarters here as long as the campaign takes."

And so it was that while he was there, he fell in love with the beautiful young daughter of the innkeeper. Her parents were flattered by his attention to Helena, for it was unusual for a young high-ranking officer in the

Roman legion to pay serious court to a maiden from such a low station in life. When he asked for her hand in marriage, they gave their consent at once. Several years later, a son was born to the young couple.

"He shall be called Constantine after his father," said Helena, as she cradled her newborn in her arms. "And indeed, may he grow up to be as great as his father."

Constantius Chlorus was indeed an able general, a favorite of Diocletian himself. The Emperor had watched him come up through the ranks, and had kept his eye on him with greater things in mind. In a time when insurrections constantly plagued the empire, Diocletian Jovius Augustus needed men he could trust. The empire had grown fat with the conquests of Gaul, Britain, and more than half of Europe, parts of Africa and all the Near East. The conquered peoples had to be restrained with solid, firm laws and strong troops, and Diocletian had done his best to make the empire secure. But his need for trusted men was never greater. And the burden of governing the vast empire was weighing heavily on him.

One day he called Constantius into his palace to talk the matter over.

"We are in need of some additional restructuring of the Roman empire," he said. "As you know, we have already divided the East and West, and Maximian Heracules shares the title of Augustus with us in Rome. He is a trusted friend, and we are well pleased with this arrangement. But Gaul, Britain and the northern provinces still need better government. They are not only harassed by the barbaric tribes from the frozen wastes beyond, but insurrection is a constant danger. We have been thinking of making two Caesars to serve under us, one under Maximian and one under ourself. Galerius, our trusted aide will be one. You, Constantius, might be the other."

Constantius stifled an inward gasp at such a sudden and high elevation. He would be Caesar? Second only to the two Augusti who reigned gloriously over the whole civilized world? Enough to make even the most sober head a little giddy!

Diocletian continued. "There is one problem as we see it. Your wife, Helena."

"My wife, Helena?" Constantius repeated, disbelieving. "She has ever been as faithful and devoted a wife as any man could ask, and never has she put any demands on me in my campaigns. May I ask, Majesty, what the problem is?"

"It's her background!" retorted Diocletian. "She's low-born and would not make a proper Caesar's wife." The Emperor had conveniently forgotten that he himself had been born of humble parents in the far-away province of Dalmatia. That was behind him now, and he had taken the name of Jupiter (Jove), the chief of the pantheon of Roman gods, as his family name. Now he was a demi-god and need not worry about his own earthly lineage.

"If you are to become Caesar, Helena will have to go. Maximian Augustus has a step-daughter, Theodora. She will make you a proper wife. As for young Constantine, we are prepared to take him into our care. If you wish to serve us in this way, see to it."

Constantius was dismissed, with his thoughts, his conscience and his ambitions.

History does not record how Helen took the news of her dismissal. By then her son, Constantine was 12 years old, old enough to be sent to the court of Diocletian to learn the ways of statecraft, and kept, some say, against his will, for many years.

That same year, 292, Constantius Chlorus was given the title of Caesar under Maximian Augustus, his new father-in-law, and put in charge of Britain, Gaul and Spain, one of the four divisions of the Empire. Maximian continued to rule Italy and Africa, Galerius was assigned to Illyricum and the Danube basin, and Diocletian continued to rule the East.

Although the official Roman position on religions was one of toleration, the Emperor's claim to divinity brought conflict between his claims and those of Jesus Christ for Christians. Persecutions against Christians were sporadic, but increasingly frequent and severe. While Constantius in Britain seemed to generally favor Christians where it was practicable, Galerius, on the other hand, seethed with hatred against them, and persuaded Diocletian in 303 to inaugurate the most violent persecution the Church had ever experienced. Even to this day the calendar of martyrs is replete with names that died in that "era of the martyrs."

When Diocletian retired in 305, Constantius was acclaimed Augustus, and shared the empire with wicked and immoral Galerius, who continued his persecution against Christians. Young Constantine finally managed to leave the court of Galerius to join his father in Britain. A year later, his father died in York, England, and Constantine was acclaimed as his successor and as Caesar by his troops. The next several years found a succession of battles and maneuvers, in which several men tried to assert supremacy as emperor. Galerius died of a dreadful disease, ending his ignominius career of persecution.

Before the final engagement with a rival, Constantine was given a vision of the cross and the "Chi Rho" (a symbol for Christ), and told that he would conquer in that sign. Believing it to be from God, he went boldly forward and won the day. Now the undisputed master of the West, Constantine joined with the eastern ruler, Licinius, in an edict which ended the terrible persecution of Christians and made it possible for the Church to emerge from the catacombs at last.

We do not know just when Helena became a Christian. It may have been at this time, for she had followed her son's fortunes with great interest, and would have been much moved by his account of the miraculous vision. It may have been during those dark days when she lived in obscure disgrace. At any rate, she was now proclaimed "Nobilissima Femina" (Most Noble Woman) by her son, who had never ceased to love and respect her. He also had her name, Flavia Julia Helena, struck on coins to spread her honor throughout the world.

By this time, St Helen was well advanced in years. A terrible family tragedy occurred a few years later (the details of which are unknown) which grieved and hurt her deeply. It was at this time that she decided to make a pilgrimage to the Holy Land, to visit the places where our Lord had lived, suffered and died. Eusebius, the great Church historian, says that her motive was to give thanks to God for His mercies to her family and to pray for His continued protection.

"I may have been declared Empress by my son," she said, "but in truth I am but a poor servant of the Lord. It is my desire to serve Him and His people in every way I can, and now the Lord has given me the means of helping many of them."

She made the most of her opportunities — distributing gifts to the poor, adorning Churches with sacred ornaments, beautifying even the most humble chapels. Prayer became her delight. She is believed to have caused two basilicas to be built — one on the Mount of Olives and one at Bethlehem. She encouraged her son in the building of churches in Rome, too, and an early tradition says that in Jerusalem she searched for the True Cross on which our Lord was crucified.

There is still a mystery about who found the True Cross, but as St Ambrose said in a sermon in 395, she worshipped not the wood itself, but the King who died on it for our sins. A later writer gave us this hymn about the Cross:

Faithful Cross! Above all other
One and only noble Tree;
None in foliage, none in blossom,
None in fruit thy peer may be;
Sweetest wood and sweetest iron:
Sweetest Weight is hung on thee.

St Helen died in the Holy Land in 330 A. D., the Lord having added years to her life, as it were, as though to compensate for the hurt and suffering of the many years of her exile. Her body was returned to Rome, and Constantine honored his mother by changing the name of her birthplace from Drepanum to Helenopolis.

In the West, her feast day is August 18, while the Eastern Churches honor her on the same feast day with her son, Constantine the Great. St Helen is usually portrayed with a crown, the model of a church, and the Holy Cross and nails.

St Etheldreda

(Audrey)

d. 679

St Etheldreda was born about 630-635 A.D., the daughter of the East Anglian king, Anna. The name "Angles" is the word from which the term "Anglo-Saxon" comes, and eventually this became "English." Several other saints came from St Etheldreda's family, St Sexburga, St Ethelburga and St Withburga. Although the names sound strange to us, they were in no way unusual for the seventh and eighth centuries.

Etheldreda felt called to remain celibate, to devote herself to God as a nun. Her parents insisted, however, that she marry a neighboring king named Tonbert. Tonbert gave her the Isle of Ely (near Cambridge) as a part of her marriage dowry, a gift that was to play an important part in her later life. Although she was now married, her husband respected her wishes, and they continued to live as brother and sister until Tonbert's death three years later, in 655.

At this point, Etheldreda went to Ely, where she hoped to continue to live out her life as a religious. This was not to be, however, for again, for political reasons, her parents prevailed upon her to marry Egfrid, the fifteen-year old king of Northumbria. Egfrid was content that Etheldreda continue to live as a nun, but about twelve years later, wanting a legal heir to his throne, he began to insist that she be a wife in more than name. Etheldreda pleaded with her husband to release her so that she might give herself to prayer and devotion in a monastery, but the king was insistent.

"Etheldreda, you are my wife. A king should have children, sons who will be able to carry on the kingdom after him. This is your duty to me, and even at this late date, you must consent to having our marriage consummated."

"But Egfrid! What am I to do? I have promised God that I would know no man, that I would be His alone! I cannot consent."

The royal couple were at a stalemate, as day after day Egfrid pressed for her consent. Finally, desperate, she made her plans to flee back to Ely, leaving in the dark of night to avoid detection. She could think of no other way out of the impasse. So with prayer to God and His Blessed Mother, she set out from Northumbria with only her trusted maid and a guard to protect them from highwaymen and brigands.

Next day word reached Egfrid that Etheldreda had fled.

"This will never do!" he shouted. "This way, we can never get this matter settled. We must bring her back at once!"

Summoning a company of soldiers, he mounted his best horse and began his pursuit. Etheldreda had already gained the distance of a night's journey, so there was no time to be lost.

By some miracle, Etheldreda and her companions managed to stay ahead of Egfrid and his men. Mile after weary mile went under their horses' feet, with but one word from the Queen: "On, we must press on!"

When they neared Ely, the familiar fens came in view. Fens were lowlands, common in eastern England, where the ground was swampy and marshy. Ely was called "The Isle of Ely" because it lay on somewhat higher ground, surrounded by these fens.

Carefully Etheldreda and her party sloshed and slogged their way across these muddy lowlands. The horses' hoofs were often stuck in the soft, squishy, black dirt, but somehow they were able to move forward.

Looking back to see if Egfrid and his men were in view, the guard noticed a very strange thing.

"Look, your majesty! The water! It's pouring in behind us, covering our tracks — even covering the path. I've never seen anything like this!"

"It's a miracle," said Etheldreda, crossing herself reverently. "God has heard my prayer and is providing a wall of safety behind me."

For a week, Egfrid and his men tried to make their way across the fens. Each time, they ran into water so deep and soil so soggy that they had to turn back. Finally, with a determined look which said, "I haven't given up yet," Egfrid said to his men, "Let's go back to Northumberland. I'll have to settle this another way."

On the way home, he went by the ancient town of York, where Constantine had once been declared Emperor of Rome, and where his cousin, Wilfred (later St Wilfred) was bishop.

"Wilfred will see it my way and convince Etheldreda to return home," he thought.

But Wilfred didn't see it his way.

"Don't you know that it's dangerous to try to dissuade someone from doing God's will?" he asked. "Etheldreda has made a vow and a commitment to God. Don't force her to break it!"

Reluctantly, Egfrid consented, and Etheldreda was permitted to receive the nun's veil from her cousin, St Ebbe, abbess of Coldingham. Returning then to Ely, Etheldreda set about establishing a monastery (or minster, as they were then called.) Hers would follow the Celtic pattern of having both nuns and monks living under her rule — living as separate communities, but sharing in the worship at the great minster church.

From that time on, Etheldreda wore only coarse woolen garments, forsaking the silks and linens she had known as a princess and queen. Eating only one meal a day, except on great feast days, she was as devout in prayer as she was diligent in work.

She became the most popular of all the Anglo-Saxon women saints. Her gift of prophecy was widely known and by it she foretold the plague that would cause her own death and that of a number of others in her monastery. During her later years, she suffered from a tumor on her neck, which she took as rightful punishment for having indulged herself in fancy necklaces in her youth. Although a surgeon removed it, the scar refused to heal. She died in 679 and was buried in a simple wooden coffin in the common cemetery of the monastery. Her sister, Sexburga, became abbess and continued her work at Ely. Etheldreda's fame and popularity continued to grow, and one day she became the most popular female saint of the whole Anglo-Saxon race. Seventeen years later, Sexburga decided that Etheldreda's body should be transferred to a more suitable shrine, because the people already regarded Etheldreda as a saint and miracles were occurring in answer to prayers at her grave in the monastery cemetery. In connection with this translation (transfer) of her body to a new tomb, two other miracles occurred. First, the men sent to find a suitable coffin, to everyone's surprise, discovered one that had been preserved since Roman times, carved out of marble, as though waiting for this special use. And then, when the wooden coffin containing Etheldreda's body was opened, the place where the tumor had been removed by the surgeon was completely healed over, with no scar left, and Etheldreda's body, dead for seventeen years, was found to be perfectly preserved with no sign of decay. Such an incorrupt condition was considered to be a verification of sainthood.

In later years, parishes throughout England used to celebrate Etheldreda's feast day with annual fairs. Her more common name by this time had been shortened to "St Audrey." One of the favorite items at such fairs was a cheap silk or lace collar, and these collars came to be known as "St Audrey's lace," corrupted to sound like "Tawdry's Lace." Thus the word "tawdry" came into our language to mean something showy, gaudy, but of no real value. How St Audrey would have laughed, for her life was one of simplicity and devotion, and had real value!

Her feast day is June 23. She is usually pictured in art with a crown and a pastoral staff, with two does, who were said to have supplied Ely with milk during a famine. Besides the great cathedral at Ely, twelve other English churches are dedicated to her.

St Etheldreda's double monastery at Ely was destroyed by the Danes in the 9th century, but a new Benedictine monastery for men was established in the 11th century and continued until the Dissolution of the Monasteries by

Henry VIII. The Cathedral, a magnificent Norman building of the 11th and 12th centuries, continues to honor her as its founder, and the Daily Offices have continued to be sung under its great vaults.

St Margaret of Scotland

1046-1093

When Margaret, a princess from Hungary, was about four or five years old, she was sent with her sister to England, to the court of Edward VI (the Confessor), to learn English ways. There she met Malcolm Canmore, a tall, sturdy young Scot of the royal house of Athol, who was preparing to return to his native country to restore his house to the Scottish throne. His battles proved successful, and in a short time he became Malcolm III, King of Scotland.

Malcolm thought no more of the child he had met at Edward's court until other circumstances brought them together again. About sixteen years later, in 1066, a date known to every English child, William the Conqueror invaded England to claim what he considered his rightful domain. The Saxon royal family fled, taking Margaret and all the others with them. The ship which they boarded for Europe ran into rough weather, and instead of landing on the continent, was blown ashore near Wearmouth in Northumberland, which was under Scottish rule. Malcolm himself was in Wearmouth at the same time, on one of his usual military missions, which were often brutal and destructive. Hearing of their misfortune, Malcolm went down to greet them and welcome them to his castle at Dunfermline.

It was the custom in those days for royal families to intermarry, in order not only to preserve the royal bloodlines, but to strengthen one's own kingdom. Malcolm wanted to secure his own power, especially against the newly arrived Normans in England. Since Margaret was from the old Saxon line, he decided that marriage to Margaret would gain him some important political ties. When he asked her hand in marriage, however, she hesitated. A devout girl from her youth, she wanted to be sure of God's will for her, so she consulted her spiritual advisors.

"I had thought, father, that perhaps God is giving me a vocation as a nun, to devote myself entire to serving Him."

"My child," said the priest, "God can use you just as much as an instrument of His will if you should marry the

King. As Queen of Scotland you would be in a position to help the entire nation. But the choice must be yours."

The marriage took place with joyful celebrations in the Chapel of Dunfermline in the year 1070. Margaret had grown to love Malcolm very deeply, and on her part, had captured his heart and affection. Recognizing her spiritual devotion and wisdom, he soon began to seek her help in guiding the internal affairs of his country. "He readily obeyed her wishes and prudent counsel in all things; whatever she refused, he refused also; whatever pleased her he also loved for love of her," reported one who knew them well.

Margaret had grown up in the faith and traditions of the western Catholic Church. Now she found herself in a rough-and-tumble country, where the traditions of the Celtic Church still held sway, sometimes in conflict with those of Rome. Using gentle persuasion, she helped to bring the people to accept practices that were in harmony with the Apostolic See, and she herself took part in many discussions of these matters. The results were new laws correcting abuses among both clergy and laity — a strengthened and purified Church. Insisting on godly learning for layfolk and for clergy, she invited groups of women to meet and study the Scriptures while they embroidered vestments and altar cloths — a faint echo of future St Margaret's Guilds for Churchwomen.

Her greatest achievement, however, was the change in Malcolm. Her confessor, the Prior of Durham, wrote of them that they would often have banquets and serve as many as three hundred poor people, especially during the seasons of Lent and Advent. They had times of prayer every day, with the reading of the gospel for themselves and their household, and together they erected hostels for strangers. Margaret introduced for the first time in Scotland, the monastic order of Benedictines, making Dunfermline a daughter house from Canterbury. In addition, the royal couple fed and cared for nine orphans and twenty-four needy adults daily, at a time when there were no orphanages or homes for the elderly.

For her part, Margaret was faithful in her private prayers, and regularly read from her Evangelistarium, a little illuminated Gospel book which can still be seen in the Bodleian Library at Oxford.

Six sons and two daughters were born to their marriage. Three of the sons followed their father in succession on the Scottish throne: Edgar, Alexander and David. David, like his mother, was revered as a saint after his death. One of their daughters, Matilda, married Henry I of England, and became known to her people as "Good Queen Maud."

In 1093, King William Rufus (meaning William the Red, because of his ruddy complexion) was ruler of England. One of the most corrupt kings in English history, "William was given to unnatural vices, blasphemy and uncurbed violence." Enmity and rivalry had continued to plague Scottish and English relationships, with border areas being often a subject of dispute and rival claims. One such incident gave William a pretext for invading what Malcolm considered his rightful domain, and war resumed. Kings themselves went to war in those days, and Malcolm led his troops, with his sons joining in the battle with him. Margaret was seriously ill and bedridden in the royal castle in Edinburgh when young Edgar returned from the battlefield.

"She must not be told of the death of my father and Edward," he said to the servants. "The shock would kill her." Margaret looked sadly at her young son's face as he approached her bed. "How are your father and brother, my son?" she asked.

He tried to smile, fighting to hold back the tears. "They are well, mother," he replied.

"Yes. I know how it is," she said softly, and closed her eyes as if to shut out everything but God. Her condition grew worse by the hour, as if her soul longed to slip away from a world which had grown old and wearisome for her. She called for a priest, and insisted on being helped into the little chapel, where she received Communion for the last time. Then, four days after the death of Malcolm and Edward, on November 16, 1093, Margaret died. Her last words were, "O Lord Jesus Christ, who by Thy death gave life to the world, deliver me from all evil."

Malcolm had ruled his nation well, but it was Margaret who had ruled the hearts of the people. Canonized in 1249, her tomb was moved to a shrine behind the high altar in the Abbey Church at Dunfermline. She was named patroness of Scotland in 1673, Scotland's only saint to be celebrated by the entire

Church in the Roman calendar. Her feast day is November 16, the anniversary of her death.

> I sing a song of the saints of God,
> Faithful and brave and true . . .
> And one was a doctor, and one was a queen
> And one was a shepherdess on the green;
> They were all of them saints of God, and I mean
> God helping, to be one, too.
>
> *(L. Scott.)*

St Henry the Emperor

973-1024

In the year of our Lord 971, a son was born to Henry, Duke of Bavaria, and his wife, Gisela, daughter of Conrad, King of Burgundy. Henry the Quarrelsome and Gisela named their firstborn Henry after his father, but early in life young Henry decided that he would be a peaceful rather than a quarrelsome ruler.

So well did Henry take to his studies at the cathedral school in Hildesheim where he was sent, that his parents began to wonder if he was perhaps better suited for the Church than for affairs of state. When he had finished at Hildesheim, he then went on to the Bishop of Regensberg for further reading and study.

In 995, when Henry was 24 years old, his father died, and the question of his vocation was settled. He was soon in office as the new Duke of Bavaria. Bavaria is located in the southeastern part of Germany, near Switzerland and the Austrian Alps. As it turned out, his education had prepared him well for leadership, and in addition had given him a life-long love for the Catholic Faith. Two years later he married Cunigund, daughter of the royal family of the neighboring kingdom of Luxembourg.

In 1002, Otto III, emperor of the Holy Roman Empire, died suddenly. Henry, last male survivor of the House of Saxony, was heir to the imperial throne. The empire at that time was a kind of loose confederation of lesser kingdoms, dukedoms and bishoprics, held together in the main by the adherence of all of them to the Catholic Faith. There were rival claims to the imperial throne, and it was about a year before final recognition came and Henry was universally acknowledged as successor to Otto. In June, 1002, Pope Benedict VIII crowned him with the triple crown in Mainz.

Henry's great aim and purpose was to unite the bickering factions that comprised the Holy Roman Empire. He was gifted in his objectives and zealous in the work of restoring peace among all the different little dukedoms and kingdoms. He was realistic enough to know that peace must be fought for, so did not hesitate to crush the internal revolts and petty feuds which arose from time to time. He also had to contend with border disputes, in addition to his right to inherit the throne of Burgundy (finally ceded to him by the French). He had to fight for control of Bohemia and Meissen in the east against the continuous rivalry of Poland, while maintaining his rights against the encroachment of his brothers-in-law in Luxembourg, to say nothing of prolonged disputes along his western frontier with Lorraine and Flanders — altogether, a lot of battles for one dedicated to peace and unity!

Through it all he sought the aid of the Church and submitted himself to its authority. He deliberately abandoned Otto's plans for a world empire. Instead, his goal was *Renovatio regni Francorum*, Renewal of the Frankish Kingdom. With the help of Pope Benedict VIII, he succeeded in filling bishops' vacancies with men who were loyal to him. Because bishops had great power in civic and political matters, this loyalty helped to unify the empire and increase the stability of society. In return, Henry showed the bishops every consideration, and richly endowed their churches.

In 1007, he founded the See of Bamberg, and with his wife, Cunigunde, endowed the cathedral and monastery there. He was a supporter of monastic reform and worked with others at ending monastic abuses. Henry placed the authority of the Church ahead of temporal government. That policy combined with his steady fulfillment of his responsibilities endeared him not only to his subjects, but to those who followed him.

On the way home from one of his campaigns in Italy in 1021, Henry became ill and stopped at St Benedict's abbey in Monte Cassino. There he experienced a miraculous healing, in spite of a chronic lameness which hampered him the rest of his life.

Henry and Cunigunde had no children. They left behind them instead a heritage of churches and monasteries which they paid for out of their personal treasures. One of the most outstanding was the great cathedral of Bamberg. He made Bamberg a center of ecclesiastical power, and furnished it with both a monastery and school. The building of the cathedral itself was begun in 1007 but was not completed until the 13th century, more than two hundred years later.

Henry died peacefully on July 16, 1024. His last efforts had been focused on settling church disputes and bringing about unity between warring factions. He and Cunigunde were buried in a richly ornamented tomb in Bamberg Cathedral in the center of Bavaria. Portraits of St Henry show him wearing a crown, carrying a scepter, and holding a miniature church.

He was canonized in 1146, and declared by St Pius X to be patron of Benedictine oblates. His feast is now celebrated on July 13.

St Elizabeth of Hungary

1207-1231

One summer evening in 1207, a minnesinger announced to Landgrave Herman of Thuringia that a baby girl had been born who was to become the wife of his son. The baby was Elizabeth, daughter of the King of Hungary, and in keeping with the prophetic announcement, she was betrothed to Ludwig, Herman's son, while they were both children. Such betrothals were a common practice among royal families of that time, a way of insuring peace between countries, by having children of both countries engaged or married to each other.

Elizabeth was only four years old when she was brought to the court of Thuringia, and ten years later, she and Ludwig IV were married. Thuringia, a separate state then, later became a part of Germany. Young Ludwig had fallen in love with his bride, who was described as beautiful, of dark complexion, serious in her ways, modest and kindly in speech, faithful in prayer, and generous to the poor.

Three children were born to the royal couple in the next six years: Herman, Sophia and Gertrude. Elizabeth would sometimes rise in the night and slip out of the room for her prayers. So concerned was she for the poor that, during a time of famine, she virtually exhausted the royal stores in supplying food to the most needy. Some of the members of her husband's court criticized her for this, Ludwig defended her actions, saying, "They will bring divine blessings on us."

In 1227, the call for a crusade to free the Holy Land from the Moslems sounded across Europe. Christians were deeply ashamed that the land where Jesus lived was now in the hands of people who did not believe in Him. Ludwig decided that he should join the crusade. Life in the 13th century was hazardous at best. A dread disease, the plague, often struck without warning. People did not know what caused it or how to avoid it. Shortly after Ludwig departed on crusade, but before he could reach the Holy Land, he contracted the plague and died. It was several months before news of his death reached Elizabeth and the Hungarian court.

"The world is dead to me, and all that was joyous in the world," she cried.

Now the jealousy and hostility of the court towards her showed its true face. Ludwig's brother, regent for Elizabeth's young son, Herman, drove her from the castle. She was given shelter with relatives for a time, but after some months, she decided to arrange for the care of her three children and devote herself to caring for the poor and the sick.

Taking the habit of the Third Order of St Francis, she underwent training in the religious life and put herself under the guidance of a spiritual director. Unfortunately, he was a very severe and strict man who frightened her and imposed heavy disciplines on her. In addition she suffered grief over the loss of her husband and her children. Nevertheless, by the grace of God, she was always obedient to what she was told to do, and kept her spirit of love and sacrifice through everything that happened.

"I am like the grass that bends under the rain, but rises up again when the rain is over," she said, speaking of the disciplines imposed on her.

She sewed for those who needed clothes, fished for food for the hungry, and in every possible way served those whose needs were greater than her own. Under the severe disciplines, however, her health soon failed. She was only twenty-four years old when she died. The nobility of her spirit and her great care for the poor and needy made her one of the most beloved saints of the German people. Her feast is celebrated on November 19.

St Louis of France

1214-1270

Born in April, 1214, Louis was the oldest surviving son of King Louis VIII and his wife, Blanche, of Castile. His mother personally instructed him in the Catholic faith, and brought him up to be a sincere lover of God.

"I love you, my dear son, as much as a mother can love her child," she said to him. "But I would rather see you dead at my feet than to see you commit a mortal sin."

He was twelve years old when he became king of France, and his mother was appointed as Regent. A forceful woman, she vigorously opposed the rebellious barons in their attempts to take advantage of the king's youth to weaken the royal power. On two occasions during this time, King Henry III of England invaded France in support of the French barons who were warring against Louis. Although he was only fifteen, Louis personally led his troops into battle each time and soundly defeated the English. Henry III beat a hasty retreat back to England. These overwhelming victories over Henry III would have enabled him to confiscate all Henry's French possessions, but Louis preferred to leave him in possession of Aquitaine and nearby areas.

At the age of nineteen, Louis married Marguerite of Provence. They were to have a happy marriage and eleven children.

In all his dealings with the barons and with Henry of England, Louis showed that he cared more for peace, reconciliation and the welfare of his subjects than for power or conquest. Forgiving the son of Hugh de la Marche, one of the barons who followed his father in rebelling against Louis, he said, "A son cannot do anything but obey his father."

Noted for keeping his word on every treaty to which he was a party, for his impartiality and justice, Louis was often asked to arbitrate disputes, even outside France. For instance, in later years, when Henry III of England was having trouble with his own barons, he called on Louis to help settle the dangerous standoff.

But Louis did not neglect his own people. He had a great love for the poor and did much to relieve their distress. Not only were they fed at his own table, but he often served them himself.

In 1244, after his victory over the English, Louis fell ill with malaria. During his sickness he made this promise to God: "If You will heal me, I will take the cross and go deliver Jerusalem from the hands of the infidels." The Holy City had just fallen into the hands of the Sultan of Egypt, and the entire Christian kingdom of Jerusalem was in a dangerous position.

Embarking with a large army, his wife and family, Louis set sail for Cypress. His mother was left to serve again as Regent for the kingdom. His plan was to capture Egyptian cities and exchange them for Jerusalem and the Christian cities of Syria which had already fallen into the hands of the Moslems.

With this in mind, he surprised and captured the coastal city of Damietta and planted the flag of St Denis on Saracen soil. He entered the city barefooted, with the queen, his brothers and the young princes. He then issued this challenge to the Sultan:

"The soldiers who march under my standards cover the plains, and my cavalry is no less redoubtable. You have but one method by which to avoid the storm that threatens you. Receive the priests who will teach you the Christian religion. Embrace it and adore the Cross; otherwise, I will pursue you everywhere."

Sending his family on to the Holy Land ahead, he and his men moved on for more Egyptian conquests. Disappointments awaited him, however, as he pushed south towards Cairo. His army was weakened by dysentery and found itself cut off from the coast by the Egyptian fleet.

First harassed and then finally surrounded by the enemy, Louis and his entire army were defeated and captured. He had to give back the city of Damietta and pay a large ransom in gold and silver to get himself and his troops released.

He joined his wife in Syria, and in spite of pleas from his barons to return to France, stayed in the Holy Land, making alliances, fortifying Christian cities, encouraging those who held them, and always trying to convert the Moslems. Only when he received news of his mother's death in 1254 did he turn back to France.

His integrity and bravery earned him immense prestige, and he took advantage of this to enact many reforms for the welfare of his people. For instance, he established a fairer system of justice which strengthened the royal government and curbed the excessive power of barons and bishops. In addition, he introduced the practice of examining witnesses in civil cases replacing the use of trial by combat. He founded the university of Paris, the oldest in Europe, as well as a hospital for the blind.

Louis was a special friend of monasticism; he befriended the new mendicant orders, the Franciscans and Dominicans, and established several monastic houses himself. Often he invited outstanding monks and theologians to dine with him; one of these was St Thomas Aquinas. In gratitude for his help to the Christians in the Holy Land, the emperor in Constantinople gave him a relic believed to be the Crown of Thorns. He revered this gift so much that he had a magnificent church built to house it, the Sainte Chapelle in Paris.

But the king's heart was still drawn to the Holy Land and the deliverance of the Christian kingdom there. Since coming back from the Sixth Crusade, he had worn a cross on his clothes to signify his intention to return. He had become more devout than ever. At a time when most Christians received Communion only occasionally, many of them only once a year, Louis made a practice of taking his children to Mass daily and teaching them their prayers and Hours himself.

In 1270, Louis took up the cross again against the urgent advice of his counselors. Age and failing health could not keep him back. He felt duty bound to make another attempt. He decided to attack Tunis, hoping to split the Moslem empire in two. The first battles yielded easy victories. Then the blow came. Louis contracted typhus, a painful and almost inevitably fatal disease. The needless schism between the Eastern and Western Churches had long concerned him, and knowing that he was dying, he called the Greek ambassadors to his bedside and urged them to be reconciled with the Roman Church.

He then sent his last message to his son, Philip, who would rule after him: "The first thing I teach you," it read, "is to mold your heart to love God; for without that no one can be saved."

On August 24, 1270, he repeated the Psalm, "Lord, I will enter into Thy house; I will worship in Thy holy temple, and will give glory to Thy name." Then he peacefully died.

With his death, the crusading army disbanded, and his body was carried back to France in a triumphal procession. Kneeling and praying, the people lined the roads as the convoy passed by. Acclaimed as a saint by the common people years before he was officially canonized in 1297, he was buried in the abbey church of St Denis, the resting place of the kings of France. He is the only king of France to be declared a saint, and was held up as the ideal of a king throughout the medieval period. Churches and cities have been named in his honor, and his feast is celebrated on August 25.

St Casmir of Poland

1458-1484

This young saint was a prince and was called "The Peace-Maker" by his fellow countrymen.

The son of King Casmir IV of Poland, Casmir was a religious boy, cheerful, with a pleasant disposition. He chose to dress plainly and was said to have avoided all signs of indulgence.

His favorite hymn, written by Bernard of Cluny, was *Omnia die dic Maria*, "All day long, sing of Mary." A copy of it was buried with him, and today it is often called "The Hymn of St Casmir."

In 1471, the nobles of neighboring Hungary, dissatisfied with their king, begged Casmir's father to permit them to make young Casmir their king. Casmir was not yet quite fifteen years old, and was not at all eager to take up the task of ruling over another country. He finally consented, only to find himself faced with a large army loyal to the unpopular Hungarian king.

"This is no way for Christian rulers to behave toward each other," said Casmir. "The shedding of blood of all these innocent people in order to satisfy the desires of a score of noble families seems wrong — and from the size of the opposing army, I think it is a hopeless cause, anyway!"

So saying, Casmir turned back towards Poland and home. Some of his generals, eager for glory and the spoils of war, argued with him.

"Sire, think of what this will mean to the glory of Poland, with father and son sitting on neighboring thrones! It's an opportunity of a lifetime." Then growing more bold, they added, "Besides that, sire, think of how angry your father is going to be when you go home without even fighting a battle."

But Casmir's mind was made up. No amount of persuasion could change his mind. "No," he said. "It is wrong. Even His holiness, the Pope, has sent an embassy to father asking him not to carry through the project. No. I will not do it."

His father, the king, was very, *very* angry.

"What's this?" he stormed. "A prince who won't go to battle? You've been thinking too much about religious things. It's affected your reason. A few months in the castle of Dobski should sober you up!"

And with that, he sent young Casmir off to the castle and to three months' imprisonment.

Still Casmir did not change his mind.

Nor was the military adventure the only subject upon which he had strong convictions. A short time later, a favorable marriage was about to be arranged between Casmir and the young daughter of none other than Emperor Frederick III, the most powerful man in Europe. Such a marriage would strengthen the bonds between the Polish kingdom and the Roman imperial power, and would be considered a great advantage to everyone, especially to Casmir's future. But Casmir had chosen another course. He felt deeply that God was calling him to live a celibate, single life, and to devote himself to studies and prayer rather than to the cares of a wife and family. Again, no amount of arguments could sway him from what he believed to be the God-inspired choice he was making.

In the fifteenth century, and up to the present one for that matter, the dread disease of tuberculosis had no known cure. It struck high and low, being no respecter of persons, and when Casmir contracted it, it was not long in taking its toll on him. He died at the age of 23 in 1484 and was buried in the Church of St Stanislaus in Vilna. Soon there were reports of miracles at his tomb, and in 1521 he was declared to be a saint by the Church. His feast day is March 4.

The kingdoms of this world have become the kingdom
of our Lord and of His Christ.
Revelation 11:15

Leaders

Remember your leaders, those who spoke to you
the word of God: consider the outcome of their life,
and imitate their faith.
Hebrews 13:7

He who is greatest among you shall be your servant;
whoever exalts himself will be humbled, and whoever
humbles himself will be exalted.
Matthew 23:11, 12

Lo! what a cloud of witnesses
Encompass us around!
Men once like us with suffering tried,
But now with glory crowned.

Let us, with zeal like theirs inspired,
Strive in the Christian race;
And freed from every weight of sin,
Their holy footsteps trace.
Paraphrase of Hebrews 12:1, 2 (1745)

St Benedict

c. 480-c. 550

Benedict moved quickly through the outlying streets of Rome. He had made his choice and he wasted no time in putting it into effect.

His family had sent him to the great city to complete his education, but the truth he discovered was not what his parents intended! The wisdom set forth in the parchment scrolls of his teachers opened a new world to the students, but what changed their minds and lives was too often the life in the taverns and dark streets of the city.

The smells of rotting food and stale flesh and wine hung in the streets. Benedict wanted to leave that behind him. Even more than the smells, he wanted to be free from the violence and temptations of his own flesh. His searching led him finally out to the wild, rocky hill-country of Subiaco. Forcing his way through the under-brush and woods up to an almost sheer face of rock, he found a stone cave. This would be his home, his school, his altar for the next three years. A neighboring monk whom he had met on the way fed him as well as he was able from his own food. He placed the food in a basket and let it down to Benedict from the top of the hill above the cave where Benedict slept.

Eventually, a group of shepherds happened to see him, and thought at first that he was a wild animal living in the cave, dressed as he was in animal skins given by his friend, the monk. But talking with him, they discovered that he possessed great wisdom and compassion as a result of his time alone with God. They told about him everywhere, and people began to seek him out with problems and questions. A group of monks nearby thought he would make a good leader, but when he joined them, they soon found that his ways were too strict for their lazy, selfish lives. Then some of them tried to kill him by offering him a poisoned drink. Benedict made the sign of the cross over the cup, and it shattered to pieces in his hand. The evil secret was revealed! That incident ended his relationship with that group of monks, and Benedict went back to the solitary life he loved.

But not for long. Soon he was constrained to organize a group of disciples who wanted to live under his direction. He went to Monte Cassino, near Naples, and founded the first Benedictine monastery. He was a very sensible and loving father to his monks. In order to help them grow and mature in their faith, he wrote a Rule to guide them. This rule is still used today by many different religious communities.

Benedict was concerned with others outside the monastery. Once there was a terrible famine in the countryside, so he gave all the food in the monastery away except five loaves. The monks were very angry at having all their food given away. Benedict said to them "You have not enough today, but tomorrow you will have too much." The next morning, 200 bushels of flour were found at the gate of the monastery.

Benedict's sister, St Scholastica, also followed the same way of life as her brother, and founded a house of sisters not far from Monte Cassino. Once each year Benedict visited her to talk over spiritual things. On their last visit, Scholastica pleaded with him in vain to stay longer. But Benedict felt that, as always, he should return to Monte Cassino after their all-too-brief visit. In desperation, Scholastica prayed that a rain storm might come to keep her brother a little longer. A storm of such violence arose that the Saint could not return to his monastery until the next day.

Two days later, Scholastica died, and Benedict saw from his monastery a white dove ascending to heaven, which he knew was a sign of her death and the ascending of her pure soul to God. She was buried in the tomb Benedict had prepared for himself at Monte Cassino.

In the year 547, sensing that his own death was drawing near, Benedict had himself carried into the chapel of the monastery, and there, supported by his monks, he received the Blessed Sacrament, standing erect. He was buried in the same tomb with his beloved sister.

The Rule of St Benedict became the model for monastic life in the West, and gained for him the title of patriarch of Western Monasticism. His rule reflects the man himself, and is one of moderation, peace, composure and single-mindedness. He always respected the individual capabilities and personalities of each monk, and described the monastic life of his rule as "a school of the Lord's service, in which we hope to order nothing harsh or rigorous." His monasteries were destined to play a vital role in the preservation of ancient learning and wisdom and the eventual revitalization and renewal of Europe. He is often portrayed with a raven sitting on his shoulder, or with a broken cup (symbolic of the poisoned wine) in his hand.

His feast is now celebrated on July 11.

St Gregory the Great

c. 540-604

St Gregory was the Pope, the Bishop of Rome. He was walking along the streets of Rome one day when he noticed several children who were being sold as slaves. They had fair skin, blue eyes, and yellow-blonde hair. The Pope asked, "Who are these children?"

"They are Angles, your holiness," came the reply. "They belong to the Angle tribes that live in Britain."

"They should not be called, *Angles*," answered Gregory, "but *angels*."

He kept thinking about these people who were not Christians and were being treated as slaves, and determined to do something about it to make them "angels."

So he sent for a good friend, Augustine, who was abbot of a nearby monastery. "You must go to the island of Britain," said the bishop, "and carry the gospel there. You can take forty monks with you, and begin a new monastery. These people, too, must be taught about the Lord and learn to worship Him."

Augustine made his preparations, took the monks and started out across France. But tales of what he would find frightened him, and back to Gregory he turned, pleading that it was too dangerous. "No. You must go," said St Gregory. "These people must hear the gospel. I will make you archbishop of all the Angles."

And so Gregory, in 597, sent the first Roman Catholic missionary to England. In addition, he struggled to put things right in the Church throughout what is now France, Germany and Holland. This was not an easy job! The people of Rome were barely able to keep themselves from starving. The rulers of other countries in Europe did not behave in a Christian manner at all. The emperor, who lived in Constantinople, was so weakened by assaults from the East and internal conflicts in the empire, that he could no longer maintain order among his subjects. Gregory greatly strengthened the West, and did everything he could to keep civilization going throughout Italy and Europe. In 593 the cruel Lombards were ravaging and pillaging the land. Gregory rallied all the help he could for other cities and towns, and when the Lombard army arrived at Rome, he himself went out to speak to the Lombard king, bargained with him and persuaded him to leave Rome in peace.

In addition to sending missionaries, starting monasteries in many places, and storing food in granaries to keep people from starving, he re-organized the Roman Church and made the office of pope stronger than it had ever been before. He was always concerned for the poor, and one of the last things he ever did was to send a warm winter cloak to a poor bishop who suffered from the cold.

Gregory was concerned to improve the worship of the Church, and arranged to have the music used in services gathered together into a system. Chant is still called "Gregorian chant," in honor of him. He also founded the famous Roman *schola cantorum* and wrote several hymns.

Although he firmly upheld the papal dignity, the title he preferred for himself was "Servant of the servants of God," which popes still use in referring to themselves.

He wrote the earliest life of St Benedict, and other important works. His feast is celebrated on March 12, and other days mark his ordination and the removal of his body to its present honored resting place in Rome.

St Ambrose

339-397

The day began peacefully enough for Ambrose, the young governor of Milan. He had completed the usual order of business — letters, messengers and a council meeting — then home for the main meal of the day. But Ambrose was worried. Trouble had started in his district with the death of the bishop of the city. The Christians there had two opposite opinions about whether Christ was really God, or only a half-god and good man. Each side was equally determined that the new bishop should represent its view. Ambrose frowned. He had not yet been baptized (not unusual for that time), but he couldn't understand why Christians couldn't agree in the truth the Gospels taught. Suddenly a messenger darted into the room where he was eating.

"Your Excellency, the people in the church are starting a riot."

"What's it all about?" said Ambrose.

"It's about the election of the next bishop! One group is shouting for their side, but others are trying to force them to be quiet. You must come quickly."

Summoning a group of soldiers, Ambrose quickly made his way to the center of town. Some of the people outside the church cried, "It's the governor!" Mounting the steps of the building, Ambrose strode inside. The crowd stilled.

"Fellow citizens," he said. "I know that you are sincere in your Christian beliefs. Well then, you must believe that it is God's will for us to live in peace and harmony with one another." He was a gifted orator and the people listened to him, spellbound. Then suddenly, someone shouted, "Ambrose for bishop!" Others took up the cry, and, to Ambrose's dismay, the entire crowd started chanting together, "Ambrose for bishop!"

Ambrose appealed to the emperor to escape their demand, but the emperor liked the idea and appointed Ambrose to the post. So at the age of thirty-five, Ambrose was baptized, hurried through the stages of ordination, and consecrated as Bishop of Milan. The year was 374. He faced many problems to begin with, but the hardest was that of restoring the church in his diocese to the simplicity of faith found in the original teaching of the apostles. The greatest enemy of that was the teaching which denied that Christ was fully God and made Him an "almost God." Called Arianism, after its originator, it had been the cause of much unrest among the Christians in many parts of the Roman empire, including Milan. Ambrose threw himself heartily into his new office. By teaching and preaching and by living a life dedicated to God, he saw the purging of Arianism from his diocese within ten years. He also gave away all his wealth to the Church. Every day he gave himself to the service of his people. He celebrated masses for them, confirmed older converts, baptized new ones. His most famous convert was none other than St Augustine of Hippo.

One day a request came from Valentinian, the Emperor, and the Emperor's mother, Justinia. "Will you go out and meet the invaders who are about to attack Italy, and persuade them not to carry out their plans?" Such a mission would be carried out at personal risk, for the attackers might very well decide to take him prisoner, hold him for ransom, or even put him to death. But Ambrose put the safety of others ahead of his own, and complied with the request — not once, but twice. Justinia knew that she could count on his cooperation, though she had constantly tried to place Arians in authority in Ambrose's diocese, including having churches surrounded by imperial troops to take possession of them.

Theodosius was emperor of the Eastern Empire, and a story from that time illustrates the complete faithfulness of Ambrose in all circumstances. The citizens of Thessalonica had rioted, and in the midst of it, the governor of the city had been killed. The Emperor was furious, and considered it a personal attack on him.

"Thessalonica must be punished, and must be made an example before the whole empire," he stormed.

He sent his soldiers and under his orders they carried out a brutal massacre of seven thousand people. When Ambrose heard of this, he first consulted with his fellow bishops, and then sent Theodosius a letter. He would neither celebrate the Holy Mysteries in the emperor's presence nor receive him at the altar until the emperor had made a public confession and penance for his crime. "What has been done at Thessalonica is unparalleled in the memory of man," he wrote. "You are a human, and temptation has overtaken you. Overcome it. I counsel, I beseech, I implore you to penance. You who have so often been merciful and pardoned the guilty, have now caused many innocent to perish. The devil wished to wrest from you the crown of piety which was your chiefest glory. Drive him from you while you can . . . I write this letter with my own hand that you also may read it alone."

The emperor could not withstand such an appeal. He stripped himself of every sign of royalty and bewailed his sin openly in the church. People wept at his willingness to publicly acknowledge his wrongdoing. The bishop and the emperor held each other in mutual affection and respect, and in fact, Theodosius died in Ambrose's arms. In his funeral oration, Ambrose spoke of his love for the emperor and urged his two sons to follow their father's example. Ambrose foretold his own death, and refused to pray for lengthening of his earthly life. "I have not so behaved myself among you to make me ashamed to live longer," he said. "But I am not afraid to die, for we have a good Master."

He died on Good Friday, 397, and his sermons have lived on as an important contribution to the Church's teaching. He also wrote catechism lessons for newly baptized Christians, setting forth sound Catholic doctrine. One of his last works was a treatise entitled, *The Goodness of Death.* He was a great lover of sacred music, and wrote hymns, at times composing them on the spot and teaching them to the people to be sung. Hymns were referred to as "Ambrosians" for many generations.

Here is a translation of one of his morning hymns still sung in churches and monastic communities:

Come, Holy Ghost, with God the Son
And God the Father, ever One;
Shed forth Thy grace within our breast,
And dwell with us, a ready Guest.

By every power, by heart and tongue
By act and deed, Thy praise be sung;
Inflame with perfect love each sense,
That others' souls may kindle thence.

O Father, that we ask be done,
Through Jesus Christ, Thine only Son,
Who, with the Holy Ghost and Thee
Doth live and reign eternally. Amen.
(Translated by John Mason Neale, 1851)

St Ambrose is famed as one of the four great Latin Doctors of the Catholic Church, along with Saints Augustine, Jerome and Gregory the Great. This means that his writings (which were in Latin) are still revered and treasured as important contributions to the Church's teachings. His feast is celebrated on December 7.

St Augustine

354-430

The sound of bare feet pounding the dusty road continued on the outskirts of the small town, though by now it was well after sundown. Still the boys raced onward, turning the corner by the orchard wall. Then one of them bumped it, lost his balance and toppled down against it. The other boys stopped, too, catching their breath. "Hey," said one of them, "Look at that ugly old pear tree. Let's steal some fruit!" It took but a moment for them to clamber over the wall and leap into the tree.

"They're hard," said one of them. "Ugh!" But the theft continued, the boys picking and throwing down pears at great speed. When they could pick no more, they seized what they could carry, and tossed them into a nearby pigsty.

The year was 365, the place was Algeria, in northern Africa, and the leader was none other than Augustine. Later he would confess this sin in a great book still read by thousands, perhaps millions, of people. It is called *Confessions*. He said, "I stole a thing of which I had plenty of my own, and of much better quality — just for the sake of stealing." Augustine continued his way of life as a boy at school, studying only when he had to, disobeying his teachers and his parents, and getting away with as much as he could. When he was 17 years old, he was sent away to Carthage, and there he became top scholar in the school of rhetoric, but he was motivated by competition and pride. To this he added other sins, living for years with a woman to whom he was not married. She bore him a son in 372.

Growing weary of life in Carthage, he decided to go to Rome, but found conditions there to be no better. So on to Milan he went, still unhappy with his life as a teacher. His mother, St Monica, continued to pray for his conversion. Following him across the sea, she caught up with him in Milan, where she expressed her concern for Augustine's soul to Bishop Ambrose. He replied, "God will save the son of so many prayers and tears."

In the meantime, Augustine grew more and more unhappy, but he said, "The enemy held my will." By now he had found that all the philosophies did not work, and when he heard Bishop Ambrose's powerful sermons, he could find no excuse for his sinful life.

In this conflict, he was in his garden one day when he heard a child's voice say, "Take and read. Take and read." He went into the house, took up a copy of St Paul's letters, and read, "Put on the Lord Jesus Christ." Taking this as a heavenly sign, he told a friend what had happened, then related it to his mother, and on Easter eve in 387 was baptized by St Ambrose. A poem he wrote on that occasion expresses his new-found joy: "Late have I loved Thee, O Beauty so ancient and so new."

After his conversion Augustine gave up his school, and a few years later returned to Africa and became a priest. In 395 he became bishop of Hippo, and in four decades in that office, he established monasteries, wrote several books and organized a common life for all the priests of his diocese. *The Rule of St Augustine* is used by several religious orders. In addition to *Confessions* he wrote *The City of God*, and his theology has had great influence from that day to this. He died in 430 just before Vandals plundered Hippo. His feast day is August 28.

St Hilda

614-680

"I had a dream one night, that when all my attempts to find my banished husband had failed, I looked under my robes and found a brilliant jewel. As I looked at it closely, the light coming from it was so bright that all of Britain was lit."

The dreamer's daughter, Hilda, was only a small baby when this happened, but Hilda became that jewel. She grew to love and serve God with her heart and mind, and many people from all over Britain came to her for advice and truth.

In the midst of the Dark Ages, 614, Hilda was born in northern Britain. Her great uncle Edwin was king of

Northumbria. They were baptized together on Easter Day when Hilda was thirteen years old.

Her sister, Hereswitha, became a nun in a convent near Paris, and when she was thirty-three years old, Hilda decided to join her sister. Travelling south, she stopped for a visit with her cousin, Anna, who was king of East Anglia. As often happened in those times, the visit was prolonged — this one lasted a year. At the end of that time St Aidan, abbot of Lindisfarne, requested Hilda to return north to a small monastery on the north bank of the Wear River, instead of continuing her journey to France. She obeyed, and soon she was asked to become abbess of Hartlepool.

It was the custom in Britain in those days for monasteries to be what was called "Double Minsters." That meant that there were two sections, one for monks, the other for nuns. They were always ruled over by an abbess, and it was this kind of abbey that Hilda was asked to rule. She had to bring order where there had been chaos, and it was her task to arrange for all the needs of those under her care.

In 657,she moved to Streanshalch on the northwest coast of Yorkshire. Later it was called Whitby, and it became famous in British history. The monks and nuns had to climb one hundred and ninety-nine steps to get from the town to the cliff where the abbey rested. The cliff dropped off very sharply seventy-five feet to the cold North Sea. A wind blows there almost every day of the year — a somewhat forbidding location for an abbey, but not too unusual in that time.

Monks and nuns, although they lived and worked completely separately, came into the Church to sing the Divine Office seven times a day. In addition, Hilda required two hours of Bible study, and both monks and nuns illuminated manuscripts and copied books, for there was no printing press yet and every book was handwritten. To add to their learning they worked at solving complicated mathematical puzzles.

The young man named Caedmon served in the abbey by taking care of the animals and the gardens. One night, in a dream, he heard a voice saying, "Caedmon, sing to me." He had never been able to sing or play any instrument.

"What shall I sing?" he asked.

"Sing to me of Creation," replied the Voice.

When Hilda heard of this, she suggested that Caedmon should become a monk. This he gladly did, and went on to become our first English Christian poet.

Hilda's wisdom and devotion made her a trusted counsellor, even to bishops and kings. When the two branches of the British Church — Celtic and Roman — decided to hold a council to decide upon some disputed questions, they chose to meet at Whitby. Besides her wisdom, Hilda had the added reputation of serving her guests well!

There were two important items for discussion. One was to decide what date Easter should be observed. The old Celtic date was different from that which Rome and the rest of Europe followed, and it so happened that the king of Northumbria was accustomed to the Celtic date, while his wife came from an area which observed the Roman date.

Hilda was host at the Council, but she was accustomed to the Celtic date of her ancestors. The king decided to go along with Wilfred, an ardent crusader for the Roman date. Hilda reluctantly agreed to accept the Synod's decision. But a short time later, on other questions, she staunchly disagreed with Wilfred. Perhaps she felt that St Wilfred could not be right in *every* decision.

Over the years, many people, including kings, bishops and princes, walked up those one hundred and ninety-nine stairs to the windblown abbey to seek Hilda's advice. So well did she train those in her charge that five of her monks went on to become bishops.

In 673, Hilda caught a burning fever, which remained with her for the next seven years. In spite of it she continued to work and tend those in her care.

On the night of her death, November 17, 680, one Sister in the abbey saw a vision of her soul ascending to heaven. Another, some thirteen miles away, witnessed a bright light coming down from heaven as angels carried her soul to rest. She was sixty-six years old, and had been a bright light in England for many years, working at spreading the light of the Word of God among the people, just as her mother had dreamed when she was a tiny infant.

Her abbey was thoroughly sacked by the Danes about 800, but it was refounded as a monastery for monks in the eleventh century, and its ruins still stand on the wind-swept shore of eastern England. Fifteen churches in England were named in her honor. Her feast is observed on November 17, the day of her death.

St Catherine of Siena

1347-1380

Even as a young child, Catherine longed to give her whole heart to God and to live completely for Him. Born in 1347, she was the youngest of 25 children. Her parents, try as they might, could not understand Catherine's desire. She was a happy, intelligent girl, and they thought it only natural that a suitable husband should be found for her. But Catherine had experienced a vision at the age of six which sealed her determination to live solely for God. She had seen a vision of our Lord seated in glory. He smiled at her, reached out His hand to bless her, and after that her heart belonged to no one else.

In their futile attempt to change her mind, her parents took away her little bedroom where she loved to meditate and pray. She was given the hardest jobs in the household each day, and became, in effect, a servant in her own home. But Catherine did everything cheerfully, in her heart doing it for the sake of Jesus. At last, her father was convinced that they should let her live as she felt called to do — a life of solitude, fasting and prayer.

Soon afterward, Catherine joined the Third Order of St Dominic — a semi-monastic way of life for lay persons who did not have a vocation as a regular religious. She began to wear the customary habit and continued her life of self-denial, but it cost her many inward trials and sufferings. This was a time of testing and purifying her faith. Many temptations came to her mind, and she had periods of feeling completely cut off from God. "O Lord," she cried, "where were You when my heart was so sorely troubled with foul and hateful temptations?" "Daughter," came the answer, "I was in your heart, strengthening you with My grace."

At the age of nineteen, Catherine began to carry her love for God out into the world to serve others. Joining her Dominican Sisters, she began to help care for the sick. People could see that she had a wonderful grace about her and in her. She did not flinch at even the most repulsive diseases, and helped many to turn to Christ in their dying moments. About this time, there was a terrible outbreak of the plague in Italy. A friend wrote of Catherine, "She was always with the plague-stricken: she prepared them for death; she buried them with her own hands. I myself witnessed the joy with which she nursed them and the wonderful effect of her words, which caused many conversions."

Despite her young age, others recognized that she was an unusually wise and discerning person. A band of followers gathered around her. It was rather like a fellowship or a family, and although she was younger than most of her "disciples," she was called "Mother" out of their love and respect.

Her sphere of influence broadened as more and more people were touched by her life and faith. Kings and political dignitaries began to ask for her advice and counsel — even in drawing up treaties and bringing peaceful resolutions to impossible situations. She was only 26 years old when she wrote to Pope Gregory, urging him to return the Papal Court to Rome from Avignon, France, where it had been for 75 years, so that the suffering and division of the Church might be healed.

Two years later, she visited Pisa, and her very presence started a religious revival.

From time to time she had to endure persecution, being accused of hypocrisy or fanaticism, but she never wavered in her determination to live for God alone. Though she was active politically and to the needs of those around her, she continued to cultivate a deep inner spiritual life. She is known as a mystic because of the many visions which came to her. She received the wounds of the Stigmata, which were apparent only to her during her lifetime, but were clearly visible to others after her death. She often experienced ecstacies, and was seen by many when she was raised off the ground during her prayers.

She was only 33 years old when she died of a stroke — possibly a result of her intense, agonizing struggle as she tried to bring unity in the Church. Her life shines out as a bright light, not only through her century, but through all time. Her last words were: "Lord, You call me to You, and I come, not in my own merits, but in Your mercy, which I ask in virtue of the most precious blood of Your dear Son. Lord, into Your hands I commend my spirit."

To her largely belongs the credit of having brought about the return of the papacy to Rome after its long absence in Avignon. In 1461 she was canonized by Pope Pius II, and in 1970 her writings were given even greater honor when she was named a Doctor of the Universal Church. Her usual emblem is the lily, and we celebrate her feast on April 29.

St Francis de Sales

1567-1622

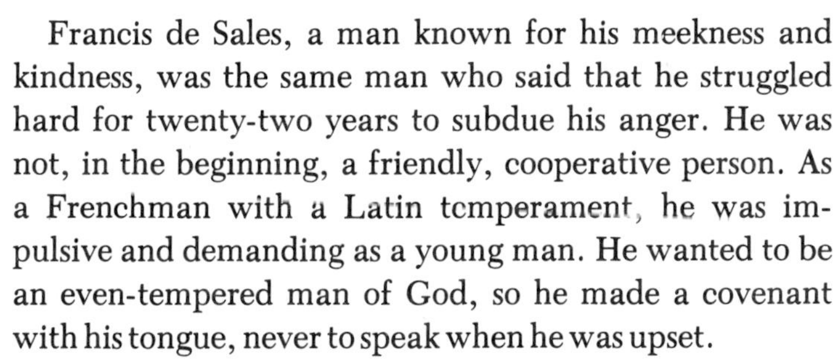

Francis de Sales, a man known for his meekness and kindness, was the same man who said that he struggled hard for twenty-two years to subdue his anger. He was not, in the beginning, a friendly, cooperative person. As a Frenchman with a Latin temperament, he was impulsive and demanding as a young man. He wanted to be an even-tempered man of God, so he made a covenant with his tongue, never to speak when he was upset.

He realized that what he must do was to make God the supreme object of his love, and toward this he persevered for many years. Many times he had to see that he was wrong, get up and ask God to help him again. He said,

LEADERS

"There is no better way of perfecting one's spiritual life, than beginning it over and over again, never thinking that one has already done enough."

Born in 1567 in Savoy, France, Francis was probably about ten or eleven years old when he chose to receive the tonsure. A tonsure is the shaving of the crown of one's head, and it indicated his intention to become a monk or a priest. His father had other ideas, however, and expected his desires to be carried out. He sent Francis to the University of Paris when he was fourteen, to a college attended by the sons of the prominent families of Savoy. Francis was sure that such a school would not be helpful in following his own vocation, so after many conflicts, he persuaded his father to send him to a Jesuit school renowned for its piety and learning. Afterward, he went on to the University of Padua and received his doctorate there.

His father planned that he should marry a lovely young woman. The senate of Savoy offered him the opportunity to become a member. On both subjects, father and son found themsevles locked in conflict. Francis still desired ordination, and this ruled out both marriage and the senate position. At first, his father said an absolute "No!" to ordination. A cousin intervened, however, and Francis was offered the position of provost of the Cathedral of Geneva. When the Pope approved this, his father reconsidered and finally gave his consent. That very day Francis entered Holy Orders.

St Francis de Sales

The baroque age, the 17th century, was a time of much strife inside and outside the Church. Many Catholics had left the Church and turned to Protestantism, while others simply dropped their faith altogether through worldly concerns. Francis was called to be a fisher of men. He worked tirelessly, encouraging people to put their faith in God and to strive toward perfection in whatever vocation they might have. In an age when people thought a close relationship with God was possible only for clergy and those in religious life, Francis began to teach and write that we are all called to a holy life, whatever our occupation. He said, "It is a mistake, a heresy, to want to exclude devoutness of life from among soldiers, from shops and offices, from royal courts, from the homes of the married," he remarked. "Religious devotion does not destroy: it perfects."

In 1602 he was made Bishop of Geneva, Switzerland. In addition to his work as administrator, preacher, and catechizer, he wrote many letters of instruction and spiritual direction especially to the aristocratic women of France who sought his help. His two most well-known books, *Treatise on the Love of God*, and *Introduction to the Devout Life*, were widely distributed. The latter, written for lay people, fulfilled a long-felt need and was soon translated into several languages. It has been treasured and read by succeeding generations. Because Francis understood his own nature and the struggles he had in overcoming temptations, he had much help for others. The tone of his writings is gentle and pleasant, because, as he often said, "More flies are attracted by a spoonful of honey than by a whole barrel of vinegar." He holds up a very high ideal, however, and his work influenced a revival of French Catholicism in his time.

"We must not lose heart," he said, "if we do not quickly reach the highest level of virtue; in order to achieve holiness, man must attack the task again and again."

His own life was proof that we must not give up when we fail. He became a master of meekness by persevering with himself. His Christlike spirit was apparent to all who met him, and people were drawn to that same Master through his life — because he was willing to choose the will of God instead of his own wishes.

A Calvinist minister in Geneva said of him, "If we honored any man as a saint, I know no one since the days of the apostles more worthy of it than this man."

He died at Lyons, in a convent founded by his friend and pupil, St Jane Frances de Chantal, in 1622. He was canonized in 1665 and in 1877 was declared a Doctor of the Church. St John Bosco was a great admirer of his, and named the order he founded to teach and train boys, The Order of St Francis de Sales (Salesians). He was further honored in 1923 when he was named patron saint of journalists and other writers. His feast is celebrated on January 24.

Confessors and Contenders

Fight the good fight of faith, take hold of the eternal
life to which you were called when you made the good
confession in the presence of many witnesses.
I Timothy 6:12

And they have conquered him [Satan] by the blood
of the Lamb and by the word of their testimony,
for they loved not their lives even unto death.
Revelation 12:11

These are they who have contended
For their Saviour's honor long,
Wrestling on till life was ended,
Following not the sinful throng:
Those, who well the fight sustained,
Triumph by the Lamb have gained!
Theobald Heinrich Schenck, 1719

St John the Baptist

First Century

John the Baptist was the forerunner of Jesus, as the prophet of old had foretold: "Behold I send my messenger before thy face, who shall prepare thy way; the voice of one crying in the wilderness: Prepare the way of the Lord." (Malachi 3:1)

Zechariah was a priest, a descendant of Aaron, and his wife Elizabeth was also descended from the priestly line. They lived in Judea, and were "righteous before God, walking in all His commandments and ordinances blameless." But they were childless, and this was a great sadness to them, for they were both getting old, and Elizabeth was well beyond the child-bearing age.

One day when Zachariah was taking his turn serving as priest in the temple, an angel appeared to him, standing on the right side of the altar. Filled with fear, Zachariah fell down before him. "Do not fear," said the angel. "Your prayer is heard and your wife Elizabeth will bear you a son, and you shall call his name John. And you will have great joy and gladness, for he will be great before the Lord . . . and he will be filled with the Holy Spirit, even from his mother's womb." The angel went on to tell that in his ministry this blessed child would turn the hearts of many to the Lord, from disobedience to righteousness.

But Zachariah was skeptical. It was too much to believe that such a good thing could happen to him and Elizabeth! "How shall I know this, for I am an old man, and my wife is advanced in years."

The angel then identified himself. "I am Gabriel," he said. "I stand in the presence of God and I was sent to you to speak this good news. And behold, you will be silent and unable to speak until these things come to pass because you have not believed my words, which will be fulfilled in good time."

When Zachariah came out form the inner sanctuary, people wondered what had happened to him, but his tongue was tied so that he could not speak. In due time, just as Gabriel had said, Elizabeth conceived and rejoiced at the prospect of bearing a child. "The Lord has looked on me to take away my reproach among men," she said.

Six months later, her young cousin, Mary of Nazareth, came to visit her. When Mary entered her house, Elizabeth heard her greet Zachariah, and the babe in her own womb leaped. "Blessed are you among women," said Elizabeth to Mary, "and blessed is the fruit of your womb! Why is this granted me, that the mother of my Lord should come to me? For when the voice of your greeting came to my ears, the babe in my womb leaped for joy! And blessed is she who believed that there would be a fulfillment of what was spoken to her from the Lord."

Mary then said the beautiful and immortal "Magnificat," which the Church has used as its own song ever since.

When Elizabeth's baby was born, she told her friends that he would be called John. But they could not understand why she would call him by that name, since none of her family or Zachariah's family were called John. So they went to Zachariah, still unable to hear or speak. Obtaining something to write on, Zachariah wrote: "His name is John." And immediately "his mouth was opened and his tongue was loosed, and he spoke, blessing God." This is the wonderful account St Luke gives us of the birth of John the Baptist.

About thirty years later, John appeared out of the wilderness dressed in a garment of camel's hair, with a leather girdle about his waist, preaching this message: "Repent, for the kingdom of heaven is at hand." Not only did he call on the people to repent, but to be baptized for the remission of their sins. Scholars tell us that when Gentiles were converted to Judaism, they were baptized for ritual cleansing, as well as being circumcised. Thus John's message, being preached to Jews, was that they were not ready for the kingdom of God without also being cleansed of their sins and converted in their hearts.

Many went out to hear him, for he was a great and powerful preacher. Religious authorities came to hear him. To them he said: "You brood of vipers! Who warned you to flee from the wrath to come? Bear fruits that befit repentance, and do not begin to say to yourselves 'We have Abraham as our father'; for I tell you, God is able from these stones to raise up children to Abraham. Even now the ax is laid at the root of the trees; every tree therefore that does not bear good fruit is cut down and thrown into the fire." When asked what they should do, he said that they should share what they had with others, tax collectors should not defraud, soldiers were to rob no one by violence or false accusations, and were to be content with what they were paid.

John called himself "the voice of one crying in the wilderness," and predicted that there was one who would come after him, mightier than he. "He is one whose sandals I am not worthy to unloose," John said. When Jesus came to be baptized, John protested that it was rather Jesus who should be baptizing him instead of the other way round. But Jesus insisted, and when He was baptized, they saw the Holy Spirit descending like a dove and resting on Him, and a voice out of heaven which said, "This is my beloved Son in whom I am well-pleased." The day after, John was with two of his own followers, Andrew and Philip, and when he saw Jesus walking along, said to them: "Behold the Lamb of God who takes away the sins of the world." And the two men left John and became disciples of Jesus.

Even old King Herod was moved by reports of what he heard about John, for he believed that John was a prophet. But John was no respecter of persons, and Herod had made an unlawful, incestuous marriage with Herodias, the wife of his own brother. John had publicly denounced Herod's sin, and Herod had him imprisoned for it. The wicked Herodias was determined to get vengeance on John for having humiliated her before the people. So the time came when at a great banquet, Salome, her daughter, was brought in to dance before her uncle (who was now her step-father). Herod was so pleased with her dance that, in oriental fashion, he offered her anything she pleased, "even half the kingdom." Salome, carefully instructed by her wicked mother, said, "Give me the head of John the Baptist here on a platter." "The king was sorry; but because of his oaths and his guests he commanded it to be given; and he sent and had John beheaded in the prison, and his head was brought on a platter and given to the girl, and she brought it to her mother." (St Matt. 14:9-12)

Our Lord said of John that he was greater than all the saints of the old law, the greatest that had been born of woman. But, He went on to remind us that "the least in the Kingdom of heaven" is greater, for in God's kingdom earthly honors do not count. John was given the important task of fulfilling the scripture and preparing the way for Christ by his message of repentance. Speaking of Jesus, John said, "He must increase, and I must decrease." That is his enduring message to every one of us, to allow Christ to increase within our hearts.

The Church celebrates the birthday of St John the Baptist on June 24, and makes memorial of the beheading on August 29. A prayer used on that day says,

"God our Father, You called John the Baptist to be the herald of Your Son's birth and death. As he gave his life in witness to truth and justice, so may we strive to profess our faith in Your Gospel. Grant this through our Lord Jesus Christ, Your Son, who lives and reigns with You and the Holy Spirit, one God, for ever and ever. Amen."

St John Chrysostom

347-407

In the setting sun of the mountains south of Antioch in Syria, about 368 AD, you might see a lonely figure climbing a crude trail leading from the valley. He is John (later to earn the name Chrysostom), going to join a group of hermits who have settled in the caves near the pass. As a brilliant law student, John made speeches that had surpassed even those of his teachers. Then at the age of 22, he had decided to be baptized. In those days, people took the meaning of this act very seriously, which involved renouncing the world. The young Christian then spent some time in an informal school for aspiring young monks, before gathering his things in a small satchel and starting up this path.

But the pampered young aristocrat worried about the absence of the comforts he is used to. "Will I be able to find the kind of food I like? Will I be able even to eat my own cooking? What about the rough work?"

At the top of the incline, however, he is warmly greeted by an older hermit. "Welcome, John. You will stay with me for a while until you get used to our life." And with that, John forgot his fears and enthusiastically plunged into a life of work, prayer and study. His muscles grew hard as they carried supplies like water and wood up the path, and his knees developed callouses from the long hours spent kneeling on the hard floor in the cave. During study times, he is said to have memorized the whole Bible.

After four years, he was ready to live in a cave alone, which he did for two years. The dampness of the cave was very harmful to his health, and his fastings and bodily severities began to weaken him, and he became dangerously ill. He returned to Antioch in 381, wrapped in his now tattered mantle.

In that city, his old friend and mentor, St Meletius, received him and ordained him as a deacon. His health improved and three years later, Bishop Flavian ordained him to the priesthood. The Antioch John knew was a bustling trade center for merchandise being carried to the Mediterranean from cities in the Far East. There was a very wealthy upper class, a small settlement of Jews, and very many poor people. Sometimes a beautiful building would be erected right next to the hovel of such a family.

John immediately concerned himself with the poor of the city, many of whom barely managed to eke out an existence. When the aged Bishop Flavian appointed him as his deputy, John made their relief his first priority. Along with that ministry, he had the responsibility of shepherding about 100,000 Christian souls in the city. He guessed that there were an equal number of pagans, too. To all of these, he preached the Word of God several times a week, often several times in a single day. He never failed to impress on those who were well off their Christian responsibility to give to those in need.

Economic conditions, already hard for many in Antioch, reached a crisis point when Emperor Theodosius I levied a new tax. The outrage of Antioch citizens knew no bounds. Grouping themselves in the center of the city, they vented their anger on the statues of the Emperor and his family, breaking them to pieces. The magistrates were helpless. After the people had calmed down, however, they were seized with terror at the thought of what the Emperor might do to them in return. Their terror was heightened by the arrival of two imperial officers who arrived from Constantinople to carry out the punishment. The only person who could help was Bishop Flavian. After all, a Christian emperor would listen to a bishop. So, despite his age and some of the worst weather of the year, Flavian set out for Constantinople to beg for mercy for his flock.

Back at Antioch, John started preaching some of his most memorable sermons concerning the incident. "What are we to fear? Death? But life to me means Christ and death is gain." These twenty-one Lenten sermons (*On the Statues*) so gripped his listeners that he became famous overnight. At the same time, the Emperor, who was touched by Flavian's appeal, granted imperial amnesty to the people. But from that time forth, Chrysostom's oratory became a great force which swayed the empire. He had rightly earned the nickname, Chrysostom, which in Greek means "Golden Mouthed."

For twelve years John continued to preach and minister at Antioch. Then, in 397, the Emperor Arcadius resolved to secure John for the post of Archbishop of Constantinople, one of the most powerful leadership positions in the Church. But John was extremely popular in Antioch, so much so, that if he were removed, there might be an uprising. Arcadius decided to turn the problem over to his good friend, the Count of the East.

Early one morning a messenger appeared at the gate of John's dwelling. "The Count desires the presence of Bishop John to visit the tombs of the martyrs," he said.

One didn't refuse an invitation like that. Seizing his cloak, John accompanied the Count and his entourage to the monuments outside the city walls. But, what was this in front of the nearest tomb? Horsemen of the Imperial Guard! Before he could protest, an officer drew John into his chariot and whisked him off to Constantinople.

John resigned himself to what seemed to be God's will, and was consecrated Archbishop on February 26, 398. Constantinople had originally been a small peninsular trading town, but when John arrived it was in the throes of half a century of drastic change. The first Christian Emperor, Constantine, had decided to move the capital of the Roman Empire there from Rome, because of the constant threat of attack under which Rome lived. The small town of Byzantium had become the imperial city of Constantinople (or New Rome). It had a magnificently strategic location, jutting out into the sea of Marmara, which facilitated the shipment of materials and workmen for the new capital. The new Archbishop would pass several of the eight public baths as he rode in, where graceful arches of 52 porticos decorated various intersections, while the Archbishop's palace enjoyed running water, thanks to the eight aquaducts supplying the city. Christianity had been active there, too, and before John died, its citizens would have a choice of fourteen churches to attend. They lived in over 4,000 homes of a size large enough to note, while a few of the aristocracy graced the city with fourteen palaces. Needless to say, Constantinople also had her very poor; since many of the shacks of these dispossessed nestled beside the new marble structures, it made their plight stand out in even bolder relief. Archbishop John immediately sought to relieve their condition. "It doesn't take all these funds to maintain my residence," he said. "Let's cut out the fancy frills and then we can help these people, and care for some of the sick as well."

Constantine had enlarged the Hippodrome, an arena for races and other performances, often the scene of immoral pagan games attended by the Emperor and thousands of people. John strenuously preached against these activities, as well as the immodesty in women's dress styles. Battling this tendency, he worked actively to found communities of devout women. His own life was lived in a strict self-denial of all luxury and ostentation, and he made enemies among some of his own clergy by imposing new disciplines among them.

It was not long before his outspoken preaching about vanity and loose living offended the Empress Eudoxia. His enemies joined with her and they succeeded in having John deposed and banished from the city. Hardly had he gone, however, when a mild earthquake shook the city, and the Empress feared she had gone too far. In a panic, she implored his recall, and soon John was back, preaching as powerfully and pointedly as ever. It was inevitable that he would again offend the Empress, and sure enough, soon he was banished again. By this time, John was old and weak, and the strain of travel was too much for him. He was still being marched away from Constantinople when, overcome by the scorching heat, he was taken to a little chapel to rest. There he saw in a night vision the martyr St Basiliscus, who said, "Courage, brother. Tomorrow we shall be together." The soldiers forced John out on the road again the next day, and marched him four or five miles before realizing that he was indeed dying. They rushed him back, and he died there in the little chapel. His last words were, "Glory be to God for all things."

The son and daughter of Eudoxia were so ashamed of their parents' treatment of John that they had his body brought back to Constantinople in 481 with great pomp, and they themselves begged God's forgiveness for their parents' sin in persecuting one of God's saints.

St John Chrysostom is recognized as one of the four great Greek doctors of the Church. His feast day is January 27, and his sermons are still read and considered among the greatest ever written.

St John Damascene

657-749

"Is this the way you forget your vows as a monk?" shouted the angry master of Mar Saba. "Instead of mourning and weeping at the death of a brother, you sit around in joy, and delight yourself by singing!"

John of Damascus said nothing. He had lived as cell-mate of his abbot for several years, and he knew that the other brothers had not welcomed anything new. They were particularly resentful of his singing and his poems.

The master continued: "As penance, you will clean up the filth around our huts with your bare hands — and you can sleep outdoors — you're not welcome here!"

Before he had become a monk, his talents had been appreciated. He had been chief tax collector in his home city of Damascus and dined regularly in the palace of the Khalif. Prince Yazid was his friend and they enjoyed discussing poetry together with Al Ahtal, the outstanding Arabic poet of his time. But one day, he and his tutor, Cosmos, obeying an inner call to serve God, had given away everything and joined the monks at Mar Saba in Jerusalem.

"Still," John reflected as he went about his disagreeable task, "God is in charge."

Not many nights later as he walked softly past the door of their little cell, the old master called him. "John, I've just dreamed a most wondrous dream," he said. "I saw the Blessed Virgin Mary, and she told me to allow you to write as many books and poems as you like. You have done enough penance. Begin tomorrow!"

Tomorrow! A hymn of praise welled up inside him.

> All the winter of our sins,
> Long and dark is flying
> From His light to whom we give
> Laud and praise undying.

Next morning, John began collecting his parchment fragments — inks and pens. He checked the scrolls he had carefully saved of other things he had written. Part of a quote from Leo the Isurian, Christian emperor of the Byzantine empire, caught his eye, ". . . in favor of overthrowing the holy and venerable images." What!? A dreary picture flashed through his mind — the magnificent Dome of the Rock without its beautiful mosaics; the inspiring icons removed from the homes of Christians and even his own cell bare of any picture of Christ or of Mary, His Blessed Mother. It was intolerable! The Christian leaders did not understand. He seized a quill and began writing "*Proskuneisis Schetikei*", "a relative worship, *not* idolatry." Words flowed from his pen as he completed the first of three teaching pamphlets refuting the arguments of those who wanted to destroy the special pictures and mosaics from the walls of churches. "They are needed to instruct those who do not know the wonderful stories of our Saviour and all His saints," he pleaded.

John wrote many other things as well: hymns, poems, lives of saints, including one of John Chrysostom, sermons, and articles on theology — even a best-selling "novel." The monk sitting on a cushion on the floor of his cell, quill in hand, did not escape the attention of the Patriarch of Jerusalem, John V. He sent for John and Cosmos and ordained them to the priesthood. Cosmos began shepherding a parish, but soon John returned to Mar Saba, where he lived until his death.

Writing was his first love, and there was much to be done. In addition to collecting books and other writings for ideas, there were pens to be sharpened, inks to be mixed and hides to be scraped into thin leather sheets of vellum or parchment. Then, of course, there was the business of revising his drafts. If his style became too flowery, or his sentences too wordy, he carefully made them simpler and more direct. His writing, he felt, should not display "levity or want of dignity."

Meanwhile, the controversy over icons raged on. The next emperor, Constantine V, began persecuting those who insisted on keeping the images. John of Damascus was put under a solemn curse and excommunicated in 740. Fortunately, this had no effect on him because he was a citizen under the protection of the Moslems and not part of the Christian empire. But John was no coward! Towards the end of his life, when he was in his eighties, he traveled right to the center of Constantinople, the capital of the Christian East, in order to preach in favor of icons. By this time his three tracts in their defense had become known and read everywhere, and had earned him the special hatred of the emperor. But John escaped any harm and continued writing from Mar Saba until his death in 749.

Although he is considered one of the greatest theologians in the history of the Church, one legend states that sometimes he was sent into Damascus to sell baskets. He was to be humbled in the city where he had once been an important official in order that good might be worked in his soul.

The Church still sings some of the joyful hymns he wrote, and in 1890 he was honored by being declared a Doctor of the Universal Church. His feast is now celebrated on December 4.

St Basil the Great

c. 330-379

Basil was born in a well-to-do Christian family in Caesarea, Macaca, the capital of Cappadocia (a province in modern Turkey), in the year 329. His family saw to it that he had the best education possible; first he was sent to the capital of the Eastern Roman Empire, Constantinople, and then to Athens to finish his studies. Athens was the university center of the late Roman Empire; its list of professors had included such notables as Cicero and Atticus. Its schools of Rhetoric propounded the last of a humane and moral paganism, and at one of them Basil studied Greek speech and literature, Greek grammar, Latin, and public speaking. With his friends, such as

Gregory of Nazianzus, he associated with only the most serious minded students. Games and festivals in the new arena constructed by Emperor Hadrian held no interest for him. Another school friend, of less happy memory, was destined to become Emperor. His name in history is Julian the Apostate.

After completing his studies in 356, Basil went back to Caesarea and taught rhetoric for several years. But something in his life failed to satisfy him. Under the influence of his sister, Macrina, he left his promising career for life as a hermit. As a sign of renouncing everything, he was baptized, and then he traveled around to several communities of hermits and ascetics in Palestine, Syria and Mesopotamia to learn about the religious life. He began on his own as a hermit on the family estates in Pontus, across the river Iris, where his mother and sister had formed a community of women. In that wild and beautiful spot, Basil devoted himself to a life of prayer and study; soon a group of followers had gathered, and with them Basil established a pattern for Eastern Monasticism.

But people needed him in Caesarea, and persuaded him to be ordained a deacon and then a priest. About a century before, Caesarea had been leveled by the Persians who defeated Emperor Valerian. Once a prosperous town, its citizens were now poor and dispossessed. The Christians in the town and throughout the whole province of Cappadocia had become divided over the Arian heresy. This belief denied both the full divinity and the full humanity of Christ. There were many of these heretics, including the Emperor Valens himself, and the Catholic Christians were having a hard time of it. Basil had to contend with the Archbishop Eusebius, who was jealous of his influence, so the saint retired again to his hermitage and began establishing other monasteries in the area.

In 365, Gregory of Nazianzus, his old friend from school, begged him to return. 'We need you to defend our clergy, church and faith against Arianism,' he said. So Basil returned and became reconciled to Eusebius by tactfully seeing to it that the Archbishop got the credit for all that he was really doing himself. Then a drought struck and soon a severe famine threatened all the citizens of Caesarea. Basil's first concern was relief for all the suffering and needy of the town. He not only organized a program to feed them, he was often seen dishing out the soup to them himself. Soon he started a church, hospital and guest house. The ministry grew into a small town called Basiliad. But Basil did not neglect his pastoral duties in the meantime; morning and evenings he preached to crowds so large he compared them to the sea.

To the rich he said, "How many shivering people could be clothed from only one of your wardrobes? And yet you turn the poor away empty-handed." To the poor he said, "You are poor? But there are others poorer than you. Don't be afraid to give . . . trust in God's goodness."

Upon the death of Eusebius, Basil was chosen Archbishop. Scarcely a year later, however, the Emperor Valens arrived in Caesarea and began a relentless persecution against orthodox Christians. But Basil would not compromise his position, either to the Emperor's prefect or to the Emperor himself. "Nothing short of violence can avail against the man," said the prefect.

The Emperor decided to banish him. Seizing a reed to sign the edict, he put it to the parchment, when the pen split in his hand! Another broke, and still another. The Emperor relented and eventually left Caesarea, never again to interfere with its church affairs.

But saints, too, can get discouraged. After the death of St Athanasius, Basil was left to champion the cause of Christian orthodoxy in the East. The Church there was torn by schisms and dissensions, and when Basil and his friends appealed to the Pope and the western bishops for help, he received scant response, apparently because of bad reports that had been given concerning him. On one occasion he cried, "For my sins I seem to be unsuccessful in everything!"

He was successful, however, in turning many people to God — criminals, prostitutes, even unjust officials. Just before he died at the age of forty nine, worn out by his austerities, disease and overwork, he received good news. The Arian heresy would no longer have the support of the imperial throne. Emperor Valens had died from wounds received in battle, and his nephew, Gratian, would be the new emperor. Gratian was a Catholic, and with him the Arian triumph came to an end in the East.

Among the thousands who mourned Basil's death were pagans, Jews and strangers, who recognized the good he had done in their city. Today in the Eastern Churches his rule is followed by almost all monks and nuns, and his name stands as one of the most illustrious of all time. His mother, Macrina, his father, sister and his younger brothers, Gregory of Nyssa and Peter of Sebaste, were all saints. His feast is now celebrated in the Western Church on January 2 along with his friend, St Gregory of Nazianzus.

St Athanasius

c. 296-373

The end of the third century was a tempestuous age for the Church. Athanasius was born in Alexandria, Egypt, in 297, and at that very time the faithful in his city were beginning to experience persecution. Athanasius was still a child when the Emperor who had determined to wipe out Christianity died and was succeeded by Constantine the Great, who stopped the persecution. Athanasius and his family were spared and he grew up receiving the best kind of education available, which included the Greek classics, philosophy, rhetoric, jurisprudence and Christian doctrine. Many of his Christian teachers bore the scars of the recent persecutions, and from them

Athanasius acquired a lasting respect for spiritual values. He even went out into the Egyptian desert to visit the famous St Antony the Hermit, and spent some time there as one of his disciples. Then, when he was only twenty-one, he was made a deacon and began service as secretary to Bishop Alexander.

About this time (323) another citizen of Alexandria, a priest named Arius, started preaching publicly that Christ was another creation of God and therefore could be the Son of God only figuratively. This teaching posed a great threat to the Church. Athanasius' bishop led the clergy of their city in condemning these doctrines and succeeded in having Arius deposed, along with his followers who were priests. Undaunted, Arius set up in Syria, and those who believed his doctrines spread the message throughout the Mediterranean. Its appeal to the intellectuals made it particularly insidious.

The Emperor Constantine reacted by asking Church leaders throughout Christendom to hold an Ecumenical Council at Nicea in 325. The young Athanasius attended as assistant to his bishop. No doubt he experienced satisfaction at their verdict: condemnation of Arianism and the formulation of the great Nicene Creed, still recited by the faithful all over the world. In fact, he may have composed the letter that the Council circulated to all the churches setting forth its decision.

He was not yet thirty years old when he succeeded Alexander as Bishop of Alexandria. The Council of Nicea had failed to crush Arianism, so despite a positive outreach to various groups of people, Athanasius found himself having to cope with all the dissension and opposition caused by this heresy.

The Emperor was persuaded by Eusebius, Bishop of Nicodemia, where he loved to vacation, to exert pressure on Athanasius to re-admit Arius to the Church. But Athanasius was steadfast in his refusal to compromise the truth. Eusebius then sought to have him deposed with false accusations put before the Emperor. When Athanasius was vindicated from these charges, Eusebius arranged to have him tried for murder, while the supposed victim was still alive and in hiding. Realizing that his condemnation had been carefully plotted, Athanasius abruptly left the assembly where he was being tried and departed for Constantinople. There he dressed as a humble beggar and accosted the Emperor in the streets. History does not record what was said, but the Emperor fully supported him and sent letters around to that effect. But the victory was shortlived, when a little while later Constantine changed his mind and banished Athanasius to Trier, a remote outpost in Gaul (now in Germany.)

For two years the Bishop communicated with his flock through letters only. Then Constantine died and his son who succeeded him restored Athanasius amid general rejoicing. However, the Bishop of Nicodemia continued his relentless attack, and again Athanasius had to leave Alexandria, this time for Rome. "Athanasius is raising up a movement against the government," said his enemies.

"Moreover, he is taking for himself food that was given to the poor."

Once again he was fully acquitted of all charges, but because another bishop had taken his see in Alexandria, the Emperor thought it best to delay in restoring him. The delay lasted, in fact, for eight years, and he was then allowed to return for a few peaceful years.

The new Emperor had been won over to Arianism, and decided to crush Athanasius once and for all. He had him condemned before several Councils and then exiled his supporters. Meanwhile, Athanasius held on with the support of his clergy and people until one night, soldiers forced open the door of his church and killed and wounded some of the congregation. Somehow he escaped and went into hiding in the Egyptian desert. There, amid the desert monks whom he had long loved and admired, he wrote the *Life of St Antony*, the spiritual mentor of his youth.

After the death of Constantius and the murder of the bishop who had usurped his see, Athanasius felt it safe to return. But new trouble awaited with the rise of the new Emperor, Julian the Apostate, who again banished the champion of the Catholic Faith in Egypt. Once more Athanasius made his way to his hiding place in the desert, where he remained until Julian's untimely death. Once again he went back to Alexandria.

Finally, after five banishments, he was allowed to possess his office in peace. In all he had spent seventeen years in exile. But, by standing for the truth amid terrible persecution and unjust accusations, Athanasius made his life a testimony to the divinity of Jesus Christ. Cardinal Newman called him "a principle instrument after the apostles for conveying the sacred truths of Christianity to the world." No saint could have a more praiseworthy epitaph than that. His feast is observed on May 2.

St Teresa of Avila

1515-1582

On the plateaus of north central Spain, late one January afternoon in 1565, you might see two lonely carriages toiling along a miry trail, buffeted by the windy gusts sweeping from stormy skies. The drivers urge the horses on as the first carriage swerves into a flooded ford and pauses before the current. Slowly the carriage sinks into the mud. The driver cracks a whip to get the horses going. The passengers inside strain out the windows. Their leader, impatient with that, opens the door and steps to the threshold. She is a Carmelite nun, Mother Teresa of Avila. The other travelers are a priest,

Fr. Gracian, and seven other nuns. Teresa alights, and before Fr. Gracian can help her, slips into the knee deep flood.

"O Lord," she sighs in exasperation. "If this is the way you treat your friends, it's no wonder you have so few of them!"

They had been heading towards Burgos when storms and flooding made the passage through the fords all but impassable. But undaunted, she and her party managed to make it to the nearest inn that night. Several months later, she completed her 17th and final foundation at their destination. Everyone loved traveling with her, tired and sick though she was on this trip. She managed to encourage their little band with her stories and humor. Even the drivers loved the delicacies she secured and handed up to them after they had been silent so the nuns could say their Offices.

Who was this woman who had been called to persist in the face of the kind of difficulties St Paul described when he said, "We are troubled on every side, yet not in despair, persecuted but not forsaken, cast down, but not destroyed"?

As a small child, Teresa had been fascinated by eternity. "For ever and ever and ever," she repeated. In fact, she even suggested to her brother, "Let's run away to the country of the Moors. There we shall be beheaded and live forever in heaven."

When she reached her teens, however, her interests became more this-worldly: romantic tales, the latest styles in jewelry, dress and perfumes; tidbits of gossip from an older friend. But she had already tired of the life she was leading when her father placed her in a near-by finishing school. "Pray for me," she asked the nuns who directed the students. "Have a mass said for me that I might enter a state where I can serve God."

After eighteen months there, she was forced to leave because of a serious illness. When partly recovered, she visited the home of a godly uncle.

"Here, read this aloud," he said, pulling a copy of Jerome's *Epistles* from the shelf. She began reading, and then came to the passage, "All things are nothing." The words haunted her even after she had resumed her busy life. Somehow marriage had no appeal to her, but as she considered everything, she found, "I could not incline my will towards being a nun." But "little by little," as she entered her twenties, she forced herself to embrace that life as "the best and safest state." At the age of twenty-one, in 1536, she entered the Carmelite house of the Incarnation at Avila.

Because her father absolutely disapproved of her decision and because of her own mixed feelings, she experienced, as she wrote later, "such great distress that I do not think it will be greater when I die." After a week there, however, she was amazed at finding a new joy. Then her precarious health broke down again just after her profession, and she was forced to return home for treatment. There she lapsed into a coma, followed by partial paralysis that lasted almost three years. Her conviction of God's call on her grew.

"Please let me return," she begged, though she had to be carried through the door of the convent. Day by day she continued to thank God for her healing, and gradually she was restored to full health.

Life at Incarnation was very lax. There were no strict rules about the matter of silence or when the nuns had to be at the convent. People of all sorts could visit the parlor while many of the sisters enjoyed prolonged stays with relatives and friends. Some of them did not even try to keep what simple rules there were. In this atmosphere, Teresa's interior life suffered; she stopped practicing mental prayer until a priest urged her to continue with it. For ten years she rode a stormy sea of conflict between the worldly pleasures of parlor visits with the distractions she found and the inner call to prayer. Eventually, she turned to the Jesuit fathers for help.

"Be careful about the socializing you do," said one of them.

"But I can't just give up all my friends," said Teresa.

"Though friendship is a good thing, not all your friendships are helpful," the father advised."Why don't you pray about it?"

Although the counsel seemed like an impossible task, she was obedient and did pray. One day she prayed, "Come, Holy Spirit to the heart Thou hast made." Suddenly, a Voice within said, "I will not have you hold conversation with men but with angels." The awareness of

God's presence filled her and never left; now she was free to have only the friends God chose for her.

From that point, Teresa continued to receive special revelations. She submitted them to her confessor and learned men, but with that, her conflicts took on a different turn.

"We have thought over everything you said God had showed you. We think you should be very careful," they said. "It could be that the devil is misleading you."

Teresa wept bitterly. "I suppose my sins must be blinding me to the real truth," she thought. But the experiences continued, despite her resistance. Again, she turned to her friends, the Jesuits. "If God wants to lift you up in His Spirit, don't resist," was their counsel.

Teresa then entered joyfully into these experiences. Often she would see Christ with her spiritual eyes after she had received the Blessed Sacrament. Sometimes she received the revealing of His real Presence on the Cross. Once she sensed a beautiful cherub with a golden spear beside her. Again and again he thrust this spear deep into her heart. The pain made her moan, "and yet the pain was so surpassingly sweet that I longed to keep it forever," she wrote. All of a sudden, she saw her life in a different way. "Either let me die or let me suffer," she cried. "I want no other thing for myself." God answered this prayer in a most unexpected way. (She had been a nun for twenty-four years when this happened.)

Initially, the other sisters had been jealous of her unusual experiences and the kind of life she led. But after observing her for several years, some of them had sought to follow her methods of devotion. They talked frequently together with Teresa; one of the problems they shared was the difficulty of having a stricter prayer life at the Incarnation. As they were talking about this one day, her niece suggested, "Let's all go away from here and organize a solitary life for ourselves like the hermits did." The idea took root and Teresa decided to discuss the possibility with her spiritual advisors and with some wealthy friends.

"Your plan is an excellent one," they said, "but how will you do it? How will you obtain all the necessary permissions? And what about the problem of raising money to buy a house?

When this discouraged her, the Lord Himself directed Teresa to work wholeheartedly toward a new convent and to name it in honor of St Joseph. Teresa went ahead and got the Provincial to approve. Then the storm broke.

"You have no love for our Convent!" the Incarnation nuns said angrily.

Worried town officials said, "Avila cannot support *two* Carmelite houses, especially when one has no financial support behind it!" In the midst of the uproar, the Provincial withdrew his consent and the matter lay dormant for almost a year.

Then a new rector came to the Incarnation Convent, a Jesuit. He encouraged the project, so Teresa made all the arrangements and secured the Provincial's approval for a second time. This time, she even got permission for them to live without an endowment of any kind: they would have to trust God completely for every need.

On St Bartholomew's Eve, August 24, 1562, Teresa and four nuns stole down the streets of Avila to begin their new life. Before anyone was up, they had set up an altar and rung the bell for morning mass. But the secret could not be kept long. The prioress at the Incarnation was sympathetic; the Provincial, after reprimanding Teresa for going ahead without him, also supported the new venture. But opposition from the town officials and other Carmelites was noisier than ever. For two years the controversy raged, until Teresa finally secured the approval of the Papal nuncio.

What was it like to be a nun at St Joseph's? Discarding their linens, the nuns wore only the coarsest of woolens and rope sandals for their feet. Between chanting the monastic hours, they worked alone in their cells to avoid idle chatter. But sisters could talk together during recreation, and the silence did not mean the absence of gaiety. Gloomy saints were not to Teresa's liking! Further, she taught, being able to pray well is not more important than tenderheartedness or the willingness to serve at the lowliest task. "To practice humility," she said, "means knowing yourself in absolute truthfulness."

It was not long before the holiness of these nuns attracted the notice of the general of the Order, Fr. Rubea. After visiting them he wrote to Teresa, "You must set up houses like this everywhere in Castile." And with that mandate, Teresa began her mission of establishing 16 more houses of the Reformed observance. She was fifty-two years old, "with scarcely a *blanca* in my pocket."

That very summer, August 1567, three creaking carts rolled out of Avila at daybreak. They contained a few nuns and the essentials to start a new house at Medina del Campo. Teresa's travels had begun.

Malagar, Valladolid, Toledo — with every foundation came difficulties of all sorts: midnight arrivals to tumbledown shacks, coaches jouncing over rutted mountain passes, opposition from other convents and sometimes town officials, donors who took back their gifts — even legal harassments against their beginnings. Her prayer for suffering was being answered.

In January, 1571, she had to stop her work of making foundations for three years. Trouble at her original convent, Incarnation, prompted the Apostolic Visitor to assign Teresa there, but this time as its prioress! One hundred and thirty discontented nuns — and now the thing they had dreaded was happening: they were going to be reformed! "What have we done that we cannot even elect our own prioress?" they wailed. They formed a human wall to block Teresa's entrance, while the few who wanted her there tried to push them aside. Finally police had to be called to restore order so Teresa could lead the way into the choir.

Later, in the chapter room, she absentmindedly took her old seat. Her infectious laugh rang out. Soon everyone was laughing as she rose and made her entrance again, this time carrying a statue of Our Lady and placing it on the prioress' seat. "I want her to be your prioress," she said. "I am here only to serve you and make things as pleasant as I can."

With that, she began seeing to it that all the nuns had enough to eat. She appealed to every wealthy friend in the city and even to her own sister for whatever could be had — poultry, fish, bread, — even things that nuns didn't ordinarily eat, since many of them had been ill.

Then there were the accounts. Night after night, she worked on their books; and soon they had the financial help they needed, with every debt paid to the last *reâl*. After this she began the reforms gradually and gently, treating each sister as an individual. It was not long before peace had come to the house and the nuns began living a penitential life "worthy of all admiration." In less than three years, Teresa was able to resume her travels, raising new foundations at Salamanc, Segovia, Pastrana, Beas, and then, southward to Seville.

But at Seville, she had inadvertently moved out of the region authorized by the Master General of the order. A bitter and divisive conflict followed, involving Teresa and others beyond the Carmelite Order as well. Finally she appealed to the King, Philip II. "All matters shall be arranged as you wish," said the King, as she curtsied before him. Then the king ordered that the reformed Carmelite branch become a second, entirely separate order. Now there would be *two* Carmelite orders: The

Regular or Mitigated Order, and the houses founded by Teresa, The Carmelites of the Strict or Reformed Observance.

"Now we are at peace," Teresa wrote, "having no one to disturb us in the service of our Lord."

By this time Teresa was sixty-five, free at last from "more troubles, persecutions and trials than I have space to tell." After establishing her 17th and last convent at Burgos, she had to make a side trip to Alba de Tormes. There she had to stop, being too ill to travel further. As she received the Sacrament for the last time, she exclaimed, "O my Lord, now is the time that we may see each other."

She died there on October 4, 1583. She was canonized in 1622, and her relics are treasured at Carmelite houses in both Alba and Avila.

During her life, St Teresa had written her autobiography, *Foundations*, (the story of the founding of all the first reformed communities), a book treating prayer and other subjects for nuns (*The Way of Perfection*) and a treatise on forms of prayer and meditation, *The Interior Castle*. Because of these and other writings, widely read over the centuries and greatly admired even today, she became the first woman saint to be accorded the honor of being named Doctor of the Church in 1970. Her feast is celebrated on October 15.

St Hildegarde

1098-1179

Moses, Jonah, Elijah, John the Baptist — the Bible is rich with those chosen by God to be instruments of His truth, to bring messages of hope, encouragement and correction to His people. Born in the year 1098, Hildegarde lived the first eight years of her life in Bockelheim, a tiny medieval town on the Nahe River in the southwest of present-day Germany. It was an exciting age in which to live, and she was to become one of the most effective spokeswomen of her time.

After her eighth birthday, Hildegard's parents gave her to the care of Blessed Jutta, a noblewoman whose cottage sat next to St Disibod's Abbey. In this vine-covered hermitage, Hildegarde learned reading, singing of chant in the abbey church next door, stories from the Bible, and the domestic skills that every woman of the time had to master. Other girls joined Bl. Jutta, and in a few years her house became an abbey, following the Rule of St Benedict. Under Jutta as prioress, Hildegarde donned the habit of a nun at the age of fifteen.

Her life for the next seventeen years was quite ordinary on the surface — studies, community worship and work. But inwardly, she continued to have revelations and unusual experiences which had started when she was quite young. It became habitual for her to foretell the future in the course of conversations. Some people, offended by this gift, made fun of her and thought her deluded. Their reactions made her blush and cry and she wanted to hide the revelations. Although she felt she should write down what she was receiving, she feared what people might think. Besides, she reasoned, her Latin was inadequate to the task.

Finally she opened her heart to her confessor, the monk Godfrey, and allowed him to refer the matter to his abbot. At their request, she wrote down some of her revelations concerning the love of Christ and the continuance of the kingdom of God. When the Archbishop of Mainz read them, he exclaimed, "These visions come from God!"

A secretary was then appointed for her, and at once she began to dictate her principle work, *Scivias*, or *The Knowledge of God's Way*, which contained descriptions of twenty-six visions. It took ten years to complete and it covered such subjects as the relation between God and man expressed in the Creation, Redemption and the Church, written in symbolic style and mixed with warnings and prophecies. Her manner of expression has been compared to that of Dante and William Blake. For example,

> I saw a great star, most splendid and beautiful, with a multitude of falling sparks which followed it southward . . . turning from Him, they suddenly were annihilated and turned into black coals and cast into the abyss.

In 1147, Pope Eugenius III visited her district and the Archbishop of Mainz referred her writings to him. He appointed a commission to examine them (including St Bernard of Clairvaux), and upon their recommendation, approved them and authorized her to write whatever God inspired in her. Hildegarde then began writing books on all sorts of subjects, ranging from medicine and natural history to commentaries on the Gospels and the Creed. She wrote a commentary on the Rule of St Benedict and a life of St Disibod, a dictionary for a made-up language, and even a morality play. When she felt moved by the Spirit, she addressed wrongs in kings, popes, and other church dignitaries, telling them when God was displeased with their lives. Even Emperor Conrad II received a warning to reform lest he have to blush for his deeds. She did not pretend to make these judgments on her own, however. "I am a poor earthen vessel and say these things not of myself but from the serene Light," she wrote to St Elizabeth of Schonau.

In 1136, Bl. Jutta died and Hildegarde was appointed to be prioress. The convent had outgrown its original cottage and Hildegarde felt that God was directing them to relocate to a desolate hill overlooking the Rhine (near modern Bingen). However, the neighboring monks stoutly opposed the move, since their abbey had gained most of its importance by being next to the relics of Bl. Jutta and a prioress with the reputation of Hildegarde. The dispute brought her to a bad state of health, but when the abbot finally agreed to the move, she recovered immediately. Seeing this, he withdrew all his objections and she relocated the nineteen sisters some time between 1147 and 1150.

Beginning with a dilapidated church and unfinished buildings, St Hildegarde and her nuns built a large and convenient abbey, which even included piped-in water. For their recreation, Hildegarde composed a large number of hymns, canticles and anthems, along with fifty allegorical homilies. For the rest of her life, she continued a voluminous correspondence with clergy and laity, giving prophecies and warnings. She made many journeys in the Rhine area, founding a daughter house near Rudersheim, rebuking monks and nuns who had relaxed their discipline, giving warnings to clergy, even conferring with the Emperor Frederick Barbarossa. Her fame spread so that she became known as "The Sibyl of the Rhine."

During her last year, she became involved in a dispute which must have cost her much of her failing energy. She was finally supported by the Archbishop of Mainz and fully vindicated, and shortly thereafter died peacefully on September 17, 1179.

Twice, the process of her canonization was undertaken without success. She was named in the Roman Martyrology in the 15th century, however, and her feast is kept in several German dioceses on September 17. Because of the private and dated nature of the revelations she received, they impose no obligation of belief. The Church treats them with respect but allows each person to make individual judgment concerning them.

Contending for the faith which was once for all delivered to the saints.
Jude 1:3

Patrons of Special Causes

The righteous and the wise and their deeds
are in the hand of God.
Ecclesiastes 9:1

"For I was hungry, and you gave me food, I was thirsty
and you gave me drink, I was a stranger and
you welcomed me, I was naked and you clothed me,
I was sick and you visited me, I was in prison and
you came to me. . . . Truly, I say to you, as you did it
to one of the least of these my brethren,
you did it to me."
Matthew 25:35-36, 40b

Whatever you do in word or work, do all in the name
of the Lord Jesus, giving thanks to God the Father
through Him.
Colossians 3:17
Chapter for Feast of St Joseph

St Jerome

c. 341-420

Patron of Bible Studies

It has been said many times that saints are not always easy to live with. That saying could be underscored when it comes to Jerome, for the records of his life show that he was always what we might term "a difficult person."

Born about 342 of Christian parents, Jerome was thoroughly schooled in Latin, Greek and rhetoric. He was sent from his home in Stridon, Italy, to Rome, where he fell easily into some of the sin so prevalent there, a period of which he later repented deeply. Even there, however, he did not lose entirely the piety instilled in him from childhood, and it was there that he was finally baptized, having been a catechumen until he was eighteen years old.

"It was my custom on Sunday," he wrote, "to visit with my friends . . . the tombs of the martyrs and apostles . . ." (the famous catacombs of Rome). In all, he spent eight years in the Eternal City. From there he journeyed north to the ancient town of Trier (now in Germany) to further his schooling. While in Trier, his spirit was further awakened and he experienced a deep conversion. From then on his desire was to give himself completely to God.

About 374 he went to Syria to spend some time among the hermits, having already become embroiled in some acrimonious and bitter controversy. Two friends who went with him to Antioch died, and Jerome himself became very ill with a high fever. During this illness, in a dream or vision, he felt himself to be standing before the judgment seat of Christ.

"Who are you?" he was asked.

"I am a Christian," he answered.

"No! You lie! You are a Ciceronian. For where your treasure is, there will your heart be also."

Deeply moved by this experience, Jerome made his way to the desert and spent four years in solitude, suffering many illnesses and severe temptations of the flesh. Later he wrote of how, strangely, even in the midst of racking pain or fever, his mind would be tormented with passion and desire.

It was during this time that he decided to fill his mind with a new challenge — learning Hebrew. In his typical unflattering words, he called Hebrew a language of hissing and gasping. But he was a faithful and careful student, and did not give up simply because he did not enjoy the sound. In order to support himself, he had books copied and sold them to wealthy patrons. He also wrote his famous *Life of St Paul the Hermit.*

Still eager to further his knowledge, he journeyed to Constantinople and studied with the renowned St Gregory of Nazianzus, Gregory of Nyssa and other lesser known teachers. In the process he is said to have become "probably the most learned man of his age."

It was an age when theological arguments were heated, and when people argued over such matters in the streets. Even emperors became embroiled in these disputes and bishops took different sides. Being a man of strong likes and dislikes, it was inevitable that Jerome would be drawn into these disputes. As a result, he made many enemies, and was never at a loss for words in writing against them. His letters (117 are still extant) are full of sarcasm, biting invectives and irony. A disagreement with Rufinus, a friend from boyhood, brought forth bitter words on both sides.

In 382 he went to Rome with Paulinus, Bishop of Antioch and became secretary to Pope Damasus I. In this new position he was able to help some of the noble women of Rome in the development of a more devout and ascetical way of life for them. He became a lifelong friend of Paula and her family, including her widowed mother, sister, and daughters. His attacks on the morals of the city earned him the reputation of being fanatical, and his attacks on the clergy cost him enemies in high places. To even the score, some of them began to spread rumors, suggesting that his relationship with St Paula was not a proper one. Indignant, his appeal was that before the judgment seat of Christ the truth would be known.

After the death of Pope Damasus, he could not continue his work in Rome, so he went back to the East, seeking a place to resume his life as a hermit. Soon St Paula and her followers decided to follow, and with her support, a monastery for nuns was begun near Bethlehem, and another for monks nearby under Jerome's direction. Jerome opened a school for boys in Bethlehem, and continued to give spiritual counsel to his many followers.

This period marks Jerome's most lasting and valuable contribution to the Church, the translation of the Holy Scriptures into Latin. Known as the Vulgate because it was in the language of the people, it remained the basic Bible for many centuries, from which translations into English and other languages were made for Catholics until very recent times. Between 391 and 406 he published a new translation of all the books of the Hebrew Bible, commentaries on the twelve minor Prophets and many other literary works. During the next fifteen years he produced exegetical commentaries on the major prophets (Isaiah, Jeremiah, Ezekiel and Daniel).

Jerome held the celibate state in such high regard that he sometimes belittled the state of marriage, suggesting that it is good only because it produces children who can choose to remain virgins. Although his views may seem extreme and out of balance from the modern point of view, they must be read in context of his struggles in the midst of an immoral, affluent, easy-going age. He upholds the Christian calling to put God ahead of all human loyalties, all human relationships and human pleasure. He maintained a warm and cordial relationship with St Paula and other close friends to the end. Paula and her daughter, Eustochium, became first rate Hebrew scholars themselves, and were useful assistants to him in his work of translating the Bible. It is to his credit that in a time when women were held in low regard, he championed their right to be involved in places of leadership and upheld their right and duty to follow their own hearts in their obedience to God.

In 404, he lost his great friend and fellow worker, St Paula, and a few years later he was grief-stricken to learn of the sacking of Rome by Alaric.

"I cannot help them all," he said of the distinguished ladies who were fleeing from the invaders, "but I grieve and I weep with them, and, completely given up to the duties which charity imposes on me, I have put aside my commentary on Ezekiel and almost all study. For today we must translate the words of Scripture into deeds. Instead of speaking saintly words, we must act them."

Further troubles came. Now his own monasteries at Bethlehem were attacked, causing much suffering among the monks and nuns, and added burdens to his heavy heart. Finally, worn out by his austerities and his work, his body emaciated from fasting and wrinkled with age, he fell peacefully asleep on September 30, 420, the day still kept as his feast day.

He is the patron of Bible Studies. Few people in history have made so lasting and important a contribution to the spiritual life of the Church as he did with his consecrated use of learning. Of him the words of Hebrews 11:4 seem especially appropriate: "He died, but through his faith he is still speaking."

St Monica

332-387

Patron of Mothers

The women huddled together in the crowded marketplace of Tagaste, North Africa, complaining to one another of the cruel treatment they received from their husbands. Suddenly all attention turned to one of their companions, who seemed somehow separate from the others.

"How do you do it?" they marveled. "Your husband has a more violent disposition than all ours put together, yet we never hear a word of complaint out of your mouth."

Monica smiled and told them with a twinkle in her eye that perhaps their own tongues were to blame for much of their husbands' behavior. She then shared her secret of living with her ill-tempered, pagan husband, Patricius. Having been raised in a Christian home, she had been well-trained, and had learned to bear his fits of rage with patience. She never fought back, even with words, and did not defend herself when he unjustly accused or made fun of her, but waited until he had calmed down before trying to reason with him.

Monica sought to win Patricius to the Christian faith by her godly conduct, and as a result, he loved and deeply respected his wife. Eventually he was brought into the Church by her saintly example and fervent prayers. She had the great joy of seeing him baptized just a year before he died in 371. Yet her heartaches were not over.

Her oldest son, Augustine, was seventeen and studying rhetoric at Carthage when his father died. He had a brilliant mind, and his parents had great ambitions for him. He was wayward and rebellious, however, refusing to be baptized or accept his mother's faith, and he was given to periods of laziness and reckless living. Monica's grief and anxiety about him increased when she discovered two years later that not only was he living a wicked and immoral life, but that he had joined the Manichean heresy as well. She fasted, wept and prayed for her prodigal son for many, many years, begging clergymen to argue with him and convince him of the truth. One of them told her, "The heart of the young man is at present too stubborn, but God's time will come." She persisted, and he finally said, "Go now, I beg of you: it is not possible that the son of so many tears should perish." This was nine years before Augustine's conversion, and encouraged by the bishop's words, Monica never ceased her tireless prayers, fastings and tears on her son's behalf.

Augustine was twenty-nine when he decided to go to Rome to teach rhetoric. Monica objected to the idea, but her words were to no avail. She saw only one course open to her: to go with him. But Augustine had other plans. While she spent the night praying for him in church, he stole away and sailed for Rome alone.

"I deceived her with a lie," he wrote later, "while she was weeping and praying for me."

But Monica was not so easily put off. As soon as possible she embarked for Rome herself, only to find that he had wearied of the Eternal City and had moved on to Milan. Still undaunted, she followed him to Milan. There, to her great joy, she found that Augustine had come under the influence of the great bishop, Ambrose, who had once been a Manichean himself. Monica threw herself into the life of the Church in Milan and became a devoted supporter of Ambrose, keeping long vigils of prayer for him when he was being harassed and persecuted by the Arian empress, Justinia.

August, 386, marks Augustine's conversion to the Catholic faith. His own account of his conversion has fascinated many generations, and can be found elsewhere in this book. His mother had been trying to find a suitable wife for him for many years, but she found that, instead, he was called to lead a celibate life to the glory of God.

On Easter, 387, Augustine was baptized by St Ambrose, and soon afterward he and his mother, together with his natural son and some friends who had just been baptized, left Milan to return to North Africa. They stopped at Ostia, the port of Rome, to wait for a ship. Augustine reports that he and his mother enjoyed a most moving conversation on the everlasting life of the blessed. But no one in the company except Monica herself suspected that her life was drawing to an end. She observed to Augustine quietly one day, "Son, for my own part, I now find no delight in anything in this life. I don't know what there is left for me to do or why I'm still here, now that all my hopes in this world have been accomplished. The one thing for which I desired to linger a little while in this life was to see you a Catholic and a child of heaven before I died. God has granted me more than this, making you turn your back on earthly happiness and consecrate yourself to His service. What am I doing here?"

Several days later, Monica suddenly became very ill. At one time she had been very concerned that she be buried in her own native country, by her husband's grave. But now she told her son, "Lay this body anywhere. Don't let care of it disturb you. Nothing is far from God, and I am not afraid that He will be unable to find my body to raise it with the rest. I ask only that you remember me at the altar of the Lord wherever you may be." A few days later she died. She was fifty-five years old.

In his *Confessions*, Augustine paid highest tribute to his mother, "who brought me to birth, both in her flesh, so that I was born into this temporal light, and in her heart, that I might be born into eternal light."

She has become the patron saint and pattern for all Christian mothers, and the tremendous fruit of her life and prayers is evident in the changed life of her son, St Augustine, who went on to become a great bishop and one of the greatest teachers and theologians in the history of the Church.

Her body now rests in the Church of St Agostino in Rome, and her feast in the reformed Roman calendar is on August 27.

St Clare

1194-1253

Patron of Television

If you were to visit the Church of San Giorgio in Assisi, Italy, in 1211 during Lent, you would be very lucky to find a space outside the door in which to stand. A huge crowd packed the building in order to hear a ragged preacher standing in the pulpit. One could barely see him, because he was so short, but there was no mistaking the burning intensity with which he spoke or the joy in his face. And if you looked at a group of women standing to one side, you might see a beautifully dressed maiden of about 18 years, eagerly drinking in his words.

The preacher was St Francis, and the maiden, Lady Clara Scifi of the noble di Favarone family. One could tell she had absorbed the message by the light in her face as she stood talking with him afterwards. Near them was her aunt who was both her personal chaperone and her personal confidant. This same woman accompanied her late one night as they quickly stole down the streets of Assisi to the outskirts of town. Winter was just ending, but it was still chilly as they walked another mile to the Church of the Portiuncula where Francis lived with his small group of Little Brothers. He and his brothers met them at the door of the Chapel of Our Lady of the Angels, carrying lighted tapers in their hands.

"What is it you wish?" he asked Clare, already knowing the answer.

"To give up everything, that I might live after the manner of the holy Gospel," she answered, her face radiant with joy. Then, kneeling before the altar, she put off her fine clothes and put on a robe of coarse sackcloth, tied at the waist with a rope. St Francis himself cut off her long, blonde hair. Then she was escorted to the Benedictine convent of St Paul near Bastia.

No sooner had her family discovered what she had done when they came in a body, demanding her return. Clare resisted. When they attempted to drag her away, she held to the altar so tightly that its linens slipped off. Then she uncovered her head to show that her hair had been cut.

"Christ has called me to His service, and I can belong to no other," she said firmly. Her family finally gave up, and not long afterwards, her sister, Agnes joined her.

Eventually Francis placed them in a small house near the Church of St Damian and appointed Clare the superior. Ladies who had enjoyed great riches began to be attracted to Clare's manner of life and, giving away all their possessions, came to be disciples. Even Clare's widowed mother eventually joined them.

For forty years Clare governed the convent, carrying out the life and spirit of total poverty. Pope Gregory accordingly granted them the "privilege of poverty," freeing them from the necessity of possessing any property whatever, either individually or as a group. Clare drew up a Rule which expresses this spirit. She wanted to be the servant of servants, to be beneath all. She washed the feet of the lay sisters when they returned from begging for food; she served meals, cared for the sick, and even tucked in the loose bedclothes for her tired sisters at night.

Then, in 1244, trouble struck. An army of Saracens under Emperor Frederick II came in a body to plunder Assisi. San Damiano was outside the walls, so the invaders attacked it first. But Clare, bedridden with sickness, had the sisters carry her and the Blessed Sacrament in a pyx to the wall in full view of the enemy. "I beseech You, Lord, protect these defenseless children whom I am not now able to protect." She heard a small voice reply, "I will have them always in my care."

Then she turned to the sisters and said, "Have no fear; trust in Jesus." At that very moment sudden terror seized the attackers, and they began to flee in such haste that some of them were injured trying to get away!

Having been delivered from danger, Clare and her nuns then began to pray for Assisi, and after some days of siege, the proud general and his troops gave up, and left off their attack. Assisi was saved.

For her last twenty-seven years, Clare endured much sickness. But this did not keep her from working. She made beautiful altar cloths and gave them to the churches of Assisi. When she was unable to attend Easter Mass, she was given a vision of the Host at the moment of elevation, along with other details of the entire service. This is why she is called "Patron Saint of Television."

As her fame spread, bishops, prelates, and cardinals flocked to see her and ask her counsel. Twice she was visited by Pope Innocent IV. Finally, at the age of sixty, her body was worn out, and her departure was near. She was heard to say to herself, "Go forth in peace, for you have followed the good road. Go forth without fear, for He that created you has sanctified you, has always protected you, and loves you as a mother. Blessed be Thou, O God, for having created me."

She was canonized only two years after her death, in 1255. Her feast is kept on August 11.

St Camillus de Lellis

1550-1614

Patron of Nurses and the Sick

The raucous laughter grew louder, attracting the attention of passersby near the open door of the tavern. Inside, barely visible in the dim twilight, a very tall young man hunched over the gaming table, surrounded by grinning soldiers. "Ah ha! Nines again! You lose!" said one. More laughter followed.

The young man turned suddenly and bolted for the street with the soldiers in hot pursuit. "Oh, no, you don't!" said one, grabbing his tunic. A struggle followed, with the massive youth swinging about wildly. Then, with a rip, the tunic came loose in the hands of the soldier. He surveyed it, sneering, "It doesn't really settle the debt, but we'll accept it anyway." Then, giving him a final shove, the soldiers returned to the tavern, and the young man stood in the middle of the Naples street, clothed only in his breeches.

The year was 1574, and the young man, Camillus de Lellis, six feet six inches tall, was a compulsive gambler and soldier of fortune. But this last streak of luck had run out, and having gambled away his pay, his weapons and all his savings, he had just lost the proverbial shirt off his back. What now?

He took another look at the tavern, but — no use; he had nothing left to wager. Slowly he walked down the street leading to the edge of town. Fortunately he could live off the land, and being away from his companions gave him time to think.

Once before he had lost everything . . . then he promised God . . . "Maybe now is the time," he thought as he quickened his steps and headed towards Manfredonia and the Gargano Mountains, all the way on the other side of Italy.

A narrow trail led a mile and a half up the mountains from the town below. He followed this until he reached a clearing near the top. By now the old wound on his leg was hurting him badly, and his steps grew more labored. Though it was almost dark, he could still see a small group of Capuchin friars hard at work setting the stones for their new monastery. Seeing the tall figure limping into the clearing, the guardian brother put down his tools and offered him their hospitality. Camillus gratefully accepted, and as the days went by, his leg became well enough for him to help them build. He proved to be a good mason, and the work sped along. Camillus began to see how wrong he had been, and a change took place in his heart. He was often moved to tears as he thought of his wasted life. Although it seemed natural for him to join the Capuchins, the sore on his leg prevented his profession as a friar, so after remaining as a semi-invalid among them several years, Camillus decided to go to the Hospital of San Giacomo. Bidding farewell to the brothers, he limped down the path and took the road leading to Rome.

The young man who entered as a patient and servant at San Giacomo was very different from the one who had been dismissed from there several years before for quarreling. This time he was determined to make the hospital a more cheerful, loving place. Soon he interested a group of attendants in devoting themselves to caring for the patients in a loving way, and there he remained for forty-six years, although his leg disease continued to trouble him.

While he was there, his confessor encouraged him to study for the priesthood so he could better minister to those who were dying. But Camillus had never learned to read, so the way was hard indeed. But he persevered, and after he was ordained, a Roman gentleman gave him a stipend (a salary) for life.

With two companions, he set up some short rules for his little band of helpers. Every day they made beds, served meals to the sick, and told them about the Lord who could give them joy even while suffering. Others joined them, and soon they started a hospital of their own. In spite of his many illnesses, Camillus continued to minister to those in his care. In 1591, Pope Gregory XIV gave Church approval for his congregation to become a religious order, called Ministers of the Sick.

He was a pioneer in insisting on fresh air, suitable diets, and separating patients with infectious diseases. He lived to see his order found fifteen houses and eight hospitals, with three hundred members. His priests wore red crosses on their cassocks, and members of his Order were ministering to the wounded and dying on the battlefield in 1859 when M. Henri Dunant conceived the idea of forming the Red Cross. St Camillus is patron both of nurses and of the sick. He died in 1614, and was canonized in 1746. His feast day is July 14.

St John Baptist de la Salle

1651-1719

Patron of School Teachers

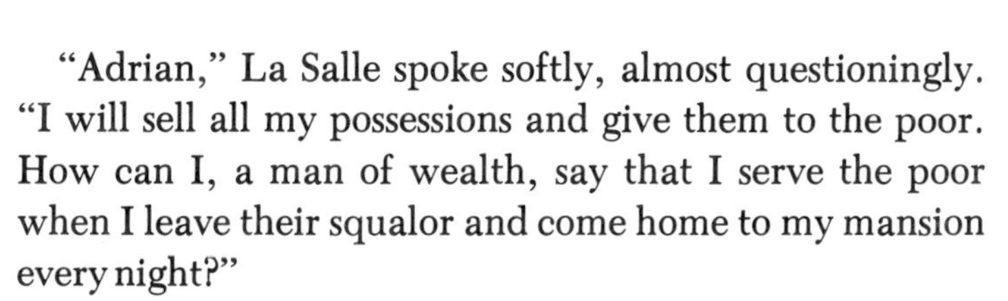

"Adrian," La Salle spoke softly, almost questioningly. "I will sell all my possessions and give them to the poor. How can I, a man of wealth, say that I serve the poor when I leave their squalor and come home to my mansion every night?"

His voice rising with determination, as if each word spoken confirmed his ideas and dispelled his fears, John Baptist went on, "I bring these brothers into my house to share my life, and I have no life but a burden of wealth that causes dissatisfaction among them. I must be as one of them, by ridding myself of all these possessions. You understand don't you, Adrian?"

Adrian had watched his friend's fervor grow from a tiny spark into a roaring fire concerning education for the poor.

Born at Rheims, France, on April 30, 1651, John de la Salle had shown an inclination for the religious life at an early age, and he was only sixteen when he became a canon. Eleven years later he was ordained to the priesthood, but even so, it was all too easy to fall into the laxity and complacency of the age. Then he met Adrian Nyel, a layman who had come to Rheims to open a school for poor boys and was drawn more and more into the vision and challenge of educating boys from poor homes. He saw that what was needed most was to raise the ideals and behavior level of the school teachers themselves if the work was to succeed. "Ushers" as they were called, were classed with hucksters and pot-boys. Teaching was not held in high repute, especially when done as a charity.

La Salle decided the best course of action was to invite the masters, seven of them, to live in his own home. Offended by the prospect of living with such ill-mannered, uncouth persons, his two brothers indignantly left. The discipline he imposed on his new wards proved too much for five of them, and they, too, left.

La Salle waited, and new teachers of a better type came, and the work grew. Too large to continue in his paternal home, he then moved what had become an infant community to more adequate quarters. The work soon absorbed his full time, so he resigned his canonry and began to contemplate giving up his considerable fortune to alleviate the suffering of the poor at a time of direst need in the Champagne area.

In a conference with twelve of his men, he established a new congregation, to be called Brothers of the Christian Schools. Members would make a vow of obedience renewable each year until they were certain about their vocation. Soon applications for admission to the new community were coming from young people. This necessitated the formation of a junior novitiate, with simpler rules and a new house with proper supervision. What resulted was the first teacher-training college in France, first at Rheims, followed later by one in Paris and another at Saint-Denis.

John Baptist de la Salle revolutionized education by having courses taught in French rather than Latin, which had been the traditional way. Instead of the classics, his students studied something that would be more practical for earning a living. There was a school for seamen and another for the sons of middle-class merchants. King James II of England, at that time in exile, requested La Salle's help in educating fifty sons of his followers from Ireland.

As his schools grew, so did criticism and persecution. The teachers of private secular institutions resented his success. Others were opposed to the idea of schooling for children of the poorer classes, and bitter complaints were made against his work. An allegation of undue severity toward novices brought an investigation by the representative of the Archbishop of Paris, and an unfavorable report resulted in more suffering. La Salle was informed that he should consider himself deposed, and he accepted the verdict without a word of protest. His brothers, however, refused to accept the proposed new superior, saying their superior was M. de la Salle, and that they would recognize no other. La Salle prevailed upon them to accept, but the matter was then dropped and he was allowed to continue in his place. A short time later, a bitter law-suit was instituted against him by people who opposed his work, and he was forced to close all his schools in the city of Paris. This, too, died down after a period, and the brothers were able not only to resume their work, but to expand it.

It was a special feature of the Brothers of the Christian Schools that no brother could become a priest and no priest could join the order. This was to insure that there would be no jealousy or rivalry between lay and clerical brothers. To this day, the order retains the same rule. Today it is the largest teaching order of the Church, working from the primary level through the universtiy level of education.

When time came to retire because of age and ill health, La Salle had Brother Bartholomew installed as superior general. He continued to teach and write, however, until his death two years later, on Good Friday, 1719.

He was canonized in 1900, and in 1950 Pope Pius XII declared him the patron of all school teachers. His work makes him one of the most important figures in the history of education. His feast is celebrated on April 7.

St Aloysius Gonzaga

1568-1591

Patron of Youth

"Boom!" The roar of the cannon startled the entire company of three thousand soldiers from their afternoon rest. Jumping to their feet, several officers ran toward the site of the sound, only to find five year old Luigi Gonzaga standing alone and unawed by the massive field piece.

"I march with my pike in the parade," smiled the boy. "And now I can shoot big guns, too."

How he had managed to load and fire the piece remained a mystery, but the firstborn son of the Marquis of Castiglione looked for all the world like the great soldier his father hoped he would become.

It was not to be, however. Little Luigi not only accompanied the soldiers in their parades. He also learned to speak their language, and his horrified tutor reproved him sternly when he repeated the words at home.

"Such language is blasphemy against God," said the tutor. "If you use such language, you dishonor God and put Him to shame." Luigi was overcome with shame himself, and determined never to use such language again.

It was at a very early age that Luigi, or Aloysius as he is better known today, began to show that he had an unusual love for God and an unusual call to sanctity. From his earliest days he had been taught to say his prayers morning and evening. When he was about seven, however, he began to recite the Office of our Lady and other devotional prayers. It was not a passing fancy, either, but a practice he kept up permanently.

At that time, sons of nobility were often made pages in the royal courts. Aloysius was assigned to the court of Francesco de Medici at Florence when he was about nine years old. There he was to learn the pure Italian of Tuscany, Latin, and court etiquette, all of which would fit Aloysius to inherit the marquisate of Castiglione one day. The court was notorious for its immoral and wicked ways, but Aloysius had found a way to protect himself from the temptations of the court. He had discovered a book on the lives of the saints, and subjected himself to the disciplines he learned from it, even to the point of keeping his eyes downcast when in the presence of women. Some have suggested that his attitude was extreme, but his confessor, St Robert Bellarmine, and three other confessors, believed that he never committed a mortal sin in his life.

Aloysius conceived the idea that he should resign from his right of inheritance in favor of his younger brother. During the next few years, first at one court and then another, he continued to develop his interest in the religious life. His practices of prayer and austerities were nothing short of heroic, and even his poor digestion and recurring kidney trouble did not prevent him from fasting three days a week and engaging in long hours of prayer and reading.

It was a book about Jesuit missionaries that inspired his decision to become a Jesuit. His father was furious when he heard of his idea, but after several changes of mind, finally agreed to allow him to become a novice. Aloysius entered the novitiate in Rome when he was seventeen years old, exclaiming as he entered his little cell, "This is my rest for ever and ever." His father died only six weeks after Aloysius entered the Society of Jesus.

Since he was an aristocrat by birth and wanted to follow Jesus' example, young Aloysius begged his superior's permission to wash dishes and do other menial tasks. These were things he had never had to do, and through them he sought the humility he could not obtain by prayers and meditation alone.

In 1591, when he was twenty-three years old, a terrible epidemic of the plague hit Rome. The Jesuits opened a hospital in which many of their members, including the father general, served the sick with their personal service. Aloysius volunteered to work among the patients and was allowed to do so in spite of his own health problems. His work was not skilled. This young man, who had grown up at court, now carried bed pans. He once conversed with the Crown Prince of Spain. Now he encouraged and comforted the dying with the gospel of the Lord he loved. This young man, who had chosen ten years earlier to follow the call of God on his life, now found happiness and peace in the opposite position of that which was his by birth. By caring for the needs of others in very practical ways, he found his life richer by far than when he had lived at court.

More and more, Aloysius was absorbed in contemplating the wonder and glory of God. Sometimes he would fall into an ecstasy at table or during recreation time. When he contracted the plague, he was overjoyed, believing that death was near. He received the last rites, but to his own and everyone's surprise, recovered. He began to wonder if his joy was a disguise for impatience to enter the joy of heaven.

His health had been fatally impaired by the plague, and it was only three months before he was almost too weak to get out of bed. Still he would struggle to make his way to his crucifix and his sacred pictures to pray. He asked his confessor, St Robert Bellarmine, if it was ever possible for one to go into the presence of God without passing through Purgatory. St Robert said that he believed it could be so, and encouraged Aloysius to hope that such a grace might be given him. His final days he spent in the glad expectation that soon he would be in God's presence. Each day he sang the *Te Deum* in thanksgiving. His superior thought he was improving greatly, but Aloysius insisted that he was going to die, and asked again for prayers for the departing. He died about midnight between June 20 and 21, 1591, with his eyes fixed on the crucifix and the name of Jesus on his lips.

He was canonized in 1726 and made patron of youth in 1729. His feast is observed on June 21.

St Vincent de Paul

1581-1660

Patron of Charitable Societies

The night air was dense with fog as a solitary figure shuffled along the garbage-strewn streets. He paused and listened to a muffled cry that was almost drowned by the night's darkness. Quickly he moved down another street. The cry was closer now, and he began to throw garbage aside until he cleared a path to an old basket covered with rags. Throwing the rags aside, he saw the source of the cry — a little baby.

"Ah, my little baby, thank your guardian angel for directing my steps, for you were truly lost in this mass of trash! You will have a full stomach tonight, and then I bet your cry will be a lot lustier!"

Picking up the child, he wrapped it in his cloak to protect it from the night air and hurriedly stepped off towards the Foundling Hospital.

"Monsieur Vincent! You bring us another one — and so late at night!" greeted the Sister of Charity.

"Ah, Sister, this one must be named after an angel, for it was his guardian angel that kept me looking long after I wanted to quit," he replied with a twinkle in his eye.

St Vincent de Paul spent his life seeking to help the poor and needy wherever they might be found. It is no accident that he would later become the Patron of Charitable Works.

Born of peasant parents in 1581, Vincent's intelligence and inclination toward the religious life were recognized early. He was sent to the Franciscans at Dax, and later to Toulouse University for his education, and was ordained at the very young age of nineteen. But at that point, he slipped easily into the prevailing mores of the day, receiving the income of a small abbey, a practice which, to say the least, was very questionable. An unpleasant incident of that period brought Vincent into a different frame of mind. His friend, with whom he was lodging, accused him of stealing a large sum of money, and, in spite of Vincent's calm denials, continued to spread the most vicious accusations about him everywhere. For six months Vincent bore this unjust slander before the true thief confessed. But change was at work in Vincent, and one of his spiritual advisors prevailed on him to become chaplain to the court of Philip de Gondi, Count of

Joigny. He was made tutor to their children and given charge of the spiritual welfare of the peasants who lived on their lands. Here he came back into contact with his own peasant roots, and he began to be aware of their physical and spiritual needs in a new way.

His work soon carried him to Paris, where he labored among the galley-slaves who were imprisoned in the Conciergerie. There he was appointed chaplain to the galleys and conducted a mission for the convicts in them. with the approval of the de Gondis, and later with an endowment from them, he was able to minister in a remarkable way to the convicts' needs. But his concerns were not limited to the poor. His benefactress, Madame de Gondi, extracted a promise from him never to cease giving her spiritual direction as long as she lived. She went on to persuade her husband to join her in establishing a company of priests who would minister to the spiritual needs of the vassals and tenants on their property. Her brother, Archbishop of Paris, gave the Collège des Bons Enfants for the use of this new community, whose members were to devote themselves to serving in small villages and out-of-the-way places, drawing their income from a common fund. St Vincent was put in charge of this house in 1625, and he himself joined the congregation after the countess died. In 1633 they were given the priory of Saint-Lazare, and this later became their mother house. From this priory they received their name, Lazarists, but they are also called Vincentians, after their founder. Before his death they numbered twenty-five houses, working in many needy parts of France and other countries.

This missionary order was not enough to exhaust the energies and concerns of this man of God. He went on to found confraternities of charity, whose task was to care for the poor and sick in each parish. This resulted, with the help of St Louise de Marillac, in the formation of the Sisters of Charity, whose aim was to serve the sick wherever they were found. Appealing to those with wealth, St Vincent banded devout women together as the Ladies of Charity, who then supported his good work with their funds and their prayers.

Even these interests did not use up his great zeal. He wrote spiritual exercises for men preparing to receive holy orders, engineered the rescue of 1200 Christian slaves from the Moors in North Africa, answered the death-bed call of King Louis XIII for help, and counselled Queen Anne of Austria on matters ecclesiastical at her request. He intervened to obtain a place for the English Benedictine nuns who had fled from their country, and fought vigorously against the Jansenist heresy. That particular teaching held that without special grace it is impossible to keep God's commandments and that His special grace is irresistible. Vincent said, "I have made the doctrine of grace the subject of my prayer for three months, and every day God has confirmed my faith that our Lord died for us all and that He desires to save the whole world." Not only did he refuse to allow those who held the Jansenist viewpoint to remain in his congregation, he worked actively to have it condemned, as it was by a Papal Bull in 1653.

His work brought him not only gratitude and applause. It was also fraught with disappointments, set-backs and criticism. In all this, he displayed a serene and peaceful frame of mind, in spite of the fact that he was, by his own admission and the witness of others, "of a bilious temperament and very subject to anger." His natural crabbiness and unpleasantness was transformed by the grace of God and the cooperation of his will into a tender and affectionate personality. Believing that humility was the greatest of virtues, he even counselled his followers not to speak of themselves or their own concerns, believing that such talk would encourage pride and self-love.

He died in 1660 at the age of eighty, having long suffered with ill health. He was canonized in 1737 by Pope Clement XII and proclaimed patron of all charitable societies by Leo XIII. The Society of St Vincent de Paul was named in his honor and sought to emulate his spirit when it was founded by Frederic Ozanam in 1833. His feast is celebrated on September 27.

Young People

Let no one despise your youth, but set the believers
an example in speech, in conduct, in love,
in faith, in purity.
I Timothy 4:12

Do not say, "I am only a youth"; for to all to whom
I send you you shall go, and whatever I command you
you shall speak. Be not afraid of them, for I am with you
to deliver you, says the Lord.
Jeremiah 1:7, 8

Young men and maidens, old men and children:
Let them praise the name of the Lord.
Psalm 148:12, 13

Shepherd of eager youth,
Guiding in love and truth
Through devious ways;
Christ our triumphant King,
We come Thy name to sing,
Hither our children bring
To shout Thy praise.
Clement of Alexander, c. 160-215

St Agnes

d. c. 303

St Agnes, one of the most popular of all the early saints, lived in the late 200's and early 300's in Rome. Because she was a very beautiful girl, many men sought her hand in marriage, even though she was very young. Her family was eager to arrange a successful marriage, according to the custom of the time — advantageous to her and to the family as well.

Agnes was not only beautiful; she loved God, and wanted to devote her whole life to serving Him. Marriage, she felt, might weaken her love for God and her ardor in serving Him with all her heart, so against everyone's advice and pressure, she refused to marry.

Although she was only about thirteen years old, her determination was very strong.

One of the young men who was very eager to marry her felt rejected and very angry at her refusal. It was a time when Christians were being persecuted by the Roman Emperor, Diocletian. He was very disturbed because so many Romans were becoming Christians, and was convinced that the old gods of Rome would bring some calamity upon the Empire if he did not turn people back to the old religion. It was a dangerous time to be a Christian, though in many places it was possible to practice the Faith quietly and go without detection. Finally, realizing that he would never gain Agnes' hand in marriage, her suitor decided to report her as a Christian to the governor. It is possible that he held out, as a last hope, that under the threats and torments which would inevitably be applied, Agnes might yet relent and consent to marriage.

At first the governor tried to persuade her to marry her suitor, using the kindest possible words. But when Agnes steadfastly refused, he began to threaten her with a terrible death. This had no effect on Agnes, and when she was finally condemned to die, St Ambrose says, "She went to the place of execution more willingly than others go to their wedding."

There is some question as to how she met her death — some say by being beheaded, and others, by having a sword pierced through her neck. Even as she was being prepared for execution, she forgave those who were persecuting her, and some of them were moved to tears at her willing acceptance of her plight.

She was buried a short distance from Rome, and from earliest times her name has been remembered in the Canon of the Mass. Because her name resembles the Latin word for lamb, "agnus," there is a custom at St Agnes Convent in Rome of shearing the wool from lambs on her feast day to make the special pallium which the Holy Father gives to each new Bishop in the Church. She has always been been regarded in the Church as a patroness of bodily purity. Her symbol is a lamb and a palm. Her feast day is January 28 in the new calendar.

St Mary Goretti

1890-1902

The story of St Mary Goretti is somewhat similar to that of St Agnes, but she lived much nearer to our time. Born in 1890, she died at the age of twelve in 1902. Her story is sad to us, but it is an important one for all Christians.

Mary lived in Italy, one of seven children in a very poor family in a little village in the Apennines. The family moved to the outskirts of Rome, hoping for a better life, and settled in the Pontine marshes, a very unhealthy area. When she was only ten years old, her father died of malaria, and in order to support the family, her mother had to go out to work. Mary was left to keep the house and care for the family during the day. Even though life was hard for the Gorettis, she tried to be helpful and cheerful. Especially she prayed often and taught her brothers and sisters their prayers also. Every Sunday she would walk two hours to go to Mass. The four times she was able to receive Communion before she died were very special for her.

The Gorettis lived with another family in the same house: a man and his son Alexander, who was about twenty years old. For a long time Alexander had been watching Mary with a desire to use her for his own sinful pleasure. One day, when no one was home, he grabbed her. Mary tore away, crying, "No! No! God does not want this!" At this, Alexander became furious. Determined to have his way, he started to threaten her.

The next day, everybody in the household was busy threshing beans. Alexander's father was resting for awhile in the shade. He had a fever because the day had been so hot. Mary was sitting on the steps, sewing. Alexander made an excuse to leave and came up the steps. He passed Mary without a word. Going inside, he rummaged through a box of junk until he found a piece of rusty metal that was sharp on one end like a dagger. Before Mary could move, the youth stepped out on the landing and grabbed her. She tried to scream, but he stuffed his handkerchief in her mouth. Still she managed to struggle and ward him off repeatedly.

Then, grabbing the dagger, Alexander thrust it into the girl again and again. He left her crumpled on the floor, unconscious. When she came to, she inched her way to the door and tried to call for help. But Alexander rushed back into the room and pierced her throat with the dagger. By this time, his father and Mary's brother had heard the commotion, and dashed up the stairs. The little brother fled in horror at what he saw. Mary was still conscious when her mother reached her a few minutes later.

"What happened?"

"Alexander did it," said Mary, still in great pain.

"But why? Why did he do it?"

"Because he wanted me to commit a horrible sin, and I would not."

When an ambulance finally got her to the nearest clinic, it was almost evening. Doctors tried to stitch up her wounds, but they couldn't save her.

"Do you forgive your murderer?" she was asked.

"I do forgive him," she replied, "and I believe that God will forgive him, too."

For two more days the martyr lived in agony, unable to take even a drop of water to relieve her thirst. She thought of Jesus on the cross and gave her suffering to Him. She kissed a picture of him repeatedly; then she became unconscious. A few hours later, she died.

For a long time, during his imprisonment, Alexander remained bitter and unrepentant. Then one night, in a dream, he saw Mary gathering flowers and offering them to him. At once his heart changed, and from then on he was a repentant man. After serving twenty-seven years in prison, he was released in time to see Mary canonized in 1950.

In declaring Mary a saint, the Church said it meant to honor all those who have kept themselves pure in the time of temptation, and even have chosen death rather than to give in to dishonor. Pope Pius XII called her "a new St Agnes." Many miracles have been attributed to her intercession.

Her feast day is July 6.

St Edmund, King and Martyr

841-869

The bishop dismounted and made his way slowly up the grassy path to a tiny croft in Fleury. He had not reached the door before a large young man bolted out, knelt before him and kissed his ring.

"My Lord Archbishop," he exclaimed, "I hope you are staying long enough this time to share a tankard or two!"

"My dear Abbo," the bishop replied. "Your hospitality is always most welcome; though I intend to make my stay short, it will not be so brief that I cannot enjoy a refreshing draught."

"It is good to hear your news," said Abbo as they went inside. "And especially to learn of King Edgar's court. I trust all is well?"

"As well as on the day the Danes finally submitted. But I am kept busy. The King sends me hither and yon with but a single purpose: rebuild and regroup the monasteries leveled by Guthrum's folk. And a huge undertaking it is." Dunstan smiled. "But what about you? How fares your tale-gathering?"

"I'm afraid it's wanting a bit. Four decades of glorious battles, the great King Alfred — but at present things are at peace . . . ." Abbo paused in thought. "But I was thinking of good St Edmund. Though it was almost a hundred years ago when he died, it seems to me his death turned the tide. What do you know of the matter?"

"I was but a boy when I first heard it," said the bishop. "But I have never forgotten the account told me by Edmund's very own standard bearer. He was an old man when I met him, yet his words are emblazoned on my mind to this day. What a Christian that young king was!"

"Aye, and a right courageous king he was." Abbo took a long draught from his tankard. "That he died at the hands of the wicked Ingwar, I know. But an account from someone who was there — I had not heard of that."

"The tale must never be forgotten. His godly life and his incorrupt body at Bury St Edmund's mark him as a great saint. He began his reign with as good an omen as any, it being Christmas Day. And that without bloodshed, he being appointed by Offa, the high King."

"I've never understood how a mere boy could reign. Why he was only fourteen years old, wasn't he? What wisdom he must have had!"

"A right godly person even then. But others took care of the harder matters, I ween. Nevertheless, he was not idle. He took time to memorize the entire Psalter, the better to join in worship in the Daily Offices, he said. He wanted to be like the great Hebrew King, David. And for fourteen years he reigned quietly and peaceably until those bloodthirsty Danes came with their long boats and took over the coast, pillaging and killing as they went. It was many a winter before we drove them out, and a hard struggle before terms of peace could be arranged."

"But didn't Ingwar offer terms to Edmund?"

"Terms! You could hardly call Ingwar's conditions of slavery any sort of terms. Edmund would have to give up half his treasure and become a vassal to that pagan. Yes, Ingwar would have accepted that. But for Edmund that would have meant giving up his faith. So he and his people fled from the castle in Suffolk and when the Danes had taken that area, he and his men made a gallant stand at Hoxne. But they were too few in number, and the cutthroats were too many. The Danes overcame them, seized the saint and tied him to a tree.

" 'Well, now do you accept our conditions?' Ingwar demanded.

"But Edmund replied, 'My faith is dearer to me than my life. I will never purchase my life by offending God.'

" 'Then you must face death.' And with that they started scourging him with whips. Afterwards they shot him with arrows, cleverly avoiding killing him. Then they hacked off his head. His standard bearer told me that when they reached the tree, his body was still tied to it, pierced with arrows like a hedgehog. But the head was missing, and they searched all the next day before they found it between the paws of a wolf who had not harmed it."

"The first miracle," said Abbo in awe.

"Through his loss, we won much," Dunstan agreed. "King Alfred started driving the enemy out just a few years later; we finally saw the last of them when I was a boy. But our Christian faith never died out, and we owe that to Edmund's sacrifice. Some of the Danes themselves were converted while they were among us."

"The tale must be preserved for others."

"Then you must write it, my friend, and add it to your collection of tales."

"Gladly," said Abbo. "I will call it 'The Passion of St Edmund'."

The year was 960 when St Dunstan related his tale to Abbo of Fleury. King Edmund had been crowned in 855 and reigned until the Danes killed him in 869. In 1010, Canute, the Christian king of Denmark, built a stone church to Edmund's honor over his tomb. The Benedictine Abbey at Bury St Edmund's became one of the strongest and most influential in the land. St Edmund's feast is celebrated on November 20.

Martyrs of Japan

16th Century, d. 1597

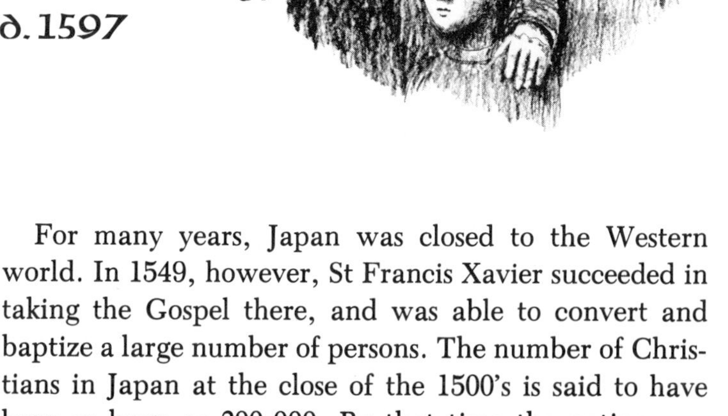

For many years, Japan was closed to the Western world. In 1549, however, St Francis Xavier succeeded in taking the Gospel there, and was able to convert and baptize a large number of persons. The number of Christians in Japan at the close of the 1500's is said to have been as large as 200,000. By that time the nation was ruled by a lord named Hideyoshi, who governed in the Emperor's name.

Hideyoshi feared the foreign missionaries and saw them as invaders, especially as the Jesuit missionaries had been extraordinarily successful in converting his lords. If the countries from which the missionaries had come should try to take over Japan, Hideyoshi worried that the converted lords might not remain loyal to him. So in 1587, he ordered all missionaries to leave Japan. A ship couldn't be secured until spring, so he decreed that they could wait on little Hirado Island. During this time he destroyed some of their churches and rectories.

The next spring, some of the foreign missionaries did indeed board a ship heading to Macao, but many sneaked back to their stations. They got the captain of the ship to send a message to Hideyoshi that there wasn't sufficient room for all of them. He tacitly acknowledged their return and did nothing. For the next ten years, an uneasy truce existed between the missionaries and Hideoyshi. Then something happened that redoubled his anger and fear about the possibility of a foreign invasion by a Christian country. A Spanish captain boasted to him that the object of the missionaries was to soften up Japan for conquest by Spain or Portugal. This enraged Hideoyshi. These foreigners must be shown that no such thing would be allowed and that he meant business!

He began by rounding up the six Spanish Franciscans who had intervened to save the Spanish ship in the crisis, along with three outstanding Japanese Christians (a priest from the aristocracy and two lay brothers). He arrested 17 others, all Japanese members of the Third Order of St Francis. To make them an object to others who might be friendly to

Christianity, he had twenty-four of them paraded through various villages with part of their left ears cut off. On February 5, 1597, he crucified all of them in a row on a hill near Nagasaki. After the crosses were raised from the ground, a separate executioner dispatched each of them with a spear, all at the same time.

Several of these martyrs, the first from the Far East, were young people who were crucified with their fathers. Saints Louis Ibarki, Antony Deyan and Thomas Kasaki were only 13 years old. They had been altar boys assisting the friars at mass. These were not the only martyrs in Japan; many others gave their lives for their faith in the years which followed before the Christian faith could be openly practiced there.

These martyrs were canonized in 1862, having been remembered with loving affection by their fellow Japanese Christians for almost two hundred years. Their Feast Day is February 6.

Martyrs of Uganda

d. 1886

Most of the saints are singled out as individuals, and we read about their lives and deaths one at a time. But there are a number of saints who were martyred in groups, and the Church remembers them for their faithfulness and bravery in the face of death.

Such a group are Saints Charles Lwanga, Joseph Mkasa and their companions, who lived in Uganda, Africa, in the latter half of the 1800's. Uganda lies in the interior of central Africa, and the first Catholic missions were established there by the White Fathers in 1879. When this happened, the local ruler was not unfriendly to the Christian missionaries, but his successor, Mwanga, became determined to root out the new religion from his country. His hatred of Christians increased when Joseph Mkasa rebuked him for his practice of unnatural vices and for his massacre of the Protestant missionaries, James Hannington and his associates.

Mkasa, who had charge of the royal pages and the royal household, had already been learning about the new faith when Mwanga came to power. When Mwanga started using his pages to gratify his lustful desires, Mkasa protested, and not long afterwards, Mwanga found a pretext to have him beheaded (November, 1885), making Joseph Mkasa the first Catholic martyr of Uganda. But his death did not wipe out Christianity as the chieftain had hoped. Instead, it flourished. The very night before Mkasa's execution, Mwanga's steward, Charles Lwanga, asked for the sacrament of baptism. He had taken Mkasa's place as overseer of the pages. More and more of the pages were being converted, which incensed the wicked ruler still more. When one of them refused his advances, Mwanga learned that a young page named Denis Ssebuggwawa had been instructing him in the Faith. In a rage, he called for Denis and ordered his throat pierced by a spear. Then he surrounded the compound with guards and called for his royal executioners. Knowing what lay ahead, Lwanga immediately baptized four of the pages, including 13-year old Kizito, whom he had repeatedly saved from the king. The next morning, Mwanga lined up all the pages and ordered the Christians to separate themselves from the others. Fifteen young men, all under twenty-five years old, stood apart from the others.

"Do you intend to remain Christians?" they were asked.

Their answer was quick: "Till death!"

"Then put them to death," was Mwanga's response. First they were imprisoned and beaten. Then Mwanga ordered them taken to a village 37 miles away to avoid an uprising among the people. During the long march, little Kizito laughed and chatted. Father Lourdel, the superior of the mission, wrote, "I was not allowed to say a word to them and had to content myself with seeing on their faces the resignation, happiness and courage of their hearts." Three of the boys were killed on the way because they could not keep up. The pages who remained were martyred on Ascension Day, June 3, 1886. They were wrapped in reed mats, rolled up and set on fire while still alive. But as the executioners chanted their murderous rituals, the voices of the young men could be heard calling on the name of Jesus and singing Christian hymns.

The persecution of Christians did not stop with this slaughter. Many other Christians, Protestant and Catholic, gave their lives for their faith. In spite of it all, the Church grew in numbers.

These martyrs, the first of Black Africa, were canonized in 1964. Their feast day is June 3.

St Thérèse of Lisieux

1873-1897

"I am only a very little soul who can offer to God only very little things," wrote St Thérèse of Lisieux, who entered a convent at the age of fifteen and lived quietly there for the rest of her short life, praying to be hidden in Jesus and forgotten by the world. And yet today she is one of the most beloved and well-known saints in the world. Countless books have been written about her; scholars and popes have acclaimed her. Hundreds upon hundreds of miracles have been attributed to her intercession, and she has been called, "the greatest saint of modern times."

Thérèse was born in 1873, the youngest child of M. Louis Martin and his wife, Zélie-Marie. M. Martin was a watchmaker in Alençon, France, where the famous lace is made, and his wife was a former lace-maker. The Martins were a devout couple, providing a godly and happy home for their daughters. Writing about it later, Thérèse said her earliest memories were of smiles and caresses. Her mother described her as a very strong-willed child, but the evidence of Thérèse's life is that she was able tc turn her strong will completely toward God. She was but four years old when her mother died, a cause of great grief for the whole family. Her father then sold his business in Alençon and moved the family to Lisieux, where an aunt helped care for the children and the home. Thérèse's older sister, Pauline, was a devout girl, and used to read to the family from a spiritual book written by Dom Guéranger, the re-founder of the famous Benedictine monastery of Solesmes. When Thérèse was nine years old, Pauline entered the Carmelite monastery (called the Carmel) at Lisieux, followed by another sister in a short time. Thérèse wanted to join then, too, but she had to wait until she was fifteen to follow her two sisters.

Her decision to become a nun was inspired by what she called her "conversion." It happened as a kind of inner vision, in which she felt that the Child Jesus filled her soul with light. After this experience, she was determined to become a sister as soon as possible, but because of her very young age could not be admitted to the novitiate. Instead, she went with her father on pilgrimage to Rome the next year in connection with the Pope's jubilee. During a public audience with Pope Leo XIII, while Thérèse knelt for his blessing, she broke the rule of silence:

"Your Holiness, in honor of your jubilee, please allow me to enter Carmel at fifteen."

The Pope blessed her, adding, "You shall enter if it is God's will."

About a month after her return home, the Bishop gave permission for Thérèse to join her two older sisters in the monastery. She was a few months past her fifteenth birthday.

In 1888, Thérèse's father suffered two strokes and from then till his death three years later, had to be confined to an asylum. Upon his death, a fourth sister, Céline, joined the other three as a Carmelite nun.

Life at Carmel was by no means easy. Meat was never eaten by the nuns, and from September to Easter they fasted on one meal a day. Thérèse's cell was totally without heat, and winters at Lisieux were very cold. And yet, she said, she was happier by far in Carmel than she had ever been in the world where she had enjoyed many comforts.

She led a rich life of prayer and had a great desire that more and more people should come to love the Lord. "Pray for me," she wrote a friend, "that I may love Jesus and make Him loved."

Thérèse never had any important position, although she served as assistant novice-mistress from 1893, helping to train other young women to become nuns. She had an ardent desire to become a missionary, but when that was impossible, she turned her concern into prayers for those who carried the Word of God into other lands.

She was instructed by her superiors to write a spiritual biography, because already they sensed that her saintliness was more than ordinary. She did this as an act of obedience, and the little book has been read by millions. She tells about what she calls her "little way" — simple obedience out of love for Jesus. She kept before her the appeal of Jesus crucified for her, and prayer was always a lifting up of her heart to him. She had absolute confidence in God and in His love for her, and she regarded everything, even the smallest task, as a way of showing Him how much she loved Him in return.

She was also known for her liveliness and wit. "There will be no laughter at recreation today," one of the nuns was heard to comment. "Sister Thérèse will not be there."

Just before Good Friday, 1895, Thérèse suffered the first serious sign of tuberculosis, from which she would die. She apparently recognized the fatal sign, and began to speak more prophetically than before. The last months of her life were marked by terrible suffering — choking, gasping for breath, coughing fits that lasted for hours, heavy perspiring and almost unbearable pain. Yet through it all she kept her faith in God, trusting that He knew best for her life and would not send her more suffering that she was able to bear. Nor did she ever lose her concern for others. The very night before her death, she was more worried about keeping the Sister who was attending her awake than she was with her own suffering. She assured everyone that she would pray for them after she was in heaven, promising to send "a shower of roses after her death." Two months before her death, she said, "I feel that I am about to enter my rest. But I feel especially that my mission is about to begin, my mission of making God loved as I love Him." She died on September 30, 1897.

Her cousin, Marie Guérin, who was a novice at Carmel under Thérèse, wrote, "I thank God for permitting me to know this little saint . . . . Hers is not an extraordinary sanctity. There is no love for extraordinary penances; no, only love for God. People in the world can imitate her sanctity, for she has tried only to do everything through love and to accept all little contradictions, all little sacrifices that come at each moment as coming from God's hands. She saw God in everything."

Canonized by Pope Pius XI in 1925, she is officially called "Thérèse-of-the-Child-Jesus," and was declared the patroness of foreign missions in 1927 and of France in 1947. Her feast is celebrated on October 1. When someone asked her what name they should call her when they prayed to her in heaven, she replied, "You will call me 'Little Thérèse.' " And so it has been ever since.

St Dominic Savio

1843-1857

The story of Dominic Savio is closely tied up with that of the great Don Bosco, for Dominic was one of the boys which the saint took under his charge at the Oratory in Turin. The year was 1854, and Dominic was twelve years old. Don Bosco was deeply impressed with Dominic's spirit, and the grace which seemed to be upon him when he became a student at his Oratory.

From the time he was a very small child, Dominic had a deep love of God and a desire to please Him above all things. His love of God made him want to try to follow Jesus in all situations, and gave him a love for the souls of others as well.

This led him to organize fellow students into a group termed The Company of the Immaculate Conception. It was their job to sweep floors, help with cleaning, and to help take care of other boys who seemed to be having problems of one kind or another. All this was before Don Bosco had founded the Order of St Francis de Sales, which would later become a world-wide missionary order. When Don Bosco founded the Salesians in 1859, all the original members of the Company of the Immaculate Conception were present except Dominic Savio, who had died two years earlier, at the age of 15.

Earlier, when two of the boys at the Oratory were going to have a duel with stones, Dominic decided that he had to intervene. There was so much hatred between the two boys that he knew that their souls were in jeopardy. He promised the boys that if they would tell him when the duel was to be held, and if they would let him accompany them, he would not report them to Don Bosco. Knowing that Dominic always kept his word, the boys agreed to let him come. On the day of the duel, Dominic told them that he was going to impose a condition on their duel, but that he wouldn't tell them what until they had arrived at the spot. Once they had arrived, the opponents selected their rocks and turned to face each other. But suddenly Dominic stood between them, directly in the line of fire, and held up a crucifix. Surely this was no way to hold a duel, and the boys shouted for him to get out of the way.

Seeing that his first plan had not worked, Dominic went up to one of the boys and knelt before him. He told the boy to say, "Christ died innocent and pardoned His enemies; but I want my revenge;" then he was to throw the first stone at him. The boy protested vigorously, so Dominic went to the other boy and said the same thing to him. This totally disarmed them both, and Dominic was able to talk to them and help them to see where they were wrong. The three of them then walked arm in arm back to the Oratory, without a stone ever having been thrown. Dominic never did tell Don Bosco what had happened, but the boys themselves did later on.

Dominic was in such a hurry to become a saint that Don Bosco sometimes had to step in and moderate the penances he imposed on himself. Don Bosco told Dominic that the best mortification he could practice was obedience and cheerful submission to God in the circumstances of his life — heat, cold, pain, illness, joy, sorrow — whatever God chose to send him. Don Bosco did not feel the need to moderate Dominic's prayer life, but he did try to protect him. Sometimes Dominic would become so totally absorbed in prayer that he would be unaware of the passing of time. Once Don Bosco went looking for him, because he had been missing all morning. He found him kneeling in a cramped position by the lectern, still praying, not realizing that Mass had ended many hours earlier. The great teacher simply told Dominic that if anyone asked where he had been, he could say that he had been with him. At such times as these, Dominic reported that it seemed as if Heaven opened above him. On another occasion, he saw a vision concerning the return of the Catholic faith to the English people. The vision was reported to Pope Pius IX, who was convinced of its authenticity.

Dominic's health, which had never been robust, began to fail rapidly in February of 1857. His condition was diagnosed as inflammation of the lungs, as pneumonia was called in those days. Treatment included bleeding, and this seems to have hastened his death. He received the last sacraments, and died with a vision of heaven opening before his eyes, saying softly, "I am seeing the most wonderful things!"

He was canonized in 1950, sixteen years after the canonization of his teacher and hero, Don Bosco. His feast day is March 9.

Remember your Creator in the days of your youth.
Ecclesiastes 12:1

National Saints

And by your descendants shall all the nations
of the earth be blessed.
Genesis 22:18

Blessed is the nation whose God is the Lord,
the people He has chosen as His heritage.
Psalm 33:12

O valiant hearts, who to your glory came
Through dust of conflict and through battle flame;
Tranquil you lie, your knightly virtue proved,
Your memory hallowed in the land you loved.
John Stanhope Arkwright, 1919

St George

d. c. 303

England

"How dare these Christians call this Jesus the Son of God? I, Diocletian, Emperor of Rome, declare that I am the son of Jupiter, the chief of all gods! And anyone who does not acknowledge this, and pay homage at my statue will be put to death!"

There was something more than madness in the emperor's words. He was worried. Worried that reports were coming in from the East and the West of restlessness, murmurings of revolt, uprisings that could endanger the whole of his empire. He would have none of it. The fire had to be stopped before it became a blaze. If a person, especially a soldier, should be allowed to worship at some altar of a foreign god, who could say what would be the next move? Rebellion and anarchy might be just around the corner!

The third century A.D. was drawing to an end. Christians had already survived several outbreaks of persecution. Their worship had to take place before the light of day, and in Rome, they worshipped in underground vaults known as the Catacombs, where the many-pronged passageways gave them safety, even against the nosey imperial guards.

In spite of the persecutions, the number of Christians continued to grow. Diocletian was determined to stamp out this dangerous heresy before it destroyed his empire.

"We have had enough of this old-womanish attitude toward these Christians. I want action! I want to see them hounded out of every city and town in the empire. And either they give up their madness in worshipping this Jesus, or they die. Is that understood?"

One young soldier understood it only too well. He had watched with increasing anxiety as one after another of his fellow Christians went to their deaths. Whatever he could do, he would do, but that was little enough. He had been able to talk to the Empress herself on one occasion, and told her about Jesus who had come from heaven to save all mankind, high and low — even empresses. And she had listened. Did it make a believer of her? He could not say. But he had never hidden his faith under a bushel. The priests had often quoted the Lord's words, "No man lights a lamp and puts it under a bushel, but on a stand, so that it gives light to every one in the house." That's what George wanted to do — give light, God's light, wherever duty should take him.

Sensing that the emperor was growing more desperate and therefore more dangerous, George feared that some of the weaker Christians might be tempted to deny their faith and give in to the emperor's demands to worship him. So he began to proclaim his faith even bolder than ever. Finally one day, a fellow-soldier said, "We've had enough of this babbler. George is a good soldier, but we can't keep on protecting him from the imperial will. If he's a Christian, he's got to face up to it and make a choice."

It wasn't long until George was arrested and put on trial. The trial was very simple — two or three witnesses who had heard him use the name of Jesus, or make the sign of the cross, or had known him to slip away to attend mass in the early hours before dawn.

"I do not deny, I freely confess that I am a believer in Jesus Christ. He is my Lord, and I belong to Him for ever."

The tribunal was not comfortable. He wanted to make a way out for this brave young man. "Acknowledge that the Emperor is the son of Jupiter. Say that, and you may go free."

"Jesus is the only-begotten Son of God. He alone is Lord."

"Then you leave me no choice. Guards! Take him to the block!"

And so an obscure and "unknown" soldier went to his death, a man we know today as St George. He was buried in a town halfway between present-day Tel Aviv and Jerusalem.

Early legends grew up around St George. One of them says that the Emperor tried to kill him three times, without success. At his hands the Empress Alexandria is said to have been converted, and many miracles were ascribed to him. Writing about him in the late 5th century, Pope St Gelasius says that his miracles were known only to God. In the Middle Ages, throughout Europe, the story of St George had become the one we know today. It is, in brief, as follows:

George was a Christian knight from Cappadocia. One day he rode through a great swampy area in which a terrible dragon lived. The entire countryside was terrified by the beast and in order to keep it from destroying the whole area, fed it with two sheep every day. Running short of sheep, the people had finally resorted to offering a human being for the dragon's daily food. On the particular day George came through, a young maiden had been selected by lot as a victim. Dressed as a bride, she bravely went to meet her fate. George, however, came just in time to see what was about to happen, attacked the dragon with his lance, and with some of the maiden's clothes made a bridle. With this she led it back to the city, "as if it had been a meek beast and debonair." George then told the people that if they would become Christians and be baptized, he would kill the dragon and rid them of its threat. They did so gladly and thousands were converted. When he was offered treasures for his service, he refused them, asking that they be given to the poor instead.

This story was written in the *Legend Aurea* by Blessed James de Voragine and translated by William Caxton, the first English printer. So popular did it become that it was told and retold, and made a point of teaching and inspiration for many. Some have suggested that this story is a christianized version of old pagan myths, and have doubted that there was a real St George at all. It seems more likely that the real saint was embellished with imaginary details, making a story that was enjoyed and believed by generations of pious people.

His legend was being told by abbots and bishops long before the Norman conquest in 1066, and Richard the Lion-Hearted came back from the Crusades in the 1190's reporting that he had seen the red cross of St George twice. Richard had great faith in St George's prayers and intercessions for him and his country and this doubtless did much to increase the popularity of this saint as patron of England. By 1415 his feast day, April 23, was made one of the chief feasts of the year, and in the 14th century, Edward III founded the Order of the Garter, making St George its patron. St George was recognized by Pope Benedict XIV as the protector of England. The cross of St George, a red cross on a white field, was made the flag of England.

St George

In the review of the calendar of saints in 1960, the Sacred Congregation of Rites removed St George's feast day from the calendar because of the untrustworthy nature of many of the stories associated with it. St George's story remains, however, a wonderful lesson of bravery, chivalry, nobility and generosity. In different guises it continues to inspire and interest us, generation after generation. Perhaps in heaven, the real St George continues to pray for those who must face danger and the test of their faith, that they may prove faithful soldiers of Christ to the end.

St Andrew

First Century

Scotland

In the Gospels, Andrew appears to be a man who was willing to take second place. That is not an easy thing for most people, so St Andrew serves as a useful reminder that it can be done.

The Gospel of Matthew introduces us to Andrew when he and his brother Simon (later called Peter) were fishing in the Sea of Galilee. Walking along the shore, Jesus said to them, "Come, follow me and I will make you fishers of men." Matthew adds, "At once they left their nets and followed him."

This is not the complete story of how Andrew met Jesus, however. John's Gospel gives us an additional glimpse of something that had apparently happened a little earlier. In this gospel we learn that Andrew was already a disciple of John the Baptist. John the Baptist had appeared from the wilderness, dressed in animal skins, announcing that the kingdom of God was at hand and that people must repent to get ready for it. When Andrew heard John preach, he was deeply moved by his message and began to obey his teaching.

All the Gospels tell how Jesus came to John the Baptist and was baptized by him in the Jordan River. It was a very moving time, for the Holy Spirit was seen coming down, as it were, in the form of a dove, resting upon the Lord, and a voice was heard out of heaven saying, "This is my beloved Son in whom I am well pleased." Everyone present knew that something wonderful was happening.

"Some time later, John was standing with two of his disciples when Jesus passed by. John looked towards Him and said, 'There is the Lamb of God.' On hearing this, the two men turned and followed Jesus. When Jesus looked about and saw that they were coming after Him, He asked, 'What are you looking for?' They said, 'Rabbi, where are you staying?' 'Come and see,' He replied. So they went and saw where He was staying and spent the rest of the day with Him. It was then about four in the afternoon." Then the Gospel adds: "One of the two who followed Jesus after hearing what John said was Andrew, Simon Peter's brother."

Andrew was so excited and moved by those two hours or so spent with Jesus that he could hardly wait to tell his brother about it. This Man, like John the Baptist, was also saying that the Kingdom of God was at hand, and that things would never be the same again. It was time to repent, to turn one's life over to God in a new way, and believe in what God was doing. So he found Simon and said, "We have found the Messiah!" The Messiah was the one foretold by the prophets of Israel who would restore all things to God. Simon knew Andrew well enough to believe that what he said was worth looking into. So together they went back to Jesus. Later, after they had been going with Jesus on His preaching and healing missions, Jesus asked them who people were saying He was. They reported, "Some say one thing, some another." "And who do you say that I am?" It was Simon, Andrew's brother, who spoke first: "You are the Messiah (Christ), the Son of the living God!"

"Blessed are you, Simon, son of John," said Jesus. "Flesh and blood has not revealed this to you, but my Father who is in heaven. And I tell you, you are Peter (a Rock), and on this rock I will build my church, and the gates of hell shall not prevail against it."

Andrew does not appear in the closest group of disciples. Peter, James and John seem to be an inner circle nearest to Jesus. Andrew appears at important points in the story, but never in first place. For instance, at the time the 5,000 men plus women and children had been listening to Jesus' teaching and were in need of food, it was Andrew who found the little boy with five barley loaves and a few little sardine-like fish, and brought them to Jesus. It was a great act of faith, but in retelling the story, who remembers that it was Andrew who engineered it by finding the little boy and bringing him to the Lord?

Near the close of the Lord's earthly ministry, some Greeks who had heard of Him came to see Him. They went to Philip (the name "Philip" is Greek, not Hebrew) and said to him, "Sir, we would see Jesus." Philip turned them over to Andrew, and together they went to tell Jesus, who replied, "The hour has come for the Son of Man to be glorified." It was apparently a signal to Him that His earthly work was almost finished. Again, Andrew disappears from the story.

Following the crucifixion and resurrection of our Lord, the apostles were scattered abroad in various directions from Jerusalem. Tradition tells us that St Andrew went on missionary journeys to Scythia, Thrace, Macedonia and Thessaly, and that he was eventually put to death in Achaia because the proconsul's wife had become a Christian through his influence. It is believed that he was crucified on a X-shaped cross, which is called a St Andrew's cross, and that he survived on the cross for several days, where he continued to preach the Gospel to all who came near.

In the 8th century a legend was widely circulated, telling how St Andrew's relics came to be in Scotland. A certain priest named Regulus, who took them in his care in Achaia, was warned in a dream to flee and carry them to a place which would be shown to him. When they reached the coast of Scotland, Regulus was shown that this was to be the resting place of the holy relics, and a church was built there to shelter them. The place today is known as St Andrew's, Scotland, and later a great cathedral bearing his name was erected there.

Some believe that the relics may actually have come by way of St Wilfred, who established great abbeys in the north of England at Ripon and Hexham in Northumberland, naming the first for St Peter and the second for his brother, St Andrew. St Bede, the historian, tells us that Wildred and Acca brought back from Rome a large number of saints' relics which they valued very highly and venerated. Some of the relics of St Andrew may later have been given to King Angus MacFergus. At any rate, the name of St Andrew came to be associated with the Christianization of the north of Scotland and eventually he was named patron of the country. His flag was a white X-shaped cross on a blue field. This flag was carried into battle against the English many times, as the English displayed their flag of St George. It is an interesting fact of history that when the two countries were finally united under one king, the British flag, the Union Jack, combined the cross of St George and the X-shaped cross of St Andrew to make its present design.

St Andrew's feast is celebrated on November 30, and there are churches which bear his name all over the world. It is well to remember the man who did not have to have first place, who was willing to let others take a place of higher honor.

St Patrick

c. 390-c. 461

Ireland

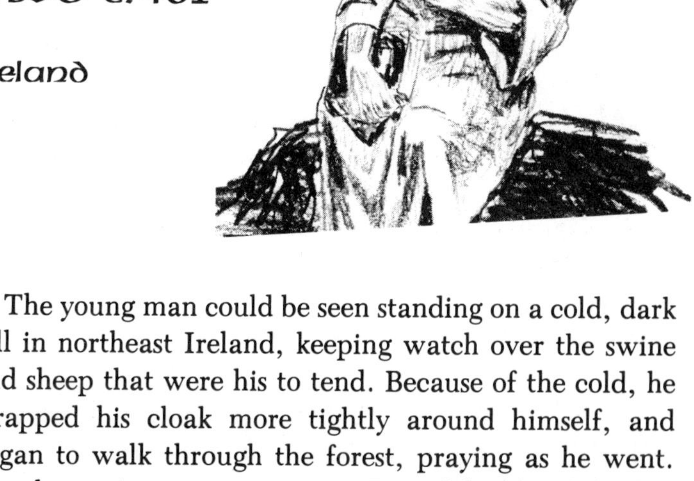

The young man could be seen standing on a cold, dark hill in northeast Ireland, keeping watch over the swine and sheep that were his to tend. Because of the cold, he wrapped his cloak more tightly around himself, and began to walk through the forest, praying as he went. For almost six years now, young Patrick had lived this life of solitude with the pigs, having no friends, no money, and not even the freedom to change his lot in life. He was a slave.

But life had not always been like this. Growing up in the late fourth century in western Britain, Patrick had enjoyed a carefree boyhood. His father, a Roman official and a deacon in the Church, had land and substance, and Patrick had been given such education as the Roman schools were able to supply. Neither deeply religious nor especially interested in learning, Patrick had drifted through life to his sixteenth year. Then it happened. Raiders from the wild island to the west swept in and seized young Patrick and carried him away. There he was put to work with the menial and unwanted task of tending the swine. Day followed dreary day, with no glimmer of hope.

Yet, strangely enough, these six lonely years on the hillsides of Ireland, had witnessed a deep change in Patrick. In his loneliness he had turned to God for comfort and had begun to pray day and night. Remembering those years later, he wrote, "Love and fear of God increased more and more in me. My faith grew and my spirit was stirred up, so that in a single day I said as many as a hundred prayers, and at night nearly as many. I used to stay in the woods and on the mountains. And before the dawn, I was awakened to pray in snow, frost and rain; nor was there any lukewarmness in me such as I sometimes feel, so fervent was the Spirit within me."

Yet there were those among the Irish who befriended him, taught him to speak some Gaelic, and from time to time fed him with the Irish stories of heroes and monsters and little folk. Yet all the time, his longing was for home and freedom.

Making sure the swine were safely rounded up and safe for the night, he made his way to a favorite rock where he often prayed. The wind was stiller now, and stars appeared in the sky as Patrick began what was now a familiar routine of talking with God. These times had become very important to him, and sometimes the whole night would be spent here on Skerry hill. It was toward dawn and Patrick had fallen asleep, when the archangel Victor appeared. Patrick held his breath as the vision spoke:

"Well do you fast and well do you pray. Soon you will see your own land again. Your ship is already waiting." Pausing only long enough to mark the place where the heavenly vision had appeared, Patrick started walking, making his way through the fields and forests to the moors and then on to the sea. The danger was great, for runaway slaves were often killed. But the memory lingered, "Soon you will see your own land."

It took several days and nights, hiding, catching a quick wink of sleep now and then in the forest, covering a distance of about two hundred miles, until he reached the coast. There a miracle awaited him. A ship sat at anchor, ready to sail for Gaul, and after a little persuasion, the captain agreed to take him aboard.

The ship landed on the coast of Brittany, and the whole crew went ashore in search of food. The winter had been long and provisions were scarce. They were near starvation, for spring was not yet fully come, and there was little to be found in field or wood.

"Friends, I am a Christian," said Patrick, "and I have been taught to pray each day to the God who made heaven and earth, 'Give us this day our daily bread.' Let us pause and kneel, for I believe that God will answer our prayers." The men looked at each other questioningly, but need made willing hearers of them, and there they knelt with him. Hardly had they risen to their feet when a familiar sound was heard.

"Swine!" shouted Patrick. "God has sent us swine to eat!" As he spoke, a herd of wild pigs came in view, and their food problems were solved. A few weeks later, Patrick was able to make his way back across the Channel to his home in Britain.

"Patrick, my son!" exclaimed his mother. "I never stopped praying for you, and now God has answered my prayers and allowed me to see your face again! And what a face! All weathered — and you've grown a beard, too! You left a mere boy, and you've come home a man."

At first Patrick was indeed happy to be home, but soon a strange thing began to happen. He found himself being awakened in the night. First, he would sit bolt upright in bed. "What were all those voices?" he wondered. Victor was there, too, calling to him — many people calling to him. They seemed to be pleading with him. Then pictures came before his eyes: Ireland, places he had known, faces of Irishmen known and unknown. Patrick would jump up, pace up and down in the room, and then all would stop.

"Dreams. Bad dreams they must be," he would mutter as he crawled back into bed. But then it would start again: voices pleading with him to return to Ireland with the truth, the gospel to save their souls. At last, convinced that God was indeed sending him a message, Patrick resolved to return to the land where he had been a slave. First, however, he needed training as a priest. For this, he went back to France to work and study as a disciple of the great St Germanus of Auxerre. He would need Church authority, too, and the support and backing of the Church if he was to go as a missionary to convert those who had once held him in slavery. Others believed with him that he had a divine commission to the Irish, and put his name forward to be appointed bishop. But he was rejected, and another man, Palladius, was sent instead. More years of waiting and discipline had to intervene before he could answer the call of the Irish voices in his dreams.

It was not until 432, when, upon the death of Palladius, Pope Celestine I sent Patrick to Ireland as bishop. Concentrating on the west and north of Ireland, where the gospel had never been preached, he established many churches and monasteries there. The Irish people were hungry to hear his truth, and he found his way into their hearts. His life was still a dangerous one, however, as the wizards and druids who worshipped the ancient gods, hated Christianity and gave him much opposition. Local kings, too, had to be won by gifts and bribes before they would permit him to work in their territories.

The lesser kings acknowledged Laogaire as the High King over them. His court at Tara was not open to

Patrick or his message. One Holy Saturday Patrick lit the Paschal fire on a hillside named Slane, across the river from Tara. This happened that year to coincide with the Feast of Tara, during which no fire could be started before Tara's fire had been lit, under penalty of death. The furious king ordered soldiers and a guard and started out for Slane to kill Patrick. When Patrick saw them, he came out to meet them, unafraid.

"Who are you? Come over here," the king shouted at him, and then ordered the soldiers to kill him.

At that very moment a fierce storm arose, with lightning, thunder and earthquakes. The soldiers suddenly became confused and started fighting among themselves. Frightened by the obvious intervention of Heaven, the High King fell at Patrick's feet and begged for mercy.

King Laogaire was not truly converted, however, and continued to plot against Patrick's life. He tried to poison him, and the envious druids, too, tried their powers on him. But Patrick's breastplate of protection was the strong name of the Trinity. He was always protected.

One day the king tried to have him murdered by a mob, and the stories say that the earth opened and swallowed the would-be killers. This ended the resistance to Patrick, and most of the people who saw these things became Christians. Loagaire was never converted, but lost his power to hinder Patrick's work.

Patrick's life was still full of perils, though. Toward the end of his life he wrote, "Daily I expect either a violent death, or to be robbed and reduced to slavery, or the occurrence of some such calamity. I have cast myself into the hands of Almighty God, for He rules everything."

In his lifetime, Patrick baptized thousands, converted chieftans, established monasteries to which Irish chieftans sent their sons and daughters for schooling. He organized Ireland under the rule of bishops, as he had learned in France. His sense of vocation and his humility in carrying it out have earned him a place of high honor among the roster of saints. In his own words he summed up his appraisal of his life and work: "I, Patrick, a sinner, am the most ignorant and of least account among the faithful, despised by many . . . I owe it to God's grace that so many people should through me be born again to Him."

Tradition says that he used the shamrock to illustrate the mystery of the Trinity — three in one, one in three. No other figure in Irish history has been so loved and revered as this simple man, who loved God with all his heart and gave himself unstintingly to serving those who needed him. He is believed to have died in 461, having lived beyond his ninetieth birthday. His feast is celebrated on March 17, and his emblem is the shamrock. His name has been a rallying point for the Irish in their long struggle for freedom from foreign rule, and he has long been considered the national saint of Ireland.

St Joan of Arc

1412-1431

France

Captain Baudricourt paced the room, arguing with himself about this strange request. Outside stood his cousin, a seventeen-year old peasant girl with a story about voices telling her to "go into France." She had said she must save her war-torn country by bringing the Dauphin, Charles, to Rheims, to be crowned king! And Baudricourt must escort her to Chinoa, where Charles was in residence.

The whole thing was absurd . . . and yet, she had an air about her of — what would he call it — conviction . . . or purpose? Furthermore, she had accurately foretold a recent loss of his in battle, including the name of the village where it had occurred. Suddenly deciding, he strode into the next room.

"Yes, I'll give you a horse and men to ride with you. And — God go with you!"

The year was 1429, and the peasant girl was Jeanne d'Arc, whom we know as Joan of Arc. To outward appearances she was an ordinary shepherdess from the village of Domremy. But for the past five years she had been seeing visions of the archangel Michael, along with other saints, urging her to lead the French armies to victory over the English and to secure the coronation of Charles the Dauphin. Finally, she could refuse them no longer, and went to see her cousin.

The armies of France were having a terrible time in 1429. They had been at war with the English for almost a hundred years, and much of France had fallen. Now they were defending the city of Orleans. If that should fall, it would be the end of the country. Morale had sunk to a new low among its citizens.

It was at this critical point that Joan approached Chinoa and sent word to the king of her arrival. Reluctantly, Charles decided to see her, but first, he devised a way to test her. He put his royal robes on one of his courtiers and mingled among the crowd of nobles.

When Joan entered, however, she walked straight to Charles without hesitation. Then she began to tell him some things that he had shared with no one but God alone. Almost convinced, the king promised her troops to deliver Orleans, but first required her to submit to an examination by a panel of Doctors and Church authorities. Several weeks passed in this manner, with Joan becoming more restless with each day's delay. The voices had told her that she had less than a year for her mission. Finally the panel concluded that she was indeed sent by God, and they dispatched her back to the king, advising him to grant her request.

Thus, at the age of seventeen, Joan found herself at the head of the French army. She proved to be a skilled organizer, with definite ideas on how the troops should conduct themselves. In setting out for Orleans, she put a vanguard of priests at the head. They carried banners and chanted hymns. Next, she followed, carrying her own white standard inscribed with the words, "Jesus Maria." She wore her white armor and went bareheaded, with her hair cut short. Before starting a battle, she required that the army go to mass and confession. In this way they made their way to Orleans, and in less than a week had re-taken the city for the French. From there, her captains pursued the English and won another battle at Patay.

Joan urgently counselled Charles to press the advantage and drive the English completely out of the country, but the king hesitated. After much cajoling, she persuaded him to go to Rheims for his coronation. On the way, they routed the English from town after town. At the ceremony in Rheims, she stood at the king's side, her banner raised high.

Instead of supporting her urgent desire to continue to press the English toward the sea, Charles now chose to return to the Loire country he loved. At first she went with him, but as the winter wore on, she began leading skirmishes with the few men Charles had left her. On one of these skirmishes, she was captured by Burgundian soldiers. Burgundy at that time was not a part of France, and was at enmity with France. They sold Joan to the English.

Now at last, the English had custody of the very upstart who was the cause of their reversals of the past year and they were delighted with their prize.

Important prisoners of war were often ransomed for large sums in those days, but the ungrateful Charles, turning his back on all that Joan had done for his cause, refused to ransom her. The English, in their turn decided to give her a trial, based on her reports of having heard and obeyed "voices." The trial lasted nine months. Charged with witchcraft, Joan defended herself bravely and shrewdly, but it was no use. They accused her of heresy and sentenced her to be burned at the stake — a little over a year after her victory at Orleans.

Before the faggots were lighted, Joan asked for a cross to be held in front of her. She died with this before her eyes, calling upon the name of Jesus. When her heart did not burn, they threw it into the Seine River along with her ashes. The year was 1431, and Joan had just passed her nineteenth birthday.

About twenty years later, Joan's mother and brothers asked that her case be reopened. The pope appointed a commission and in 1456 the verdict of heresy was rescinded and she was declared innocent. In her death, three kingdoms shared the guilt — England, France and Burgundy. Several hundred years passed before Pope Pius X declared her to be among the blessed, and she was canonized as a saint by Pope Benedict XV in 1920. A wonderful example of bravery under persecution, and of persistence in what she believed and understood to be the will of God for her, Joan of Arc was made patroness of France along with St Thérèse of Jesus. Many churches honor her memory and she has been praised in song, drama and story. Her feast is celebrated on May 30.

St Wenceslas

907-929

Czechoslovakia

Most of us have sung or heard the Christmas song, "Good King Wenceslas." It tells of a kind and generous king who gave gifts to a poor man whom he met when he was out hunting.

The story of St Wenceslas is even more exciting than the song. His story really begins with his grandmother, St Ludmilla, Duchess of Bohemia. When St Methodius arrived in Bohemia in 871, he was received at the court of the Duke and Duchess. So persuasive was he in his presentation of the Gospel, that both rulers accepted the Catholic faith and were baptized. Ludmilla became a Christian of great piety and zeal. They set about establishing Christianity in Bohemia, but in doing so, met violent opposition from many of the powerful families of the nobility.

Their hopes to see the faith further advanced were dampened when their son, Ratislav, married Drahomira, who was still practically a pagan, although she had been baptized. Drahomira was a forceful and ambitious woman, and her sympathies lay with those who still opposed the entrance of Christianity into their country. To Drahomira's great disappointment, Ratislav entrusted their young son, Wenceslas, to the care of his own mother, St Ludmilla. Ludmilla began at once to train Wenceslas to love God and to be an obedient son of the Church. He was taught to read both Latin and Slavonic, and was so faithful to his religious duties that it was remarked that he was more fitted for the cloister than the throne.

Wenceslas was only about thirteen years old when his father was killed in battle. At this point, the struggle between Ludmilla and Drahomira became acute. Drahomira was appointed regent for her minor son, and the nobles who still clung to their pagan gods saw the opportunity to turn the kingdom back to its old ways. Ludmilla was equally determined to save the country from such a disaster, and on her part, urged young Wenceslas to protect the religious welfare of his people.

The two women were now locked in a life and death struggle, with Drahomira holding the upper hand at the moment. Drahomira knew that Ludmilla's influence would be fatal to her own ambitions if she continued to influence Wenceslas, and so, with others, she instigated the murder of her mother-in-law, thinking thereby to put an end to the struggle with Christianity. The deed was carried out in the dark of night, as two "noblemen" made their way to Ludmilla's castle and strangled her.

Grief-stricken at his grandmother's murder, Wenceslas set about asserting his own judgment, and sought the counsel of Christian advisers as to how best to proceed. Drahomira continued her ambitious and reckless course, and within another year, the tables turned, and she was driven out of power. Wenceslas was acknowledged as ruler, and immediately announced that he would support God's law and His Church, and that he would endeavor to rule with justice and mercy. He even recalled his mother from her banishment, and there is no reason to think that she ever opposed him again.

Wenceslas undertook to promote the welfare of his people, to break down the iron hold of tribal rivalries in the interest of national unity, and to strengthen the ties of his people with the rest of Christian Europe. In order to avoid having his country devastated by a superior force, he decided to acknowledge the German Emperor, Henry the Fowler, as successor to Charlemagne and as his overlord. This move, although meant to save his people needless suffering, angered some of the pagans who especially resented the role Wenceslas gave the clergy as his counselors.

About this time Wenceslas married, and when a son was born, his brother, Boleslaus, realizing that he had lost his chance for inheriting the rulership decided to join those who opposed Wenceslas and wanted to be rid of him. The plot was carried out in stealth and secrecy. In September, 929, Wenceslas, then only 22 years old, was invited to go to a feast in honor of saints Cosmas and Damian. Wenceslas was warned by friends that he was in danger, but he paid no attention to them. At the banquet, he was in great peace as he proposed a toast in honor of St Michael, "whom we pray to guide us to peace and eternal joy."

Next morning as he made his way to church, he met Boleslaus and thanked him for his hospitality at the feast.

"Yesterday I did my best to serve you well, but this is my service today," retorted Boleslaus as he struck Wenceslas in the face. Stunned, Wenceslas grabbed his brother, and a struggle followed. Watching from their hiding places, Boleslaus' friends then ran out and killed Wenceslas on the spot. As he died, he looked at Boleslaus and said, "Brother, may God forgive you."

Immediately people begain to acclaim Wenceslas as a saint, and reports of miracles at his tomb continued to circulate. Boleslaus had gained the power he coveted by the murder of his brother, but was insecure enough to be frightened at this turn of events. Three years after Wenceslas' death, Boleslaus had his body transferred to the church of St Vitus in Prague. There it became a place of pilgrimage, and soon Wenceslas was considered the patron saint of the Bohemian people. His feast day is September 28.

St Stephen

c. 975-1038

Hungary

"This is going to be a great day, Vaik," said the old nurse. "Today you are going to be baptized and get a new name. From this day on, you will be a Christian, and your name will be Istvan."

The year was 985, and Vaik, oldest son of Geza, duke of the Magyars, wasn't quite sure what it all meant. The Magyars were a fierce people, who had made their living by raiding others, all the way from the Danube where they had settled, to France and Italy and the peoples of the west. But they had found out about the Christian faith in some of these raids, and Geza, Vaik's father, had decided that he and his people should adopt the Christian religion. Although it would have little effect on his father, today's baptism was destined to have a profound effect on Istvan, whom we know today as Stephen.

When he was twenty, Stephen married Gisela, a Christian duchess, sister of St Henry the Emperor, and two years later he succeeded his father as governor of the Magyars. For several years he had to struggle with rival leaders to establish his right to rule over the Magyars, whose fierce tribal loyalties threatened the unity of the nation he sought to build. Finally he was able to receive the title of first King of Hungary from Pope Silvester II. The pope even prepared a crown to be sent, and along with it some detailed instructions as to how a Christian king should behave toward the church and his subjects. Stephen's response showed such respect and reverence for all things holy that his example inspired the same attitudes in his people. The old Magyar fierceness had been replaced by a desire to walk in new ways of justice and peace. When the Pope's message had been read in the hearing of the king, the ambassador crowned him in a ceremony of great solemnity and splendor. The year was 1001, and this marks the beginning of Hungary as a Christian kingdom.

Stephen was greatly loved by his people, being readily available to hear their grievances and problems. He established churches and monasteries, some of which still exist. Furnishing the churches himself, he saw to it that the Catholic faith could be put in reach of all the people, abolishing many of the superstitious customs inherited from their old religions. Tribal loyalties and rivalries die hard, and it was necessary from time to time for Stephen to take up arms against those who opposed him. His hopes for the continuation of his Christian kingdom underwent a great blow when news reached him that his son and heir, Emeric, had been killed in a hunting accident.

"God loved him and has taken him away early," he cried. With the heir out of the way, others now saw their opportunity to seize power when Stephen would be gone. His sister, an ambitious and cruel woman, had lived in his court since the death of her husband. This was the chance she needed, and taking advantage of Stephen's painful illness and the swirling conflicts which were going on in the court, she pushed her son, Peter, forward as the chosen heir. The ensuing years held much strife and suffering for the newly Christian land.

Stephen died in 1038 at the age of sixty-three. Miracles continued to occur at his tomb, and in 1083, Pope St Gregory VII had his relics enshrined in the great Church of our Lady at Buda (Now Budapest). In 1686 his festival was appointed for September 2, commemorating the liberation of Buda from the hands of the Turks by Emperor Leopold.

Stephen unified his land and laid the foundations for the ending of tribal rivalries. Throughout his life he sought to use his office to further the cause of justice and peace by faithful adherence to the Christian faith, an outstanding model for other Christian rulers to follow.

St Sergius

c. 1314-1392

Russia

Strictly speaking, St Sergius cannot be called "patron of Russia." That ancient honor belongs to St Andrew, who is also patron of Scotland. But it can be said that St Sergius is the most beloved of all Russian saints. Sergius was born at Rostov about 1314, one of three sons of a noble family. Christened Bartholomew, he had great difficulty in his early life learning to read and write.

Driven from their home by a civil war, his parents had to leave their life of luxury and plenty to make their living by farming at Radonezh, about 50 miles northeast of Moscow. Hence we know him today as St Sergius of Radonezh.

One day Bartholomew was walking in the fields and met an old monk.

"My son, what would you like most in the world?" asked the holy man.

"Most of all, Father, I would like to be able to read and write," answered the boy. "Then I could read and study the Holy Scriptures."

"Here, take this little piece of bread," said the monk. "Chew it well; you will find it sweet, and it will bring you much joy."

Bartholomew obeyed, and found, to his great delight, that he was able to read.

His parents bravely continued to live and work as peasants. The hardships of their new life, however, took their toll on them. They died before Bartholomew reached his twentieth birthday, leaving him alone with an older brother, Stephen. Stephen's wife, too, had died.

"What are we to do?" asked Stephen. "Life has lost its meaning with my parents and my wife gone."

"Be of good cheer, brother!" said Bartholomew. "God is good, and will show us what to do, even though we have to have many sorrows and disappointments in this earthly life. For my part, I feel the longing to be a hermit, so that I may talk to God and live in constant touch with Him."

"A hermit! Yes, that's it! Why don't we both go and find a place where we can build a little hut and find peace."

And so it happened that the two of them decided to become hermits. Together they made their way to a forest at Makovka, several miles from their nearest neighbor, and built themselves first a little hut and then a tiny chapel. They were able to persuade the Archbishop of Kiev to send a priest to dedicate their little chapel to the Most Holy Trinity.

Stephen's peace was short-lived. He found that living alone did not ensure that everything would be peaceful within. Inner doubts and loneliness still assailed him, and it wasn't long before he decided to move to a monastery, leaving Sergius, as he was now called, completely alone in the little hermitage at Makovka. Like other hermits before him, Sergius experienced many spiritual battles — evil thoughts, hunger, demonic powers, dangers from wild beasts. In addition to these, Sergius had to endure the bitter cold, ice, winds, snow and rains of the Russian winter. He made friends of the bears and regarded fire and light as his friends, echoing many of the same sentiments we hear in St Francis. Unlike Francis, however, Sergius was a large, strong man rather than a frail, emaciated one.

Before long, word of this holy man began to spread, and people began to seek him out. Gradually they came, not only to talk and listen, but to stay and learn from his way of life. Others built little huts nearby, and when they numbered twelve, they asked that he might become their abbot. The bishop agreed and Sergius was duly ordained. Their numbers continued to grow until a little village could be seen where once only a tiny hut had stood among the forest trees.

At this point, the story of St Sergius takes an unhappy turn. Stephen decided to come back to the hermitage, and a decision about the form of life the monastery should follow had to be made. Up to this time the monks had lived as hermits, each in his separate hut, following the pattern that St Antony of Egypt had laid out many centuries before. Sergius decided that the Community needed a more cohesive form of community life. Some of the brothers objected to his decision. Unfortunately, Stephen joined with those who disagreed with Sergius' decision. Rather than be party to controversy, Sergius quietly left to settle down some miles away at Kerzhach, near the monastery of Makrish. So many of his monks followed him to the new monastery, that in a few years the original settlement at Makovka was in a state of crisis. The Metropolitan of Moscow intervened and sent Sergius word asking him to go back to his old monastery. Appointing an abbot to care for his new foundation, Sergius returned to a tearful and joyful welcome from his brothers, having been away four years.

It was a period of critical importance in Russian history, and because he was known for his wisdom and ability to make peace between disagreeing parties, Sergius was frequently consulted by responsible people both in the Church and in government. The greatest crisis came in the confrontation between the forces of

Dimitry, Prince of Moscow and Khan Mamai, leader of the Tartar overlords. The Tartars were infamous for their brutal cruelty, and it was known that if Dimitry's forces should lose, Russia would suffer more than ever under their iron rule. Dimitry went to Sergius to ask his advice.

"It is your duty, sir, to care for the flock which God has entrusted to you. Go forth against the heathen, and conquer in the might of God's arm. And may you return in safety, giving God the glory," was the saint's reply.

At the last moment, seeing how strong the enemy was, Dimitry hesitated. Just at that moment a new message came from Sergius: "Do not fear, sir. Go forward with faith against the foe's ferocity. God will be with you."

Dimitry's forces won the day. The Tartars were defeated and scattered. Back at the monastery, Sergius and his brethren were in earnest prayer. Within an hour of the victory, with no human communication, by the divine gift of knowledge, Sergius announced that Dimitry had won the day.

Sergius' biographer says that the saint was reluctant to talk about the miracles which were worked at his hand. He did relate, however, a vision given him of the Blessed Virgin, who appeared to him with the apostles Peter and John, assuring him that his monastery would greatly flourish in the years ahead.

Six months before his death, Sergius, given to know that the end was approaching, resigned from his office, appointed a successor, and then became ill for the first time in his life. He died at the Monastery of the Holy Trinity on September 25, 1392, being about seventy-eight years old, and was canonized in Russia before 1449.

His warm personality, combined with his unwavering faith and his unquestioned holiness brought people to him, high and low, rich and poor. He was generous and always ready to help the sick and suffering. For him, following Jesus meant caring for others and putting their needs ahead of his own. "The people saw in him a chosen man of God, on whom the grace of the Spirit visibly rested. Many of them still go as pilgrims to his shrine in the Trinity monastery of Zagorsk." In 1917, the monastery was closed. The bolshevists removed Sergius' body from its honored place in the principal church there and placed it in an "anti-religious museum." In 1945, however, the Soviet government gave permission to the Russian Orthodox authorities to reopen the monastery and his relics were restored.

His feast is celebrated on September 25, the anniversary of his death.

By its light shall the nations walk;
and the kings of the earth shall bring
their glory into it.
Revelation 22:24

Great Mystics

I was in the Spirit on the Lord's day, and I heard
behind me a loud voice like a trumpet saying,
"Write what you see . . . ."
Revelation 1:10, 11a

I know a man in Christ who fourteen years ago
was caught up to the third heaven — whether in the body
or out of the body, I do not know, God knows . . .
and he heard things that cannot be told,
which man may not utter . . . .
II Corinthians 12:2-4

And your young men will see visions
and your old men will dream dreams.
Joel 2:28

Jesus, whom now veiled, I by faith descry,
What my soul doth thirst for, do not, Lord, deny,
That Thy face unveiled, I at last may see,
With the blissful vision blest, my God, of Thee.
St Thomas Aquinas, c. 1260

St Antony of Egypt

251-356

"Go, sell what you have, and give to the poor, and you will have treasure in heaven."

The words sounded in the ear of twenty-year old Antony as a direct message from God. He had gone to church in search of some peace and direction for his life. His parents had died, leaving him and his younger sister orphaned, and he did not know which way to turn. This sounded like a divine direction.

Returning home, he said to his sister, "I believe that God would have me give away some of the land we have been left, sell the rest, and keep only enough money to take care of us."

And so he did. Things were working out quite well, though many of his friends thought him a little strange. Then one day, as he sat in Church, another word came strongly into his heart. "Take no thought for the morrow."

"I have gone only half way," he said to himself. "I'm still looking out for my own security and life. I must do more."

He arranged for his sister to enter a house of maidens where she would be cared for, gave away the rest of his wealth, and went out into the Egyptian desert near Memphis, to live as a hermit.

His life as a hermit was made up of prayer, manual labor, and reading. In order to learn how best to serve God, he eagerly went to older men who were also living the same kind of life, and asked for their advice on how to live a holy life. All the time, Antony himself was growing in grace and holiness. Gradually the word spread that here was one who was especially gifted in helping people with their problems.

But life in the desert was not easy. There were devils to be fought, troubling doubts about all the good he might have done if he had not given all his money away. Then the devil began to put impure thoughts into his mind day and night — even appearing to him in the form of a beautiful woman to tempt him to sin. When this did not work, the devil changed into other forms to frighten him, and on one occasion at least, beat Antony so badly that he almost died. But God assured Antony that He was with him, and told him that his fame would spread through the whole world because he had remained true to Him.

When Antony was fifty-four years old, he came out of his solitary mountain hermitage and started his first monastery, in order to help others who were having a hard time trying to live a holy life. He told the monks, "The devil dreads fasting, prayer, humility and good works."

In 311, a persecution against Christians was raging. In order to encourage others to remain true to Christ, he left his monastery and went to Alexandria for a time. Again, in 355, he came back to Alexandria to battle the Arians, whose heretical doctrines were wreaking havoc in the Church. Because of his clear, impelling logic, even philosophers were impressed. His spiritual power, demonstrated in miracles and wonders, was a factor in converting many to the Faith.

He always ate very little, sometimes only a little bread every three or four days. Yet he was not sick, he had good eyesight and firm teeth, and lived to be 105 years old! Even the emperor sought his prayers and his advice. He is regarded as the patriarch of monks and the patron saint of domestic animals. His temptations have been portrayed by several artists, among the most famous of which was painted by Grunewald. A pig is often seen in pictures with him. His feast day is January 17.

St Mechtilde of Hackenborne

1240-1298

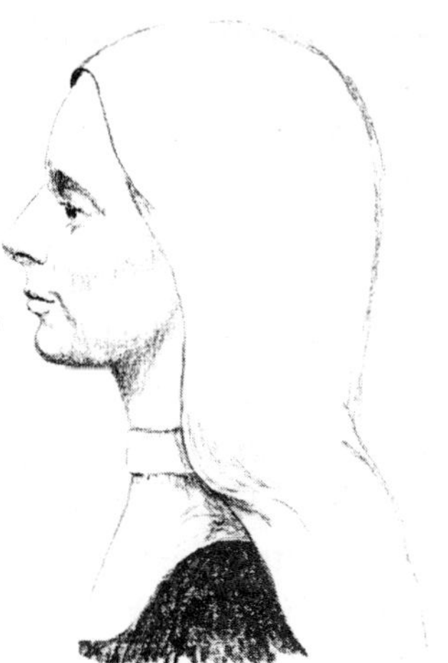

When Mechtilde was just seven, her parents brought her to stay with her sister, to be educated in the cloister school. Her sister, Gertrude of Hackenborn, carefully supervised her and helped train her excellent voice.

After she became Abbess, Gertrude moved her monastery to Helfta (near Eisleben), and Mechtilde followed her and took her vows as a nun. There she continued singing as choir mistress and directed the new cloister school. In that capacity she received in 1261, a new student, a five year old, also named Gertrude. Outwardly, Mechtilde's life was like that of any contemplative nun of her time: silence except during stated times, regular attendance at the day and night Offices, where she led the chanting, and classes with her students. But inwardly, she was receiving many revelations from God.

The child Gertrude grew up in that Helfta cloister, and she, too, was receiving many extraordinary visions and graces from the Lord. When she was twenty-six, and Mechtilde was fifty, Mechtilde began to confide her experiences to Gertrude. Regularly they would talk together, and then Gertrude would go and write everything down. For seven years Gertrude did this secretly. Then Mechtilde discovered what had been going on! At first she was greatly distressed, but then began to feel that perhaps this was God's will and inspiration that the writing should be done. Together, then, the two nuns wrote and edited what became the *Liber Specialis Gratiae, The Book of Special Graces.* Mechtilde's contribution is joyful and warm. She stresses devotion to the Heart of Christ and the use of all the senses to praise God. The whole is based on the liturgical year and centers on the person and nature of our Lord Jesus Christ.

Seven years later, on November 19, 1298, the Lord called her to Himself. As she died, "she offered the Lord her heart, plunging it into His." Although St Mechtilde has never been canonized, her feast is permitted to numerous houses of Benedictine nuns. Writing of her later, St Gertrude the Great said, "There has never before been anyone like her in our monastery, and I fear there never will be again." Her feast day is November 19.

St John of the Cross

1542-1591

For a long time St Teresa of Avila had dreamed of extending her reforms into the Carmelite Order for men. But this did not become possible until she met a young friar studying at the University of Salamanca, who later became known as John of the Cross. He offered himself to her as a recruit at once.

Teresa was delighted; she had no doubts whatsoever about him. Later she would comment, "He always was a saint." John wanted to get started immediately, but it took almost a year to find a small *casita* for men. They started in Dureulo, one of the poorest villages in Spain, in a shack that was barely a lean-to. But John and one other brother cleaned it thoroughly and found great joy in observing strictly the old Carmelite rule: fasting, many hours of prayer, thin, worn clothing, and sleeping on the ground with a stone for a pillow.

In a few years, the original brothers were asked to start a new foundation at Mancera. John was then appointed rector at Alcala, a college of the university there. In 1571, just four years after entering the order, Teresa requested that John come to be the spiritual director at the convent at Avila, where she was just getting her reforms under way.

Life at Avila, however, was not peaceful. The reformed Carmelites were vigorously opposed by those who did not want the old rules introduced again. The Vicar-General began to take stern measures against them, but when the Avila nuns refused to have any other abbess but Teresa, he excommunicated them all and forbade John to administer the Sacrament. Prior Maldonato (of the unreformed Carmelite friars in Toledo, of the monastery where John had previously lived) ordered John to return to his original monastery. John refused. So the prior, accompanied by civil officers, broke down the door of John's hut and carried him away to Toledo. There, the Carmelite Vicar-General ordered him to give up the reforms, but again John refused, maintaining that he had received his authority from the Pope's representative.

Upon that, the Vicar ordered him beaten regularly, and John carried the scars of these beatings with him the rest of his life. For nine months he was kept in a small cell with no light except one tiny window that was so high up that he had to stand on a stool to read his daily offices (prayers). His comment later was, "God gave me a high idea of the value of suffering when I was imprisoned in Toledo."

As spring warmed into summer, John sat in his cell enduring stifling air day after day, a diet of highly seasoned food, and little water. By midsummer he could only lie on the floor of the cell. Then one day the door opened, and Prior Maldonato entered the cell and stirred John with his foot. John rose and apologized for his bodily weakness which kept him from rising more quickly in the presence of his superior. The prior asked him what he had been thinking about.

"It's our Lady's feast tomorrow, and it would be such a joy to serve Mass," said John.

"Not in my time," retorted the Prior, and with that slammed the door and locked it behind him.

That night the Blessed Mother appeared to him in his cell. "Be of good courage," she said. "Your difficulties will soon be over."

A few days later, she appeared again, and showed him a certain window overlooking the river Tagus. "Go that way and I will help you," she said.

John had aready been at work unscrewing the lock, and that night after supper, he made a crude rope of clothes and blankets. Then, while the rest of the monastery slept, he slipped down the halls to the window.

Crossing a room where two visiting friars were sleeping, he quietly wedged the bedding on the window bar, crept over the sill and slid down. At the end of his "rope," he dangled for a moment, then dropped the remaining ten feet, and rolled and slid down the embankment towards the river, and with his last remaining strength managed to scale a neighboring wall. This turned out to be that of a convent of Reformed Carmelites, so the sisters took him in and spirited him away to another friary, where he was safe. Because King Philip's intervention helped settle disputes in the Order, John was spared further harassment, and the two branches of Carmelites eventually became two separate orders.

After the death of St Teresa in 1582, John became prior at Granada, and was then elected to the governing body of the reformed Carmelites. An unfortuate quarrel erupted among that group, and John was stripped of all his offices and exiled to a remote friary. In the midst of this he became very ill. He chose to stay at the monastery of Ubeda, where the prior treated him inhumanely and denied him the extra care and food he needed. When the guilty prior was corrected by the Vicar-General, he repented, but it was too late. John died on December 14, 1591.

John was a poet, and his works are still admired and read today. His most famous book is *Dark Night of the Soul.* He was canonized in 1726, and declared a Doctor of the Church in 1926. His feast day is December 14.

St Catherine of Genoa

1447-1510

Caterinetta Adorno, a beautiful young woman from Genoa, Italy, paced the lovely garden in front of her palazzo. With a growing sense of despair, she realized that life had come to a complete dead-end for her. Her depression mounted, except for the small glow of faith she kept alive despite outward circumstances. She brooded over her inescapable situation: at sixteen years of age, she had been forced into an arranged marriage to Julian Adorno, a man badly suited to her in every way. In addition to being undisciplined and temperamental, he had been unfaithful to her and frequently absent from home. The fact that her upper class family, the Frieschis, had powerful connections, including the pope, was no help at all. Nor was the fact that she had been surrounded by luxury all her life. Her earlier desire to enter the convent had been smashed, and added to that she had been trapped into a marriage that left her lonely and frustrated.

This had been going on for ten years, and for the last five of them she had done her best to enter into the gaiety and pleasures of the Genoan society, but it was all in vain. The emptiness of it continued to overwhelm her.

Then, on the first day of spring, 1473, all of this suddenly changed. While making her confession, she was suddenly overwhelmed with the sense of God's vast love. It lifted her above all her miseries into a new life. It was not a fleeting emotion that she felt. Rather, it was a lasting sense of the depth of God's presence. Over and over she said to herself, "No more world! No more sins! If I had in my possession a thousand worlds, I would cast it all away."

Several days later she saw a vision of Jesus carrying His cross. This filled her anew with a realization of her unworthiness. What could she do for her sins, when He had done so much? "O Lord," she cried out, "if it is necessary, I would be willing even to confess my sins in public!" A few days later, as she received the Blessed Sacrament, her experience of God in it was so deep and rich that she continued the practice every day for the rest of her life. Joyfully, she entered into a new life of prayer and fasting, although she had no spiritual director to guide her.

Julian's extravagance had brought him to the edge of bankruptcy. In that needy state, in answer to Catherine's prayers, he turned to God and was converted. Not only did he repent of his past ways, but he immediately joined the Third Order of St Francis and embraced the spirit of poverty, giving away much of their remaining wealth, keeping only enough to live on, forcing them to move to a small house in one of the poorest sections of the city, near the hospital of Pammatone. Now both of them gave themselves freely to the care of the sick and needy.

In 1479, they decided to move into the hospital itself, living in two small rooms and working without pay. For the next twenty years, first as a nurse, and then as administrative head, Catherine gave herself completely, along with her husband, to the care of the poor and dying. Caring for the sick and dying during the plague of 1493, which afflicted four-fifths of the population, Catherine herself nearly died.

Julian died a few years later after a long and painful illness. Catherine then sought a spiritual director, and found one in Fr. Cattaneo Marrabotto, who was a great help to her. With his encouragement, she and a wealthy attorney, Hector Vernozza, and some other friends formed the Fraternity of Divine Love. The object of the group was not merely spiritual development, but was to provide an organized means for caring for the poor. They agreed together to go to confession monthly and to receive the Blessed Sacrament at least four times a year, although

Catherine continued to do so daily. Members assisted orphans, provided for the needy, consoled prisoners, nursed the sick in hospitals, and helped young delinquents. Later, similar groups were formed throughout Italy. Because the members were largely from the wealthy and upper class, they kept the Fraternity a secret so that the poor would not distrust them.

Fr. Marrabotto felt that Catherine's experiences would help others who were longing for a more meaningful spiritual life. He encouraged her to share her insights, and before long, followers from every class in the city came to hear her.

"Lift sin from a person's shoulders," she would say, "then God can act." They listened with rapt attention as she explained, "God has no better thing to do than to come and dwell within you. But in order for Him to do it, you must be purified by the fire of His love. You must not wait for purgatory for this! Yes, the fire there is as horrible as hell, and for us here, too, it burns when God cleanses us. But don't let that discourage you. It will free you and make you pure so you can see Him. So you see, the pain isn't really pain at all, because every little glimpse we get of God is so much more wonderful than any of the pain. More than that, seeing and knowing God this way goes beyond any joy we can imagine."

As she talked about her inner experiences and the joy of coming to know God more fully, some who heard her were inspired to write these thoughts down. Vernazza and Marrabotto faithfully collected her sayings, which became two of the most outstanding works on mysticism: *Treatise on Purgatory* and *Spiritual Dialogues*.

Her contemplative and visionary experiences never caused her to lose her down-to-earth practicality. She is one of many examples of the religious contemplative who combines spiritual concerns with competence in human affairs. As hospital administrator, she kept its accounts down to the last "penny." Very few details in the care of the patients escaped her notice.

For the last nine years of her life, she suffered from a disease which became more and more agonizing. Even though it made it impossible to do her work for periods of time, she continued to serve the hospital almost to the end. She died in 1510, and her canonization took place in 1737, on the same day as St Vincent de Paul. Her feast is celebrated on September 15.

"I tell you, John, the vision was as clear as you are to me at this moment. I was going back home after Holy Communion at the Capuchin church, deeply lost in recollection, when at a street corner I was suddenly uplifted in spirit, and saw myself dressed in a black tunic with a white cross on the breast. Below the cross in white letters was the holy name of Jesus, and I heard a voice saying, 'This signifies how pure and spotless that heart should be which must bear the holy name of Jesus engraved on it.' And I knew, John, that this would mean entering into His sufferings in some way I cannot explain."

John Baptist Daneo looked at his brother Paul Francis. Whatever this strange vision would mean for his brother, John knew that he, too, would be included, for the two were all but inseparable.

The year was 1720, and Paul Francis was twenty-six years old. From earliest childhood he had been taught to love God and, as a child, his mother had soothed his own hurts and pains by having him look at a crucifix to remind him how much greater were the pains Jesus had borne for him. The Passion of Christ had been a life-long reality to him.

"What can it all mean?" asked John. "Five years ago, when you went away to fight against the Turks, you found that the life of a soldier was not for you. You didn't mind the marches and the drilling, but the roistering and gambling made you feel far from God, and you decided you should be a soldier of Christ instead."

"Yes, I remember," said Paul. "And in the meantime I have read St Francis de Sales' *Treatise on the Love of God* over and over, and some of the works of John of the Cross. God knows what a fool I made of myself when I made a vow to do what anyone told me. When you and the others began to give me orders that contradicted each other, I saw the folly of that and renounced *that* vow and repented of having made it!"

"That gruff old priest you chose as your first spiritual director made being a soldier of Christ a real challenge," recalled John. "Remember when he used to reprimand you so loudly in the confessional that others waiting their turn would tremble in their seats?"

"Yes, and the time he passed me by when I knelt for Holy Communion. I was truly grieved by that, but realized that it was for my humiliation and good. He was the director I needed then," mused Paul. "This past year here at Castellazo, when we have been able to teach catechism to children and to work with St Anthony's Confraternity, has been a real blessing. It has given me time for prayer and how I have enjoyed those hours before the Blessed Sacrament, and the walks with the other lads after Vespers, as we talked about spiritual things! Yes, it has been a good year, but, somehow, I think there is more. And I don't know what it is. Does God want me to be a hermit? Sometimes I think He does, and that I would be well suited. Or should I be a missionary? I long to help others find the love of God active in their lives. But I do not dare presume. I must wait for God's way to be made more clear."

Sometime later another vision was granted. This time the Blessed Virgin appeared to him, clothed in the same black tunic he had seen before, and within the heart were the words *Jesu XPI Passio* with three nails. She told him that he should found a Congregation in which members would be clothed thus, mourning the Passion and Death of her dear Son.

It was not long before the Bishop of Allesandria (near Genoa, Italy) gave permission for Paul to wear the black penitential habit he had seen in the vision. The emblem, however, was not to be worn until approval had been given by the Holy See. The Bishop sent him back to Castellazo, where for the next forty days he was on retreat in a small, damp, ill-lighted room. It was the dead of winter, and his only food was bread and water, his bed a handful of straw on the bare floor. Here was his desert; here, like Benedict in Subiaco, he fought through his thoughts, temptations and struggles. And here too, he wrote the rules of his Order that was yet to be, rules that remain essentially intact to this day, completing the task in five days. In his opening lines, he says

> ". . . Let it be known that when I was writing, I wrote as quickly as if some one were dictating to me: I felt the words were coming from my heart. . ."

In his eagerness to get started on his new work, Paul, with the Bishop's letter of commendation, sailed from Genoa for Rome to seek approval of the Holy See. On September 8, the wind died away and the boat lay helpless in sight of a lofty headland called Monte Argentaro. As soon as Paul heard the name, he remembered a word which had come as he was praying months earlier. "Paul," the Virgin had said, "come to Monte Argentaro, for I am there alone." He resolved to learn more about this beautiful mount facing the blue Mediterranean.

Clad in his rough black tunic, barefooted and hatless, he went directly to the Pontifical Palace and asked if he could see the Pope. The chamberlain took one look at him and barked, "Be off at once!" and slammed the door.

Paul turned away, bewildered but not defeated. He went to the Basilica of St Mary Major and there before a picture of the Virgin, vowed to spread devotion to Jesus Crucified. Then he packed up his precious Rule and set out for Monte Argentaro.

He found everything he had sought on Monte Argentaro — even an abandoned hermitage, the Hermitage of the Annunciation. But what was he doing without John Baptist, still waiting in Castellazo to hear from him? So in a short time, John was with him, with permission to wear the penitential habit. And there for more than a year the two brothers led an eremitical life of extreme hardship, but great spiritual peace. Their food consisted of water from the spring, a little fresh salad, a few beans and wild grapes, bread, sometimes brought by friendly neighbors down the mountain, and fish occasionally sent up from a coastal village nearby. Many hours they spent in prayer, penance, solitude and silence. At midnight, they rose for Matins and were awakened by the song of birds at dawn. They sometimes practiced extreme penance, occasionally to excess. Paul wrote of it later, "I soon suspected some move of the devil in that, for I was performing those penances without orders from my spiritual director, and therefore without the merit of obedience."

Throughout his life Paul continued to practice unusual penances, which he believed God required of him. One can only judge from the fruit of his commitment — the thousands of hardened hearts he was able to move to a new love for Christ.

The next years were filled with perseverance and multiplied hardships. Pope Benedict XIII gave him oral permission to gather companions in 1725, but life on Monte Argentaro was too severe and demanding for some of the recruits, and they soon left. Paul and John then went back to Rome, where they worked in the Hospital of St Gallican. In 1727 Pope Benedict ordained both of them as priests in order to facilitate their work among the sick and dying. A change in hospital administration required everyone to perform medical chores, even to assist at operations! Paul, unable to bear the crude surgical methods then in use, soon fell ill, and realizing that it was wrong to try to keep them longer, their patron, Cardinal Corrandi, obtained permission of the Pope for them to return to Monte Argentaro. Paul was now thirty-three, and his dream was still unfulfilled.

It was at this time that the missions began for which Paul of the Cross became famous. The first was a short Paschal retreat at the little town of Portercole at the foot of Monte Argentaro. The area of his work was one of extreme poverty and many difficulties. Three political kingdoms vied for superiority, Austria, Spain and the Papal States, and at times Paul crossed enemy lines to minister to the armies lined up in open warfare against each other. Many times his work carried him through areas infested by thieves and robbers, across malaria-ridden swamps. The people to whom he preached were, for the most part, rude and uncultured, yet he was able to move them to tears and repentance by his preaching.

As his fame spread, other churchmen came to see his methods and to hear his appeal. They, too, were often moved to tears and open confession of their lack of care and faithfulness to the people they served.

Once, as he and his little band moved through a dangerous area, a heavily armed bandit stepped out of the bushes to confront them. "Father Paul, come with me!" said the bandit.

Paul shrugged his shoulders and followed the man into the woods. When he asked the man what he wanted, the bandit answered grimly, "Forward! Into the woods!"

Paul was now truly alarmed and prayed for God's protection. Then the bandit wheeled around, "Father, I want to go to confession!" he blurted.

Mildly rebuking him, Paul said, "My son, you should have told me sooner. Wait here while I tell my companions." Then he hurried back to hear the man's confession.

His preaching was done in a serious demeanor. He felt that the missionaries should always behave before people in a way that would elicit respect and a sense of reverence. They were to avoid frivolity and the temptation to make people laugh. In the first part of his message, he seemed stern, even severe, as he talked about the righteous wrath of God against sinners, and the sure hell that awaits the unrepentant. But as the message continued, his face lightened, and he began to speak of the tender love of Christ, shown in his suffering and death. A senior officer of the Spanish army said to him, "Father

Paul, I have been under fire during the war. I have faced the enemy's guns, and I have never been afraid. But when you are preaching, I tremble . . . ." A bandit who heard him confessed, "When I hear you, I shake from head to foot."

One young woman, living a harmless but frivolous life, decided to come to hear him preach. At the time she was suffering from a toothache. Paul was preaching on the eternal truths when, all of a sudden, he pointed in her direction and cried, "You who cannot stand the pain of a simple toothache, how do you expect to support the pains of hell you deserve?" She was startled into a new awareness of her need for repentance, and began a life-long association with him as her spiritual director, reaching a marked and unusual degree of spiritual illumination and maturity.

His work was always under attack from one quarter or another. Enemies both within and without the Church rose up, and those which hurt most were those within the Church. Even St Leonard of Port Maurice lent himself to opposing Paul of the Cross, something he deeply regretted later on. The Passionist Congregation was accused of violating restrictions which prohibited them from locating too near other mendicant orders. Other accusations went along — too severe, too lax, too much zeal. Sometimes bishops closed their dioceses to him and his missionaries, and whispers reached all the way to the Vatican, where finally, in utter frustration, the Pope launched his own investigation of the charges being brought against him. Through it all, Paul's attitude was one of patience and trust in the ultimate vindication of truth. But others, determined to defend his good work, sometimes acted against his will in carrying the cause before the Church tribunals. His own motto was: *Suffer and be silent.*

Eventually the work of the Passionists was indeed vindicated with the approval of the Rule by Benedict XIV in 1741 and 1746. To be sure, there were still problems to be solved in relation to other Orders, but Paul and John were able to begin new foundations and carry the work of the missions forward. Through it all, John had been Paul's chief counselor and corrector. Given to some bluntness, he never hesitated to correct his older brother, and Paul loved him for it. It was because of the bond between them that John's final illness came as another heavy cross for Paul, who was himself suffering from arthritis and gout, brought on, at least in part, by his heavy austerities and penances of earlier years. At last, however, he was able to limp into his brother's cell, to ask him about his soul, knowing that John was nearing death.

"If our time be come, let us die manfully," said John.

Again, he had words of advice and wisdom for his brother. "Be slow to accept candidates, and still slower to have them ordained. You will never be many indeed, but you will be an elect people, well fit to promote God's glory."

When he had received his final absolution, Paul asked him if anything troubled him. John's answer, in characteristic brevity, was, "*Sto quietissimo* — I am at perfect peace." His brother led the Community in chanting the *Salve Regina* as John's soul went out to meet its eternal reward.

The future of the Passionists was further assured and strengthened a few years later by Pope Clement XIV. Cardinal Ganganelli had been a long-time friend of Paul, and had said to him, "If ever I am in a position to confer a favor upon your person which I love, or upon your new-born Institute which I venerate, it will be an obligation and a privilege to give you proof of my utter devotion and my constant affection." That promise was fulfilled in 1769 when, as Clement XIV, he issued his Papal Bull granting the Passionist Congregation all the favors accorded to the great Orders of the Church and placing it under the special protection of the Apostolic See.

In this latest period of the life of our saint, the trials and dark nights of spiritual dryness being largely past, Paul experienced some of the most remarkable mystical experiences ever reported. Asked about one of them, he exclaimed, "Never shall I tell what I have seen," but the joy in his face spoke volumes. "Oh how much did I understand then about the Power, Wisdom and Goodness of God, and the other divine attributes, but I cannot speak of them, for there are no words to express them!" His very heart had been enlarged as a result of his deep desire to have the Passion of our Lord engraved upon it. A doctor testified that in an examination of him when he was sick, three ribs were displaced on the left side, and this enlargement resulted in much discomfort and infirmity. "Pray to Jesus Christ," he had written friends, "that He may show His mercy towards me, and that He may impress His holy Passion upon my heart." Eye witnesses reported a number of supernatural experiences in which our Lord and His blessed Mother were seen in moving conversation with the saint. Toward the end, his conversation was occupied with the joys of Paradise.

About a year before he died, the Community was summoned to his bedside, and one by one they came into the little room. He gave them the text of his little sermon to them: *God forbid that I should glory save in the Cross of Our Lord Jesus Christ, by which the world is crucified to me and I to the world.* And then he drove home his point: "O sons of the Cross and Passion, you must be crucified to the world; you must detest all that the world loves and embrace all that the world hates." And then, gasping for breath, he added "I leave you two maxims: First, never complain, never cherish resentment, never justify yourself. Secondly, work, suffer and be silent."

On October 18, 1775, Paul received the Viaticum for the last time. As Vespers approached, he spoke calmly to the infirmarian: "My death is very near. Call Fr. John Mary (his confessor) for me to recommend my soul."

Pointing to the crucifix beside his bed, he said, "There are all my hopes — the Passion of Jesus Christ. . . ."

Fr. John Mary entered and saw that the moment of his departure was near. He summoned the Community, and a priest began to read quietly the Passion according to St John. The crucifix was held before Paul's eyes as his breathing grew more gentle, Then, as the words were read,"Father the hour is come. Glorify Thy Son, that Thy Son may glorify Thee," Fr. Paul's eyes closed in eternal rest.

He was canonized in 1867 by Pope Pius IX. The Passionist Fathers continue his work of missions, seeking to bring others to know and love the One whom he served so well. His feast is on October 19.

St Catherine Labouré

1806-1876

On the evening of May 2, 1806, as the Angelus bells rang out over the French countryside, people stopped for a moment to pray, as their ancestors had done for centuries before them. But in the obscure little village of Fains-les-moutiers, the Labouré family were rejoicing over the birth of their ninth child, their second daughter, Catherine, and never even heard the bells.

Very little is known about Catherine's childhood. Her parents were well educated, as were her older brothers and sister, but Catherine and her younger sister received no education. It was not until Catherine entered the religious life that she learned to read and write. She was very close to her mother, a devout woman with a life-long love for God. When Catherine was nine years old, her mother died, and she longed for someone to fill the empty place left in her heart. She turned in her grief to the Blessed Virgin, asking her to be her mother, and from that time on, Catherine never doubted that Mary truly was a mother to her.

When Catherine was twelve years old, it became necessary for her to take over the management of her father's household with the help of her younger sister, Tonine, who was ten. This was no small task, since in addition to having the care of their father and an invalid brother, with all the cooking, cleaning, mending and sewing, there were thirteen hired men who lived with them. Just being sure that they always had enough of everything to provide for such a household was a formidable job. But Catherine's will was equal to it, and with Tonine's help, the house ran smoothly for the next ten years.

All through those ten years, Catherine felt that she was being called to enter the religious life. At the age of twenty-two, assured that Tonine was able and willing to assume full responsibility for the household, she asked her father's permission to leave home to enter the convent. But M. Labouré was not willing to have this daughter, who had served him so well, leave him. His answer was an emphatic, "No!"

She remained obediently at home, but her heart was no longer in it, and the difference was obvious. Her father decided that she needed to stay in Paris a while, so sent her to live with one of her brothers. Here, too, she was so obviously unhappy that after a year's time, the family prevailed upon her father to give her the permission she sought to become a nun.

She entered the Sisters of Charity of St Vincent de Paul in Paris in 1831. Her three months' postulancy passed quickly as she gave herself wholeheartedly to her new life. Soon after her entry into the novitiate, Catherine began to receive visions and the interpretation of them as well. But on the night of July 18, 1830, she received the greatest blessing of her lifetime. Her life-long desire to see the Blessed Mother was granted. She had been asleep for about two hours, when she was awakened by a little child who told her to come to the chapel where the Virgin awaited her. The chapel was brightly lit as if for midnight Mass, but Catherine saw no sign of the Virgin. After a little while the mysterious child announced that the Virgin was there, and looking up, Catherine heard the sound of rustling silk and saw a Lady coming down the altar steps. Her initial doubts about who the Lady was soon vanished, and Catherine threw herself down before her and looked up into her eyes.

She was then told that God had a mission for her and would assist her in carrying it out. The Virgin went on to tell Catherine of the terrible things that would befall France and the world, and to assure her that the Sisters of Charity would be protected. After a little time, the

Virgin was gone, and the child took Catherine back to her bed.

A few months later, Catherine was at evening prayers with her Sisters, when once again she heard the sound of rustling silk. Looking up she saw a vision of the Blessed Virgin with rays of glory streaming from her. Catherine then received a commission to have a medal struck showing the vision just as she had seen it. There would be abundant grace for all who would wear it in faith. But Catherine was instructed to tell no one but her confessor, Father Aladel, about the visions. He alone had to decide on the reliability and truth of what she had said, and see to it that the Virgin's instructions were carried out. It was almost two years before he finally convinced the panel of inquiry which had been set up by the Archbishop of Paris, of the reality of Catherine's visions. The medal was struck in 1832, and in the next six years his book telling of the medal and its origin sold more than 130,000 copies. The popularity of the medal continued to increase, and many thousands more have sought the intercession of Our Lady of the Miraculous Medal, and have been grateful for healings and miracles that have occurred.

For the next forty-six years, Catherine lived in almost complete obscurity, carrying out her duties as a Sister of Charity, caring for the aged men who lived at the Hospice run by the Sisters, and in charge of the convent's chickens. Her superiors spoke of her as "rather insignificant," "matter-of-fact and unexcitable." Not until shortly before her death did she reveal to her Superior that she had been the Sister of the apparitions. She had not used the visions to exalt herself or gain special favors from her Sisters. Rather, she lived a life of obedience and service to others.

At her funeral in December, 1876, there was an outburst of spontaneous recognition that she was indeed a saint, and a child of twelve, crippled from birth, was instantly healed at her grave soon afterward. Although her life had been lived in obscurity, God looks on the heart, and eventually the Church came to recognize and honor the quality of her devotion and the holiness of her life. She was canonized in 1947, and her feast is observed on November 28.

St Margaret Mary Alacoque

1647-1690

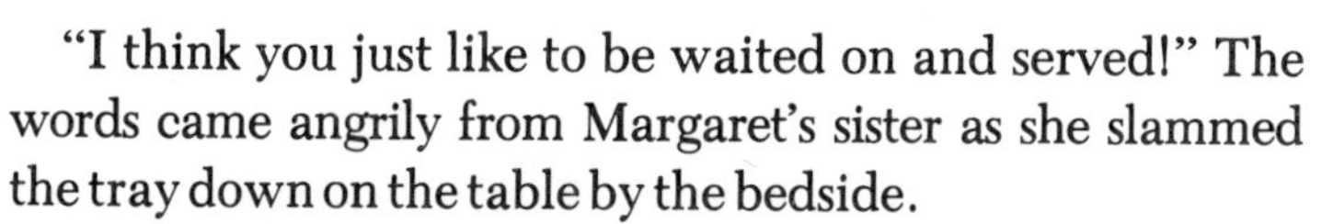

"I think you just like to be waited on and served!" The words came angrily from Margaret's sister as she slammed the tray down on the table by the bedside.

Margaret said nothing, but tears quickly flooded her eyes again. She had been home from the Poor Clares' school for only a week, and her joints were still swollen from a painful rheumatoid condition which left her weak and hardly able to move.

"You're just like Mother," the sister went on, bustling around the bedroom. "It's hard enough to run this house, without the two of you always demanding my attention!"

Margaret's father had died two years before when she was only eight. During the time she had been sent away to school, many changes had taken place in the home. Her mother was no longer in charge. Instead, her sister and other relatives had moved in and dominated the household with their own ideas and plans. At ten years of age, Margaret could only look on, feel the pain, and pray. She wrote later that concerning those years, "The heaviest of my crosses was my inability to lighten the crosses laid on my mother."

There she remained, and although her rheumatoid condition gradually improved, it kept her bedridden until she was fifteen years old. There was much talk about whom she might marry, and Margaret herself wondered just what kind of future she might have. The dances and other social affairs, although she entered into them, left her empty and dissatisfied. Her place in the home was little more than that of a servant. More and more, Margaret wanted to answer her vocation to become a nun. But it was not until she was twenty-four years old that, having overcome the objections of her family, her brother Chrysostom furnished her with a dowry, so that she could enter the Convent of the Visitation at Paray-le-Monial, in the provence of Burgundy, France. The date was June, 1671.

Between 1625 and 1690, two others besides Margaret Mary were experiencing new revelations and understandings of the heart of Jesus, and in addition, the Protestant chaplain to Oliver Cromwell in England, Thomas

Goodwin, published a book entitled *The Heart of Christ towards Sinners on Earth*, reflecting much of the same spirit. Margaret Mary's revelations came in the form of four visions of Jesus she received between 1673 and 1675. As she knelt before the Blessed Sacrament in the chapel, Jesus invited her to lean upon His breast, as St John had done at the Last Supper. "It was as though our Lord took her heart and put it within His own, returning it burning with divine love into her breast." From then on, she felt a mission to honor His Sacred Heart of love in the form of a human heart. But the Lord warned her to do everything only in obedience to those set over her.

When she told her Superior about the vision and the instructions the Lord had given, she was forbidden to do any of the things spoken of in the vision.

"I withdrew in great peace," Margaret Mary wrote later. But she became very ill almost immediately.

"If God cures you," said the Superior, "I shall take it as a proof that all you experience comes from Him, and I will allow you to do what our Lord wishes in honor of His Sacred Heart."

Others in the Convent were not so willing to believe in the visions, and through the years following, Margaret Mary had many times of persecution and humiliation. An examination by theological experts concluded that she was deluded, but she continued to believe that she was a willing sacrifice, and that her sufferings were in part a reparation for the insults Jesus still received from the world and for the ingratitude of her sister nuns. A new spiritual director came to the Community, Fr. Claud La Colombiere, who was much influenced by her visions, and later, in England complained that there was no "Sister Alacoque" there!

By her faithful adherence to the visions and the instructions she received, Margaret Mary was able to introduce devotion to the Sacred Heart, first in her own convent among the novices whom she was training, and later into other houses of Visitation sisters. Eventually a chapel was built in honor of the Sacred Heart, and the devotion gradually spread throughout France.

Her visions and teachings on the Sacred Heart, along with those of others, contributed much to the devotional life of Catholics, and in 1856 a special feast of the Sacred Heart of Jesus was made universal.

She was only forty-three years old when she became ill again. The doctors did not think it was anything serious, but she said, "I shall not live, for I have nothing left to suffer." Within the week, she died, saying, "I need nothing but God and to lose myself in the heart of Jesus."

She was canonized in 1920, and her feast is celebrated on October 17.

CHRONOLOGY

This brief "time line" will help you to place the various saints in their historical setting, in relation to some of the secular events and developments in the history of the Church. Early dates are all approximate. The letter "c" also means "about" such and such a date.

World Events	Dates	Church Events
	4 BC	Birth of Jesus
Rule of Herod the Great	37-4 BC	
Augustus Caesar, Emperor	27-4 BC	
	27 AD	John the Baptist's ministry
	+ 30 AD	Jesus' Crucifixion and Resurrection Holy Spirit poured out on Pentecost
	+ 34-35	Martyrdom of St Stephen
	c. 35	Conversion of St Paul
Herod Agrippa persecutes early Christians at Jerusalem	44	Missionary activity of St Paul
	+ 45	Martyrdom of St James of Jerusalem
Rome burns, Nero's persecution of Christians begins	+ 64	Martyrdom of Sts Peter and Paul
	c. 69	St Polycarp b.
Jerusalem destroyed by Titus	70	Jesus' prediction of temple destruction fulfilled
Pompeii buried under lava	79	
Trajan Emperor of Rome	98-117	
	c. 100	Justin Martyr b.
Christianity made a crime in Eastern Roman Empire Trajan crushes Jewish revolt	116	Renewed persecution of Clergy
	140	Marcion heresy spreads among Christians
	+ 155	St Polycarp burned at stake
	+ 165	St Justin Martyr killed
	195	Conversion of Tertullian, champion of orthodoxy
	200	Canon of Holy Scriptures forming

World Events	Dates	Church Events
	+ 215	St Clement of Alexandria dies
Decius, Emperor of Rome	250	Decian persecution of Church
	c.250	St Helen b.
	251	St Antony of Egypt b.
	+ 254	Origen dies. Great Eastern theologian, but never canonized
	c. 296	St Athanasius b.
	|	St Antony and St Pachomius pioneer desert monasticism
Diocletian Emperor	300	Severe persecution of Christians especially in the Eastern Empire
	+ 303	St George and St Agnes martyred (and many others)
Constantine adopts Christianity Unites empire under him	312	Persecution of Christians stops
	|	Arian heresy abounds, denying the full divinity of Christ
	325	Council of Nicea upholds Catholic faith (Nicene Creed)
	c. 330	St Basil b., St Helen d.
	c. 332	St Monica b.
	336	Arius dies
Constantine dies. Empire divided.	337	
	339	St Ambrose b.
	340	Old Roman creed, basis of "Apostles' creed"
	c. 342	St Ambrose b., St Jerome b.
	347	St John Chrysostom b.
	354	St Augustine b.
	+ 356	St Antony of Egypt d.
Julian the Apostate Emperor	361-363	
Theodosius becomes Eastern Emperor	370	
	+ 373	St Athanasius d.
	+ 379	St Basil d.

World Events	Dates	Church Events
	+ 387	St Monica d.
Theodosius makes public penance under St Ambrose's direction	c. 390	St Patrick b. in England
	+ 397	St Ambrose d.
	+ 407	St John Chrysostom d.
	407	Spread of monasticism by Sts Jerome, Basil and Martin of Tours
Fall of Rome to Alaric the Hun Barbarian rule of the West	410	Jerome's translation of Bible into Latin (Vulgate)
	413-426	St Augustine writes *City of God*
	+ 420	St Jerome d.
	+ 430	St Augustine d.
Vandals take Hippo, Augustine's city	431	Council of Ephesus to settle dispute over person of Christ
	432-461	St Patrick's ministry in Ireland
Attila the Hun defeated by Vandals	451	Council of Chalcedon to further clarify Church's teaching
Rome sacked by Vandals	455	
	+ c. 461	St Patrick d.
	+ 461	St Leo the Great (Pope) d.
	c. 480	St Benedict of Nursia b.
Clovis, king of the Franks	496	Baptism of Clovis
	c. 521	St Columba b., St Kenneth (525)
Justinian, Emperor of East	527	
		Work of St Benedict, Father of Western monasticism. Monte Cassino founded, 529. Benedictine *Rule*
	540	St Gregory the Great b.
	543	St Columban b.
	+ 550	St Benedict d.
Mohammed b.	570	
	590-605	Gregory the Great, Pope
	596-597	St Augustine of Canterbury sent to England by Gregory the Great
	+ 597	St Columba d.

World Events	Dates	Church Events
	+ c. 600	St Kenneth d.
	+ 604	St Gregory the Great d.
	614	St Hilda b.
	+ 615	St Columban d.
Mohammed's flight to Mecca begins Commonwealth of Islam	522	Moslem threat to Church begins
	c. 630	St Etheldreda b.
	657	St John of Damascus b. "Greatest theologian of the Eastern Church in medieval times."
	664	Synod of Whitby unites Roman and Celtic Church in Britain
	673	Venerable Bede b.
	675	St Boniface of Mainz b.
	+ 679	St Etheldreda d.
	+ 680	St Hilda d.
	690	British missionaries active in evangelizing the European continent
Arabs invade Spain from N. Africa	711	
	726	Iconoclastic controversy (dispute over use of images in Church)
Charles Martel turns back Moslem attacks at Tours	732	
	+ 735	The Venerable Bede d.
	+ 749	St John of Damascus d.
	+ 754	St Boniface martyred
Pepin the Short est. Papal States	756	
Charlemagne's Victories	772-776	Papacy still growing in power
First Danish raid on England	787	
Charlemagne crowned emperor by Pope Leo III	800	
Moslems invade Asia Minor	791-809	
Reign of Louis the Pious	814-840	
King Edmund of East Anglica b.	841	
	842	End of Iconclastic controversy

World Events	Dates	Church Events
	+ 869	St Edmund martyred
	907	St Wencesias b.
	910	Foundation of Abbey at Cluny Monastic reforms begins
	+ 929	St Wenceslas murdered
Otto revives Roman empire	962	
St Henry the Emperor b.	973	
St Stephen of Hungary b.	975	
Reign of St Vladimir in Russia	980-1015	
St Henry the Emperor d.	+ 1024	
St Stephen of Hungary d.	+ 1038	
St Margaret of Scotland b.	1046	
	1054	Great Schism between Eastern and Western Christendom
Crusades		Gothic Architecture developed
St Margaret and Malcolm of Scotland	1045-93	
William the Conqueror wins Battle of Hastings: Norman rule of England	1066	Norman style churches built in England
St Margaret of Scotland d.	+ 1093	
	1090	St Bernard of Clairvaux b.
	1098	St Hildegarde b.
Second Crusade	1147	St Bernard preaches crusade
	+ 1153	St Bernard d.
	c. 1160	St Benezet b.
Oxford University beginnings	1167	
	+ 1179	St Hildegarde d.
	1181	St Francis of Assisi b.
	+ 1184	St Benezet d.
	1194	St Clare b.
	1195	St Anthony of Padua b.
University of Paris chartered	1205	
St Elizabeth of Hungary b.	1207	
England under papal interdict	1208	No Mass allowed in England
St Louis of France b.	1214	
Magna Carta in England	1215	Dominican Order approved
	c. 1218	St Zita b.

World Events	Dates	Church Events
	1221	St Bonaventure b.
	1223	Franciscans chartered
	1225	St Thomas Aquinas b.
	+ 1226	St Francis of Assisi d.
St Elizabeth of Hungary d.	+ 1231	St Anthony of Padua d.
Mongol Conquest of Russia (1237-1241)	1241	St Mechtilde of Hackenborn b.
	+ 1253	St Clare d.
St Louis of France d.	+ 1270	
	+ 1274	St Bonaventure d.
	+ 1274	St Thomas Aquinas d.
	+ 1278	St Zita d.
	+ 1298	St Mechtilde d.
	1314	St Sergius b.
	1347	St Catherine of Siena b.
Famine followed by Black Death ravages Europe, esp. Italy	1348	
Dimitri defeats Tartars in Russia	+ 1380	St Catherine of Siena d.
	+ 1392	St Sergius d.
	1412	St Joan of Arc b.
Henry V of England reconquers Normandy, Battle of Agincourt	1415	
	1414-1418	Council of Constance, John Hus burned at stake for heresy
	1417	St Nicholas of Flue b.
	1427	Thomas à Kempis writes *Imitation of Christ*
English begin seige of Orleans	1428	
St Joan of Arc burned at stake	+ 1431	
	1447	St Catherine of Genoa b.
War of Roses in England (1455-1485)	|	
	1456	Gutenberg prints first Bible Joan of Arc's name cleared
St Casmir of Poland b.	1458	
Byzantine Empire falls to Turks	1453	
Ferdinand & Isabella unite Spain	1469	
	+ 1471	Thomas à Kempis d.

World Events	Dates	Church Events
Turks defeat Venice	1479	
	1483	Martin Luther b.
St Casmir of Poland d.	+ 1484	
	+ 1487	Brother Klaus d. (Nicholas of Flue)
Columbus discovers New World	1492	
	+ 1498	Savonarola burned at stake for heresy
	1506	Erasmus publishes Greek New Testament
		St Francis Xavier b.
	1508	Michaelangelo begins ceiling of Sistine Chapel
Henry VIII becomes King of England	1509	
	+ 1510	St Catherine of Genoa d.
	1515	St Teresa of Avila b.
	1517	Luther's "Ninety-five Theses" symbolize beginning of Protestant Reform
	1530	Diet of Augsburg defines Lutheranism
	+ 1531	Zwingli, Swiss reformer, killed in battle
England enacts "Act of Supremacy"	1534	Church of England officially separated from Roman rule
	1536	John Calvin's *Institutes*
Henry VIII suppresses monasteries	1539	
	1540	Society of Jesus (Jesuits) founded
	1542	St John of the Cross b.
	1545	Council of Trent begins Counter-Reformation
	+ 1546	Luther d.
Henry VIII d.	1547	
Act of Uniformity in England	1549	First Book of Common Prayer issued
	1550	St Camillus de Lellis b.

World Events	Dates	Church Events
	+ 1551	St Francis Xavier d.
Mary Tudor restores Catholicism to England	1553-58	
	+ 1556	St Ignatius of Loyola d.
Elizabeth I, Queen of England	1558	Church of England re-separates
	+ 1561	John Menno, founder of Mennonites d.
	1567	St Francis de Sales b.
	1568	St Aloysius Gonzaga B.
French war against Huguenots	1562-98	
Massacre of Huguenots in France	+ 1572	John Knox, Scot Reformer, d.
Moors defeat Portugal	1578	
Sir Francis Drake circles the globe	1580	
	1581	St Vincent de Paul b.
	+ 1582	St Teresa of Avila d.
	1586	St Rose of Lima b.
Spanish Armada defeated by England	1588	
	+ 1591	St John of the Cross d.
	+ 1591	St Aloysius Gonzaga d.
	+ 1597	Martyrs of Japan
Edict of Nantes, toleration for French Huguenots	1598	
First permanent English colony at Jamestown, Virginia	1607	
	1609-10	Douay Version of Bible issued
	1611	King James Version of Bible
	+ 1614	St Camillus de Lellis d.
	+ 1617	St Rose of Lima d.
Thirty Year War in Germany	1618-48	
Pilgrims land at Plymouth	1620	
	+ 1622	St Francis de Sales d.
Puritans found Massachusetts Bay	1630	Massive persecution of Puritans
English Civil War: Commonwealth established	1640	Puritans in control of Church of England
	1645	Book of Common Prayer suppressed
	1647	St Margaret Mary Alacoque b.

World Events	Dates	Church Events
	1651	St John Baptist de la Salle b.
	+ 1660	St Vincent de Paul d.
Restoration of English monarchy	1660	Non-conformists jailed for preaching
	+ 1662	St Francis de Sales d.
	1668	St Aloysius Gonzaga b.
	1678	John Bunyan publishes *Pilgrim's Progress*
Edict of Nantes revoked, 100,00 Huguenots flee from France	1685	
"The Glorious Revolution" places William and Mary on English throne	1688	
	+ 1691	St Aloysius Gonzaga d.
	1694	St Paul of the Cross b.
	+ 1696	St Margaret Mary Alacoque d.
	+ 1719	St John Baptist de la Salle d.
	1734-40	Great Awakening in America (religious revival)
	1739	Beginnings of Methodism in England
	+ 1758	Jonathan Edwards, Puritan preacher and theologian, d.
	1773	Abolition of the Society of Jesus
	1774	St Elizabeth Seton b.
	+ 1775	St Paul of the Cross d.
American Revolutionary War	1776-1783	
U. S. Constitution	1787	
French Revolution	+ 1789	John Wesley, father of Methodism d.
Napoleon rises to power (1795)		Protestant Episcopal Church founded in U.S.
		John Carroll, First Roman Catholic Bishop in U. S. appointed
Concordat between Napoleon and Pope Pius VIII (French troop occupy Rome in 1809)	1801	

World Events	Dates	Church Events
	1806	St Catherine Labouré b.
	1810	First American Foreign Mission Board established
	1814	Jesuits reestablished by Pius VII
Napoleon defeated at Waterloo	1815	St John Bosco b.
	+ 1821	St Elizabeth Seton d.
Catholic Emancipation Act in England	1829	
	1833	Oxford Movement (Anglo-Catholic) in Church of England
	1843	St Dominic Savio b.
	1845	John Henry Newman (later Cardinal) enters Roman Catholic Church
Louis Napoleon seizes power in France (1851) Crimean War begins	1854	Dogma of Immaculate Conception proclaimed by Pope Pius IX
	+ 1857	St Dominic Savio d.
American Civil War	1861-1865	
Karl Marx writes *Das Capital* advocating Communism	1867	
Italy unified under Victor Immanuel	1870	Vatican I proclaims papal infalliblity
	+ 1870	Dr. David Livingstone, missionary, d.
German Empire established (1871)	1873	St Thérèse of Lisieux b.
Africa divided betw. European Colonial Powers (1878)	+ 1876	St Catherine Labouré d.
	+ 1886	Martyrs of Uganda
	+ 1888	St John Bosco d.
	+ 1897	St Thérèse of Lisieux d.
	1890	St Mary Goretti b.
Spanish American War frees Cuba (1898)	+ 1902	St Mary Goretti martyred
	1907-08	Pope Pius XI attacks modernism in the Church

INDEX